GUIDED READING:

What's New, and What's Next?

Michael P. Ford

capstone
professional

Guided Reading: What's New, and What's Next?
By Michael P. Ford
© Copyright 2016. Michael P. Ford. All rights reserved.

Cover Design: Richard Parker
Book Design: Charmaine Whitman

Library of Congress Cataloging-in-Publication Data
Names: Ford, Michael P., author.
Title: Guided reading : what's new, and what's next? / by Michael P. Ford.
Description: North Mankato, MN : Maupin House Pub., Inc. by Capstone
  Professional, 2016. | Includes bibliographical references.
Identifiers: LCCN 2015032374 |
ISBN 978-1-4966-0527-6 (pbk.)
ISBN 978-1-4966-0528-3 (ebook PDF)
ISBN 978-1-4966-0529-0 (ebook)
Subjects: LCSH: Guided reading. | Reading (Primary)
Classification: LCC LB1050.377 .F67 2016 | DDC 372.41/62—dc23
LC record available at http://lccn.loc.gov/2015032374

Image Credits:
Newscom: ACESTOCK Stock Connection, 138, BSIP, 136 (bottom), Ingram
Publishing, Cover, KidStock Blend Images, 135; Shutterstock: Monkey Business
Images, 136 (top), 139, Tracy Whiteside, 148; The Image Works: Ellen B. Senisi,
140, The Star-Ledger/Patti Sapone, 134; Wisconsin Department of Public
Instruction. (2010). Wisconsin response to intervention: A guided document., 177
Design Elements: Shutterstock

Capstone Professional publishes professional resources for K–12 educators.
Contact us for tailored, in-school training or to schedule an author for a workshop
or conference. Visit www.capstonepd.com for free lesson plan downloads.

This book includes websites that were operational at the time it went to press.

Maupin House Publishing, Inc. by Capstone Professional
1710 Roe Crest Drive
North Mankato, MN 56003
www.capstonepd.com
888-262-6135
info@capstonepd.com

To Dr. Michael F. Opitz

There has been no better long-time collaborator, colleague, and friend.

ACKNOWLEDGMENTS   While this is my first book as sole author, I did not complete the project alone. I would like to acknowledge my attentive Capstone editor Karen Soll, who invited and embraced this project. I want to thank those whose previous collaborations influenced my thinking and writing in this book: Michael Opitz, Kathryn Glasswell, James Erekson, Joanne Caldwell, Mary Jo Fresch, Kathy Champeau, and Norm Andrews. My thinking on intervention was heavily influenced by the work of the Oshkosh Area School District, and I appreciate my colleague, K–6 reading coordinator Deb Zarling, who first shared these resources. Thanks also to Tom Schiele whose invitation to present on the topic of guided reading caused the initial organization of my thinking on this topic and became the outline for this book. Finally, my thanks to Pat Scanlan for her never-ending support.

Table of Contents

Introduction 7

CHAPTER ONE:
Where Have We Been, and Where Are We with Guided Reading Practices? 13

CHAPTER TWO:
Why Is Guided Reading Still Important? What Is the Purpose of Guided Reading? 33

CHAPTER THREE:
How Does Guided Reading Fit into the Rest of the Literacy Program? 55

CHAPTER FOUR:
How Should Texts Be Selected for Guided Reading? 73

CHAPTER FIVE:
How Do We Support Different Types of Learners During Guided Reading? 91

CHAPTER SIX:
What Is the Rest of the Class Doing During Guided Reading? 133

CHAPTER SEVEN:
How Is Guided Reading Positioned for Intervention? 161

Appendix 179

Resources 199

Guided Reading: What's New, and What's Next?

Introduction

> "The exciting romance with guided reading is well underway."
>
> *Fountas and Pinnell, 2012*

During the summer of 2014, I was invited to present at a professional development conference in Las Vegas. The conference attracted more than 6,000 educators, and many joined a tract I presented for called "I Teach First Grade." While I was asked to present on what I thought were three contemporary hot topics, such as helping students handle complex texts, integrating nonfiction in literacy programs, and using accessible assessments to document the progress of learners, a session I conducted entitled "Guided Reading: What's New?" drew the largest number of educators—almost four times as many as the others.

It surprised me that so many educators were still interested in learning more about guided reading. In an era of constantly identifying *what's hot* and *what's not*, I thought guided reading had been pushed to the back burner. It seems to be the focus of minimal scholarly attention, but it still dominates literacy programs, especially primary classrooms. In fact, in these times of increasing demands from Response to Intervention (RtI) frameworks and college and career readiness standards, small group instruction including guided reading is now carrying the responsibility of providing interventions to accelerate the growth of all readers. Models of small group reading instruction seem particularly critical for readers who need our help the most.

While models of guided reading have existed for many decades, they re-emerged in 1996 with the popularity of Fountas and Pinnell's text *Guided Reading: Good First Teaching for All Children*. Ranked first by relevance in a Google search on "guided reading" and cited more than 1,000 times, it is clear this is the most influential resource in shaping what we now know as guided reading. A number of how-to resource books emerged subsequently to support teachers. One of those was a text I co-authored with Michael F. Opitz (2001) called *Reaching Readers: Flexible and Innovative Strategies for Guided Reading,* written in part to expand the vision of guided reading and to encourage teachers to break out of an orthodoxy that had developed around the practice. Since that time, less has been written about guided reading. *The Next Step in Guided Reading* by Jan Richardson was published in 2009 and has been embraced by many educators looking for more direction. *Preventing Misguided Reading* by

Burkins and Kroft has a more recent publication date (2010) and offers a more critical view of the practice. In their observations, they warned:

> Misinterpreted instructional methods run the risk of abandonment. Education is littered with the remains of educational trends lost in translation. Often, the reality is that we compromised the fidelity of their implementation. So, critics assemble and declare that the approach doesn't work, as researchers and publishers line up to set a new program in place. We see this trend surfacing with guided reading, and we lament the energy and resources that districts may expend in totally revamping literacy instruction that may simply need adjusting (xv).

Perhaps the time does seem right to refocus some attention on improving small group instruction including guided reading within current literacy programs. When I prepared my presentation for the summer conference, I organized it around seven key guidelines to frame not only what was new in guided reading but, more important, what was working and what needed to be improved. The content was positively received by the audience and indicated to me an existing need to help educators look critically at this practice that has had almost two decades of implementation. So when Karen Soll from Capstone Professional approached me about doing a new book, I suggested looking at guided reading and thinking about how to position it for a more productive role in today's literacy programs.

That discussion led to this book. Although this teacher resource book is grounded in critical theory, research, and issues, I focus primarily on practical ideas to improve small group instruction, including guided reading within literacy programs. It is framed around seven key questions, and each chapter answers each by presenting a discussion of the issues and illustrating practical ideas educators can implement within their literacy programs. Reproducible forms and support materials are also available to readers within the chapters and in the Appendices.

The seven key questions that frame each of the chapters are:

1 CHAPTER ONE:
Where Have We Been, and Where Are We with Guided Reading Practices?

This chapter builds on research about the history of guided reading that Michael Opitz and I did for the chapter "Guided Reading: Now and Then" in Mary Jo Fresch's book *An Essential History of Current Reading Practices* published in 2008 by the International Reading Association. A version of this chapter was also published as the article "Looking Back to Move Forward with Guided Reading" in the journal *Reading Horizons* in 2011. To look ahead, the chapter presents results from a national survey of guided reading practices Opitz and I conducted that was published in *Literacy Research and Instruction* in 2008 as an article called "A National Survey of Guided Reading Practices: What We Can Learn from Primary Teachers."

2 CHAPTER TWO:
Why Is Guided Reading Still Important? What Is the Purpose of Guided Reading?

When the conversation in the reading community shifts to new topics, or at least new ways of talking about old topics, it is important that we don't throw out the baby with the bathwater. In this chapter, I will provide the theory and research supporting the use of guided reading. It is important to be able to articulate why guided reading is still relevant in literacy programs. This chapter also includes suggestions for an assessment, which can be used as a baseline.

3 CHAPTER THREE:
How Does Guided Reading Fit into the Rest of the Literacy Program?

Often, guided reading is relied on to carry the responsibility of addressing all instructional needs for the students that it serves. Exclusively using or over relying on guided reading in this manner will result in an imbalanced comprehensive literacy program, and the instruction will fall short of what it needs to do. Guided reading needs to be supported by other aspects of the literacy program. This chapter discusses how to better align guided reading within a comprehensive literacy program.

4 CHAPTER FOUR:
How Should Texts Be Selected for Guided Reading?

In looking at issues and ideas for using texts during guided reading for this chapter, I revisited work that I conducted with Kathryn Glasswell. This work was first published in *The Reading Teacher* in 2010 in the article "Teaching Flexibly with Leveled Texts: Bringing More Power to Your Reading Block," and related work was published in the article "Let's Start Leveling about Leveling" in *Language Arts* in 2011. I also provide a review of some guided reading programs commercially available.

5 CHAPTER FIVE:
How Do We Support Different Types of Learners During Guided Reading?

In this chapter, I look at a number of sources to discuss ways of structuring the guided reading sessions for different types of learners. I avoid presenting one right way to structure the lesson for all learners. Conversely, I recommend different formats to consider when planning and conducting effective sessions that support different learners and different purposes.

6 CHAPTER SIX:
What Is the Rest of the Class Doing During Guided Reading?

This question has been a focus of my attention since first writing about guided reading with Michael Opitz in 2001 in our book *Reaching Readers: Flexible and Innovative Strategies for Guided Reading* with a chapter focused on "Organization and Management." We wrote two articles for *The Reading Teacher* on independent work away from the teachers: "What Do I Do with the Rest of the Kids? Ideas for Meaningful Independent Activities During Small Group Guided Reading" (2004) and "Using Centers to Engage Children During Guided Reading Time: Intensifying Learning Experiences Away from the Teacher" (2002). This work informed my thinking as I wrote Chapter Six.

7 CHAPTER SEVEN:
How Is Guided Reading Positioned for Intervention?

....

If there is one area that has quickly surfaced in the discussion of guided reading since the first generation of resources emerged, it is the role of guided reading in RtI frameworks. The final chapter includes information on what guided reading looks like when it is not just used as universal class instruction but as an additional layer for intervention.

I hope that K–5 classroom teachers and those individuals who support K–5 literacy instruction (including but not limited to reading teachers, special education teachers, interventionists, coaches, and/or administrators) will find this to be a valuable resource. Teachers can use it to individually direct their professional development or position it for professional development across a group of educators.

It's time to look at guided reading. What's new, and what's next?

CHAPTER ONE:
Where Have We Been, and Where Are We with Guided Reading Practices?

> We need to be cautious when an educational practice, like guided reading, begins to develop the trappings of an orthodoxy ... teachers find themselves struggling to make the "conventional wisdom ideal" fit their unique contexts and classrooms.
>
> *Opitz and Ford, 2001*

One year after Fountas and Pinnell published *Guided Reading: Good First Teaching for All Children* in 1996, Cassidy identified, for the first time, a list of *hot* and *not hot* topics in literacy. The 26 reading topics were based on recommendations by experts in the field. It is interesting to look at the list. Guided reading was not on it. (See Figure 1A on page 14.) Grouping issues were only represented as *whole class instruction*. Within a year after developing the list, *whole class instruction* was already identified by more than 75 percent of the respondents as *not hot*. While the topic "came to the forefront with literature-based instruction and heterogeneous grouping," the authors pointed out that it was "never strongly advocated by the profession" (Cassidy & Wenrich, 1998/1999, 405).

Perhaps this would make way for guided reading. It did not. As far as the experts in the field were concerned, grouping issues were on the back burner at best. In fact, grouping issues were not even on the stove. In hindsight, reflecting on nearly 15 years of conducting the survey, Cassidy and Ortlieb (2013) more recently identified grouping practices as a topic *that was never hot but....* While never acquiring enough attention from the experts to rise to the top of the list in any one year, the researchers did suggest that grouping "deserved more attention in the past" and also warranted "more attention now and in the future" (24). This chapter will bring light to grouping practices in the past and present, including small group instructional models like guided reading.

Figure 1A: The Original List of Topics Considered for the First What's Hot/What's Not Survey

1. Automaticity	10. Literature-based instruction	19. Schema Theory
2. Balanced reading instruction	11. Motivation	20. Skills instruction
3. Basal readers and anthologies	12. Phonemic awareness	21. Spelling
4. Comprehension	13. Phonics	22. Standards for language arts
5. Constructivism	14. Portfolio assessment	23. Strategy instruction
6. Direct Instruction	15. Process writing	**24. Whole-class instruction**
7. Early intervention	16. Push-in programs	25. Whole language
8. Emergent literacy	17. Reader engagement	26. Word knowledge/ vocabulary
9. English as a second language	18. Reading Recovery	

Reading instruction was often exclusively carried out in homogenous small groups. Typically there were three groups—one at, one below, and one above grade level.

The history of guided reading has always been entangled with the history of grouping practices. It's important to remember that, historically, small group instruction dominated most classroom literacy programs. Reading instruction was often exclusively carried out in homogenous small groups. Typically there were three groups—one at, one below, and one above grade level. Student groups were determined with less precision than they seemed—usually by the administration of a group assessment with an arbitrary cutoff point determining who was at, below, or above the standard. Or they may have occurred individually by reading a selection in the anthology where lots, some, or no errors determined placement. Groups were often labeled in subtle or not too subtle ways to reflect the level. (Remember the bluebirds, robins, and crows?) The structure was so pervasive that it would have been seen in almost any elementary classroom reading program (Caldwell & Ford, 2002).

Then, in 1985, the landmark federal document *Becoming a Nation of Readers: Report from the Commission of Reading* (BANOR) was published. Sponsored by the National Institute of Education, BANOR revealed what many already knew: There was no positive research base for the exclusive use of homogenous small groups that so dominated elementary classroom reading programs. The widespread dissemination and popular embrace of BANOR led to many shifts in reading pedagogical practices, including rethinking the exclusive use of homogenous small groups. BANOR was probably the first popular resource that called into question the value of ability grouping.

> In theory, ability grouping allows teachers to pace instruction at a more-nearly-optimum rate for children at every level than would be possible in whole class teaching. In fact, the evidence suggests that ability grouping may improve the achievement of the fast child but not the slow child (89).

People sat up and took notice when BANOR actually pointed out: "Some scholars have argued that it is not so much ability that determines the future attainment of a young child, but the reading group into which the child is initially placed (90)." BANOR concluded: "Because of the serious problems inherent in ability grouping…educators should explore other options for reading instruction (91)." While BANOR did suggest a more flexible type of grouping and recommended changing the membership, purpose, and instruction in the continued use of small groups, the recommendation most educators latched on to was: "One option is more use of the whole class instruction (91)."

When the pendulum swings in education, it often swings to extremes. This happened with grouping. Following the release of BANOR, small group instruction disappeared from many classrooms. Whole class instruction began to be the main component of many commercial reading programs and their materials. Again, the inherent flaws of whole group instruction were magnified when it became not part of an overall flexible grouping plan but was used virtually exclusively as the grouping plan. The set of concerns related to the exclusive use of homogenous small groups was just replaced with a new set of concerns related to the exclusive use of heterogeneous whole class instruction (Ford & Opitz, 2011). Teachers quickly became frustrated as they tried to meet the needs of diverse students using the same text for all in whole group settings. Models actually emerged about how to differentiate within these whole class structures (Paratore, 1990). These models showed how to integrate the use of small groups to guide readers directly and indirectly by varying levels of support when using single texts. This was long before anyone was talking about "teaching up" with the use of complex texts (Tomlinson & Moon, 2013). In the end, however, most teachers kept their classrooms and texts whole and marched all students through the same instruction at the same time (Caldwell & Ford, 2002).

Not surprising, within a few years many educators looked for an alternative to yet another less-than-satisfying grouping practice. They struggled to meet the specific needs of all learners within these whole class models. They needed models that would allow instruction to target learners more effectively. The pendulum swung back, and suddenly small groups re-emerged in classroom literacy programs. If you have been around long enough, you have seen classroom practices come and go and come again. Of course, the concern is always when the field returns to a practice from the past, will its thinking be informed by new research and expertise that has emerged? Will this new vision of small group reading be any different from the bluebirds, robins, and crows of the past? Could we return to small group reading without returning to the problems that caused us to move away from it in the first place? Conceiving of small group reading as guided reading seemed to suggest a new vision and direction.

The new vision of small group reading instruction as guided reading was informed significantly by Fountas and Pinnell (1996, 2001), who drew on their work with individual and small group intervention programs, including what they had seen in New Zealand classrooms. Classrooms Down Under had been promoting the use of guided reading years before its widespread use in the states. In *The Foundations of Literacy*, Holdaway (1979) described guided reading as "a form of group instruction in which we introduce children to the techniques of reading new or unseen

Again, the inherent flaws of whole group instruction were magnified when it became not part of an overall flexible grouping plan but was used virtually exclusively as the grouping plan.

material for personal satisfaction and understanding (142)." He contrasted it with small groups of students reading round-robin style, critiquing the damaging features of this traditional approach. Looking at Holdaway's description of guided reading, it is easy to see the impact on models that crossed the ocean: "…all of the children read the entire unit to themselves whether they are reading aloud in the early stages or silently as competence grows. The group should be at a similar level and all capable of reading with at least 95% accuracy (142)." This shaped the vision of Fountas and Pinnell, who went back to the United States and proposed small groups of similar students reading complete texts with levels of accuracy to provide opportunities for targeted instruction.

Similarly, in her classic text *Reading To, With, and By Children*, Margaret Mooney (1990) discussed guided reading as "a careful match of text and children to ensure each child … is able to enjoy and control the story throughout the first reading (45)." She argued for the need for flexibility in small group instruction and instruction that led to independence. Mooney clearly pointed out that this was not just a new name for old models of instruction. This was a new way of conceiving small group instruction. Mooney even delineated instructional models of guided reading for emergent, early level, and fluency stage readers.

Proposed as a classroom practice that would provide **good first teaching for all children**, *guided reading became a possible structure for reducing the number of children who would need individual interventions or, at least, provide classroom instruction that could support and build on the work done in those individual intervention programs.*

You can see the influence in the New Zealand models of guided reading discussed by Fountas and Pinnell. Proposed as a classroom practice that would provide *good first teaching for all children*, guided reading became a possible structure for reducing the number of children who would need individual interventions or, at least, provide classroom instruction that could support and build on the work done in those individual intervention programs. Fountas and Pinnell originally (1996) identified the following essential elements of guided reading:

- Teacher works with children in small groups who *are similar* in their development and are able to read about the same level of text. (Notice they didn't say the children had to be *exactly* the same.)

- Teacher introduces the stories and assists children's reading in ways that help to develop reading strategies, so children can reach the goal of being able to read independently and silently.

- Each child reads whole texts with an emphasis on reading increasingly challenging books over time.

- Children are grouped and regrouped in a dynamic process that involves ongoing observation and assessment.

In their 2012 article, they discuss a few changes in the infusion of guided reading, such as differentiated instruction, conducting benchmark assessment conferences, using running records to determine reading levels, using gradients to select books, giving attention to the elements of proficient reading, using elements of the guided reading lesson, and building classroom libraries.

In looking across multiple sources and voices defining guided reading, Michael Opitz and I (2008) identified eight common principles that framed guided reading instruction:

1. Guided reading starts with the belief that all children have the ability to become literate and requires that teachers determine what the child already knows and what the child needs to learn to design instruction accordingly (Soderman, Gregory & McCarty, 2005).

2. All children need to be taught by a skilled teacher during guided reading in order to maximize their full potential in reading (Snow, Burns & Griffin, 1998).

3. The purpose of guided reading is to help children internalize specific strategies they can use independently to successfully read a text. They are able to monitor themselves and choose from a range of strategies because they have developed a self-extending system (Clay, 1991).

4. Children learn to read by reading. It is important that independent and instructional level texts are used in guided reading to help children become competent readers (Allington, 2001).

5. Guided reading is designed to help children construct meaning, exposing them to higher-level thinking activities especially as they engage in discussions about the texts they read. (Gambrell & Almasi, 1996).

6. Guided reading should help children become metacognitive: knowing what they know; the why and how of reading (Brown & Palinscar, 1982; Raphael, 1982).

7. Children need to experience joy and delight as a result of the reading experience. We are not only teaching children to read, we are also teaching children to be readers (Gambrell, 1996; Watson, 1997).

8. The successful guided reading lesson relies on a three-part lesson plan (Before/During/After Reading) with one focal point for the overall lesson and the use of specific teaching strategies at each phase of the lesson (Hornsby, 2000).

We are not only teaching children to read, we are also teaching children to be readers.

Many others have defined essential elements of guided reading; however, all tend to agree that guided reading is planned, intentional, focused instruction where the teacher helps students, usually in small group settings, learn more about the reading process (Ford & Opitz, 2011). Fountas and Pinnell (1996) described it as "an instructional context for supporting each reader's development of effective strategies for processing novel texts at increasingly challenging levels of difficulty (25)."

If these eight common principles were operationalized, how would this new vision of small group reading differ from the previous models? Some differences would be very visible. The materials at the heart of guided reading would be different from materials we had used in the past. Small group reading instruction that focused on homogenous settings relied on basal reading materials, such as stories in the grade-level anthologies that made up the reading series. After the pendulum moved back to small group instruction that included guided reading, teachers utilized whole texts, usually from sets of leveled texts. Interestingly, as leveled texts became popular, basal companies began to package sets of leveled texts in their programs so the textbook series would lend itself to the guided reading practices that were emerging in classrooms.

Other changes would be less obvious. From the outside, guided reading groups would be based on the students' reading levels. For some, they would look like the old ability groups of the past. They have a similar makeup and size. So what would be different? Actually, if a teacher sees reading levels as primarily a tool to identify, sort, and group children, then guided reading groups may be more like the small groups of the past, especially the more static those groups become. When students identify themselves and the texts they read using levels as labels, we are close to returning to the past flaws of homogenous small group instruction.

A more subtle difference is reflected in the eight common principles. The difference is mostly manifested in the instruction that the teacher provides during the small group. Fountas and Pinnell observed: "Guided reading has shifted the lens in the teaching of reading to a focus on a deeper understanding of how readers build effective processing systems over time and an examination of the critical role of texts and expert teaching in the process" (p. 4). The instruction of guided reading groups is informed more from transactional models of learning rather than the transmission-oriented models of the past. The bottom line in guided reading is that the teacher is teaching *learners*, not just *texts*.

In the past, teachers often felt compelled to cover material—teach texts. In Durkin's (1978) classic study, small group instruction was basal driven. Teacher-directed, round-robin, oral reading followed by literal-level questions was more often than not the type of instruction used. There was very little guided reading taking place in these groups. Children were marched through each story with little regard to what the child needed or desired. The thought in transmission models is that the student brings little to the table, so it all must be taught directly. These pedagogic models were rooted in theories of reading as a set of skills that were mastered in a bottom-up approach from small parts to whole in a linear fashion. For the most part, one size of instruction fits all with these models.

The eight principles would suggest another vision of instruction using transactional models. By selecting the use of the term "guided" to describe these reading groups, instruction is less about teachers transmitting information and more about teachers coaching the students. This is a critical difference in conceptualizing small group instruction. In fact, Taylor and her colleagues have suggested that it may be the most critical difference. In their study, schools were identified as least effective, moderately effective, and most effective at improving reading performance and achievement by traditional measures when serving similar students. *Coaching during reading* was the one practice that seemed to occur with significantly greater frequency in the most effective schools

> The bottom line in guided reading is that the teacher is teaching **learners, not just texts**.

(Taylor, Pearson, Clark & Walpole, 1999). If we also look at the earliest gradual release of responsibility models, demonstrations were described as a form of explicit instruction in which the teacher had more responsibility than the learner (Pearson & Gallagher, 1983). In guided instruction, the learner shares the responsibility with the teacher. Sometimes the teacher leads the students, and other times the students lead the teacher.

The best metaphor for thinking about the instruction during guided reading would be scaffolding. Teachers would take time to know where their students are at and where they need to be in order to build scaffolds that support the students as they move from one point to the other. Scaffolding would require teachers to plan sensitive, responsive instruction to provide the bridge between those two points. Boyle and Peregoy (1998) listed five criteria defining literacy scaffolds. Scaffolds:

- Are applied to reading and writing activities aimed at functional, meaningful communication found in entire texts;

- Make use of language and discourse patterns that repeat themselves and are therefore predictable;

- Provide a model, offered by the teacher or by peers, for comprehending and providing particular written language patterns;

- Support students in comprehending and producing written language at a level slightly beyond their competence in the absence of the scaffold;

- And are temporary and may be dispensed with when the student is ready to work without them (p. 152).

In other words, we could potentially prevent the return to problems of the past by moving to a type of small group instruction that is based less on skill-coverage and more on strategy-based constructivism as the key focus. We would shift from just covering materials, to instead teaching learners. Or as Burkins and Croft (2010) suggested, we would be holding *guided reading sessions* not just teaching *guided reading lessons*. The key objective is that teachers would be less concerned about covering lessons and more concerned in using the sessions to help learners become more proficient as readers.

> *The key objective is that teachers would be less concerned about covering lessons and more concerned in using the sessions to help learners become more proficient as readers.*

Where Are We at with Guided Reading Practices?

If principles such as these informed our return to small group instruction, then the vision of guided reading would be quite different from the homogenous small groups of the past.

Is that what happened? Nearly 20 years have passed since Fountas and Pinnell published their book on guided reading. That is enough time to stand back and see whether that vision of guided reading has been achieved. We do know that in the past, certain hot topics in the reading community have meant a variety of things to different educators (Bergeron, 1990). Variations in understandings often lead to significant differences in how practices get implemented. Two extreme responses can be observed. The first is dogmatism—a rigid orthodoxy toward one right way to do things, no matter the context, learners, or texts.

> We need to be cautious when an educational practice like guided reading begins to develop the trappings of an *orthodoxy*. A *one-size-fits-all* viewpoint begins to shape practice, and teachers find themselves struggling to make the "conventional wisdom ideal" fit their unique contexts and classrooms (Opitz & Ford, 2001, p. 1).

Burkins and Croft (2010) were still warning about how rigid adherence can lead "to forced fits and instructional confusion" (p. xviii) more than a decade after *Guided Reading* was published. On the other hand, the other extreme response might be labeled as a *hinterland effect*, in which some see and label whatever they are currently doing as the new practice even when it is clearly not. Neither extreme is desirable. This may be why even Fountas and Pinnell (2012) suggested the reality of guided reading is that "continuous professional learning is needed to ensure that this instructional approach is powerful" (p. 4). The intent of this book is to add to that professional learning.

My colleague Michael Opitz and I (2008) conducted one of the few national surveys of primary teachers for a sense of what the landscape related to guided reading practices was. We surveyed more than 1,500 K–2 teachers nationwide to get a sense of their understandings and practices related to guided reading. At that point in time, it allowed us to see what we really knew about what teachers understood and did in their efforts to implement guided reading. The survey focused on five critical questions:

1.   What is the purpose of guided reading groups?

2.   What grouping techniques should be used?

3.   What texts should be used?

4.   How is instruction planned with and away from the teacher?

5.   How are learners assessed during guided reading?

Since that study, others have surveyed teachers about guided reading practices, including Ferguson and Wilson (2009), who worked with 40 K–5 teachers from schools in southwest Texas. Reeves (2011) surveyed 28 teachers at an urban school in western New York prepared to teach the specific model of guided reading reflected in the materials by Fountas and Pinnell. Their survey results will also be incorporated into this analysis of current guided reading practices.

I have included a modified version of the original Ford and Opitz survey in this book. (See the Guided Reading Practices Survey, starting on page 180 in the Appendix.) Readers may want to complete the survey to reflect on their current guided reading practices. This will allow them to self-evaluate where they are with guided reading and reflect on what they would need to do to move their practices forward. Interestingly, when we aggregated results, we noticed that there were some key areas teachers may need to look at in order to move guided reading forward. These included confusion about the purposes of guided reading, considerable variation in grouping techniques, a tendency toward static membership in groups, over-reliance on narrative texts, inconsistent use of instructional-level texts, extensive use of centers and seat work, and frequent use of informal assessments (Ford & Opitz, 2008). I want to point out that the responses are from teachers, 91 percent of which said they were very or well informed about guided reading. These were teachers that knew about guided reading. So let's look more specifically at each of the previously identified questions to get a sense of where teachers were in their knowledge and use of guided reading practices.

What Is the Purpose of Guided Reading Groups?

Purpose clearly needs to drive decision-making with any instructional practice teachers might be using. Teachers were asked to identify what they felt was the purpose of guided reading. Four purposes were listed, and teachers were restricted to choosing one option: 1) provide demonstrations of skills, strategies, responses, and/or procedures; 2) provide interventions around scaffolded instruction for students; 3) facilitate a group response among students around a shared text; or 4) facilitate a group response among students around multiple texts. Two-thirds of the teachers identified providing demonstrations as the primary focus of guided reading. Eighteen percent of the teachers identified scaffolded instruction as the key purpose of guided reading. The remaining teachers saw facilitation of response to a shared text (12 percent) and across multiple texts (3 percent) as the primary focus. When also asked whether guided reading was linked to other aspects of their literacy programs, two-thirds of the teachers reported that they linked their guided reading to other classroom instruction, including shared and independent reading, writing instruction, and content-area instruction. The others reported that they did not connect their guided reading instruction to other classroom instruction.

Some (Opitz & Ford, 2001; Routman, 2000) have argued that in an expanded vision of guided reading, all four reasons stated above may be important reasons for using small groups during reading programs. This may be especially true if the teacher is working with older students (Fawson & Reutzel, 2000). In primary classrooms, however, the purpose of guided reading often focuses on providing scaffolded instruction for students. Since most of the teachers responding were primary teachers, the results of this survey were a bit surprising. More teachers saw providing demonstrations rather than scaffolded instruction as the primary purpose of guided reading. This surfaces a concern about how the nature of the teacher-learner relationship is conceived by teachers during guided reading.

Burkins and Croft (2010) actually stated that the direct teaching of skills and strategies should be largely outside guided reading. Referencing Clay, they describe guided reading as the arena in which skills and strategies that have already been taught and demonstrated are actually used by the learners under the watchful eye of the teacher. Explicit instruction often is a quick detour to get the students back on the road to reading the text. Remember that in a gradual release of responsibility model, demonstrations were described as an explicit form of instruction in which the teacher has a more active role than the learner. Scaffolded instruction suggests a form of instruction in which the learner is actively involved with teacher. "Guided" suggests a type of instruction that would be less about modeling and more about coaching. It's less about the teacher showing a child how to use a strategy and more about providing support as the child uses the strategy. If the outcome of guided reading is to teach for transfer and independent regulation, scaffolded instruction is crucial. Yes, teachable moments are seized to provide explicit instruction to the students, but they are usually planned to follow the lead of the students as they operate with the texts.

Sometimes teachers repeat demonstrations used in large groups during guided reading to provide a small group of students who need another look at the strategy extra exposure. This makes sense. Why provide review to all students (or no students) when just a few students need an additional dose of the large group instruction? If one-third of the teachers, however, were not connecting their guided reading to other classroom instruction and using their small groups primarily as a time to provide initial demonstrations to students, it surfaced a concern about whether this is the most powerful way to use guided reading.

Finally, fostering response within and across texts is also an important issue. What is the role of discussion during the guided reading session? Does the focus of guiding extend beyond just "reading" the text to also include talking about the text? Initially, many teachers argued that constraints precluded planning for and implementing both guided reading and response discussion groups (like those seen in literature circles) in classroom reading programs. Abandoning one for the sake of the other, however, seemed less productive than discussing how to bring elements of both practices together during small group reading instruction. The danger in guided reading instruction that never included response was that the reader's attention may be narrowly focused at the micro-level of the text (words, sentence-level comprehension, literal understandings), and looking at text beyond this level may be ignored. Repeated instruction at the micro-level may lead some readers to believe that is the primary purpose of reading, and they may not be well equipped to handle text when they need to move beyond that.

As we look at the landscape of guided reading now, the question we need to ask is: Do teachers clearly understand the primary purposes of guided reading? In the time since this survey was conducted, have teachers gained additional expertise? Do K–2 teachers still view guided reading as an opportunity to demonstrate skills and strategies rather

Repeated instruction at the micro-level may lead some readers to believe that is the primary purpose of reading, and they may not be well equipped to handle text when they need to move beyond that.

than to provide scaffolded instruction? If so, how do we help teachers fully understand the difference between these two purposes? In a recent conversation with area literacy coaches, they surfaced their frustration that many of the teachers with whom they worked saw guided reading as something that is done. Perhaps with the packaging and presenting of guided reading as a program, this is not a surprising conclusion. But if teachers are primarily back to teaching a program versus teaching the learners in front of them, re-examining the instructional purposes of guided reading may be a critical issue. There is a difference between using "parts of a guided reading lesson and using guided reading to bring readers from where they are to as far as we can take them in a given school year" (Fountas & Pinnell, 2012, p. 4).

The responses regarding curricular integration bring additional questions to the surface. Have practices changed since this survey? If students benefit from seeing connections among different components of their literacy program, do teachers make those connections during guided reading? Certain experts have laid out plans to connect typical elements of a literacy block like read-aloud, shared reading, and independent reading with guided reading (Burkins and Croft, 2010). In today's classrooms, however, guided reading is often treated as separate block within an instructional organizational format or even relegated to a block outside the regular classroom program. When guided reading is driven by a set of materials separate from other core materials being used in the reading program, should we be surprised that many teachers might view guided reading as something separate from other instruction? Should we be surprised that students may not transfer what is learned during guided reading to other parts of the school day? If we are not teaching for transfer, are we only teaching for the moments at the guided reading table?

If we are not teaching for transfer, are we only teaching for the moments at the guided reading table?

Do current conceptualizations of guided reading include elements of response beyond the word level? The role of facilitating response as a part of the guided reading lesson is a critical aspect of instruction. Teachers in the primary grades need to see this as one purpose of guided reading if students are to see meaning-making beyond the word level. Though it is clear that some teachers see accuracy as the driving force for guided reading, discussion of the text is clearly identified within the structure of more recently published guided reading lessons (Fountas & Pinnell, 2012).

What Grouping Techniques Should Be Used?

If there was one overarching theme related to grouping techniques, it was variability. Most teachers reported using four small groups during guided reading, though there was significant variation. At least one-fifth of the teachers reported using five or more guided reading groups, while another fifth reported using one or two groups. While at one time, some experts did use the term to describe large group reading experiences within their structures (Cunningham, Hall & Cunningham, 2000), is it truly guided when a teacher is only using one group? Probably, but only if it was a very small class or a very similar group of children. Teachers predominantly used homogenous grouping in forming groups. When indicating all the ways they grouped students (so results could exceed 100 percent), the results showed that 60 percent grouped students homogeneously based on developmental levels, 40 percent by needs, and six percent by other methods. It should be noted that 22 percent of the teachers also reported using heterogeneous grouping during guided reading.

On average, guided reading groups included six students. Teachers met with their groups on average 22 minutes at 3.3 times a week. Again, results showed great variation. Over one-fourth reported meeting with their groups every day, while another fourth reported meeting with their groups once or twice a week. A critical dimension in guided reading was the dynamic nature of the grouping arrangements versus the static nature of the grouping arrangements of the past. Twenty-five percent of the teachers said they changed their groups at least weekly, and 13 percent said at least monthly. The majority (53 percent), however, reported changing their groups less than once a month. An additional 12 percent reported they never changed the membership of their groups.

What is most apparent in these results—and most problematic for those supporting teachers in implementing and improving their use of guided reading—is the variation reported in these grouping techniques. It was interesting to note that even when teachers were prepared to implement guided reading using the same model and materials, variation still existed (Reeves, 2011). Take the variation in the number of groups used during guided reading, for example. If some teachers are attempting to juggle five or more groups while others are using one or two groups, professional development needs will certainly be quite different. Add to that the variation in the frequency of meeting with groups. Some teachers are struggling to meet with each group every day. Others are meeting with groups once or twice a week, falling short of what some have suggested would be a more powerful implementation of this practice. If those teachers are in the same building or district, staff development will need to be tailored to provide support in different ways. The former may need to explore management and organization ideas as they work to meet with each group and keep other students engaged on a daily basis. The latter may need help fully embracing techniques for greater differentiation during guided reading.

Another concern is the implementation of guided reading that results in fairly static group membership. The survey responses appear to indicate that we have yet to achieve necessary dynamic grouping arrangements. As teachers rediscover the value of homogenous small groups in reading programs, they must be careful not to return to what got us in trouble in the past—the inflexible use of homogenous small groups. Guided reading proponents suggest that groups be flexible and fluid. Student membership should be constantly re-evaluated and groups re-formed as needed. Teachers already working to implement a vision of guided reading with more dynamic grouping arrangements may need to have support in successfully doing this; while teachers who have not embraced

As teachers rediscover the value of homogenous small groups in reading programs, they must be careful not to return to what got us in trouble in the past—the inflexible use of homogenous small groups. Guided reading proponents suggest that groups be flexible and fluid.

this aspect may need help in seeing how to make static arrangements more flexible.

The only issue that saw less variation was how teachers grouped their students. Since most guidelines suggest working with groups of students who are more alike than they are different, grouping students by levels and/or needs seems to capture the spirit of guided reading. It is important that teachers see the difference between grouping by level and grouping by need. In a classic example described by Clay (1993), two children who have read the same level book with the same degree of accuracy and with the same miscues could be quite different in their strategy needs. While guided reading advocates stress a better match between readers and texts, this often is interpreted to mean no matter what the purpose is for small group instruction, the children are always grouped by levels. In Chapter Four of this book, the topic of leveling will be looked at more closely. One concern about leveling is that it simplifies a very complex relationship among the text, reader, and context, often ignoring factors (social dynamics between learners, affective factors like interest in selected topic or text) that should be considered when forming groups. On the other hand, complex leveling systems with many discrete levels of texts and readers complicate the simple idea of matching increasingly challenging texts with readers, which is at the heart of guided reading (Glasswell & Ford, 2011). Teachers end up with frustrating situations in trying to manage many discrete levels of readers and texts in their classrooms. Those conducting staff development need to shift some of the attention away from leveling and toward other grouping issues. One shift might be to focus on other ways to flexibly group children besides using levels exclusively (Opitz & Ford, 2001; Boushey & Moser, 2009).

These findings lead to questions about the best ways of helping teachers to understand the why and how of grouping students. Clearly, group membership needs to be determined by the purpose for forming the group in the first place. Educators often seem overly concerned with the quantity issues—how many groups, how many kids in each, how long with each, how frequently they should be changed, etc. One significant question that needs attention is this: How do we shift focus from quantity issues to quality of instruction issues? The main challenge is how to help teachers understand that purpose is what should guide group formation, membership, and duration. Instead of just worrying about how many students should be in a group, the focus can shift to which students have a similar need that can be addressed in the group.

Instead of just worrying about how many students should be in a group, the focus can shift to which students have a similar need that can be addressed in the group.

What Texts Should Be Used?

The types of books used in guided reading are different from the reading materials used in small groups in the past. Teachers were asked to indicate all the different types of texts they used during guided reading. (Percentages will exceed 100 percent.) Fifty-six percent of the teachers reported using "little books" (initial, stand-alone, leveled texts from collections by the Wright Group and Rigby), 43 percent used trade books, and 24 percent used supplemental basal materials. But some of the materials used for guided reading were the same as the past. Thirty-two percent of teachers reported using basal textbooks. Teachers reported having access to an average of 400–500 texts. Teachers reported that two-thirds of the texts used in programs were narrative stories. While 36 percent of teachers use texts for their classrooms only, most share texts with other teachers in order to build collections needed for guided reading. Thirty-nine percent also share materials across their grade level, 23 percent across the primary grades, and 22 percent share texts within an entire school. Numerous leveling systems are now used in classifying books. In this survey, almost half the teachers reported using the levels identified by their basal reading systems. With regard to text selection, 83 percent of the teachers reported choosing texts used by the students during guided reading. Additionally, teachers reported that all students read texts at their instructional level 58 percent of the time.

The survey reflects the importance of access to many different types of texts when implementing a guided reading program. Currently, this seems to be limited in at least one way—narrative stories dominate. Working toward a better balance between narrative and informational texts remains a critical goal for improving guided reading. Different texts are written with different text structures, and exposing students to these structures puts them in a better position to comprehend a variety of texts in and out of school. The shortage of exposure to informational texts in primary classrooms (Duke & Bennett-Armistead, 2003; Kletzien & Mariam, 2004) and the impact on performance and achievement as seen in recent international comparisons (National Center for Education Statistics, 2003) could be addressed by helping those who use guided reading understand the variety of texts at their disposal and the importance of using this variety.

While some advocated the use of guided reading as a means for preparing students to choose their own texts (Cunningham, Hall & Cunningham, 2000; Opitz & Ford, 2001; Routman, 2000), most of the teachers chose the texts used by students. Since guidelines recommend this level of control, that was not surprising. What was surprising to observe was that teachers reported students read texts at their instructional level only a little more than half of the time. This finding is particularly troubling given that the main reason teachers are often encouraged to select the texts is that they are more knowledgeable of what the students need. This percentage certainly indicates there is still room for improvement. Guided reading was designed as a return to small group reading instruction to address the overuse of whole group instruction, during which many students were not reading texts at their instructional level. If adding guided reading doesn't lead to students spending more time with instructional-level texts, then that aspect of the program still needs to be addressed.

How do we help teachers move toward the greater use of informational texts during guided reading? If the College and Career Readiness Standards have impacted things in one significant way, it has been to call attention to the need for more nonfiction. An increasing number of nonfiction titles, even for younger and struggling readers, are available for use in guided reading programs. Some publishers have even intentionally paired narrative stories with informational texts to encourage this balance. There are also many other available texts in electronic and alternative formats, such as classroom newspapers and magazines. Teachers may need some instruction on how these texts can be used in guided reading. Likewise, they may need to see how guided reading can be integrated in content-area texts. But perhaps needs go beyond access to materials. Teachers who are used to teaching with narrative genres may need to be supported as they prepare instruction for nonfiction genres. This could very well become the focus of staff development for some teachers.

Secondly, if most teachers are selecting the texts used by students, why aren't teachers choosing texts that are at the instructional levels of their students? While we acknowledge the complexity of the interaction between the reader and the text, authors of guided reading programs use leveling systems that help teachers match a student to a text at his or her instructional level. For those supporting teachers implementing guided reading programs, we must consider whether teachers need help identifying the levels of texts they are using, assessing the performance levels of the students with whom they are working, or both.

How Is Instruction Planned with and Away from the Teacher?

The teachers reported that they had a fairly substantial two-hour language arts block with a little more than a third of the time devoted to guided reading. The teachers reported a total of 90–120 minutes in their language arts blocks. They estimated that about 37 percent of the time was devoted to guided reading (33–44 minutes). Ferguson and Wilson (2009) discovered that teachers in the primary grades tend to use guided reading on a daily basis, though that was not true for many intermediate-grade teachers. When asked about the integration of skill instruction with guided reading, teachers reported that they spent four days a week teaching explicit skills for about 25 minutes each day. Teachers reported teaching skills before (75 percent), during (69 percent), and/or after the guided reading session (47 percent).

Given that teachers reported having a two-hour block of time for language arts, what amount of time was spent with the teacher and how much time were students left to fend for themselves? If teachers are typically meeting with four groups for about 22 minutes per group, that would mean that teachers meet with each group three to four times a week. Students would receive 66–88 minutes of instruction each week if the teacher rotated systematically through the groups. On the other hand, it must be remembered that students are spending at least some of their time away from the teacher every day. In fact, students may spend up to 132 minutes a week away from the teacher while the teacher is working directly with small groups. In this rotation, the students would also spend up to two days a week without any direct contact with the teacher in the small group.

So what are students doing when they are not working directly with the teacher? Survey results suggest that most teachers rely on either the use of centers (72 percent) and/or the use of independent seat work (62 percent) to engage students when they are not working with the teacher. Some teachers (35 percent) reported having access to another adult who worked with students in a separate guided reading group. Others (30 percent) combined guided reading with reader's/writer's workshop so that students were engaged in independent reading and writing while others were working with the teacher in small groups. Only five percent reported using inquiry projects as a means to engage learners away from the teacher. The most popular centers included a listening post (68 percent), writing corner (53 percent), working with words station (49 percent), computer (48 percent), reading corner (46 percent), reading and writing the room (36 percent), math center (34 percent), art projects (32 percent), buddy reading (31 percent), and pocket chart activities (22 percent).

It was clear from this survey that teachers benefited from a significant block of time for their language arts instruction. They did not find it difficult to give adequate attention to skill instruction while implementing guided reading programs. While there are some concerns about the actual decisions being made to provide guided reading instruction directly at the table with the teacher, the data remind us that the critical factor for a successful guided reading program may not be what is happening with the teacher, but instead what is happening away from the teacher. Teachers surveyed by Ferguson and Wilson (2009) indicated that one of the major constraints of guided reading was that students were unable to work independently away from the teacher. One-fourth of the teachers surveyed by Reeves (2011) also felt this was the major limitation of guided reading.

An instructional practice that almost guarantees students will spend more time away from the teacher than with the teacher needs to be conceptualized in two dimensions. One dimension entails planning for what is done with small guided reading groups at the table. The second dimension entails planning for what indirectly guides groups and individuals when they are not with the teacher. Both dimensions work together to better ensure that the power of instruction away from the teacher rivals the power of instruction with the teacher. That is, if teachers increase the number of small guided reading groups, the potential of increasing the time that students spend away from the teacher is a given. The greater the percentage of time spent away from the teacher, the greater the need for powerful instruction away from the small group. Any practice that results in questionable instruction during the majority of its allocated time needs to be re-examined.

Unfortunately, the whole notion of instruction away from the teacher was often marginalized in early professional resources about guided reading implementation. So much attention was given to what the teacher was supposed to do during the guided reading lesson that little attention was given to what the students were supposed to do when they weren't with the teacher. This looms as a significant factor in good professional development that is provided to teachers trying to successfully implement guided reading programs. Early on, Kane (1995) suggested that this may be the number one key to successful implementation. If the teacher does not have a structure in place that allows him or her to work attentively with small groups and individuals during guided reading, this aspect of classroom management could negatively impact the quality of instruction being provided. This suggests that teachers need professional development that includes not only how to directly support students during guided reading groups, but also how to indirectly support the remaining students working away from the teacher.

So what do they do with the rest of the kids? That's usually the number one question by teachers. One reasonable response focuses on helping teachers see how other parallel classroom processes like reader's/writer's workshop might be integrated within the guided reading block and provide students with literacy activities as they work away from the teacher. Regardless of the answer, teachers need to understand the importance of instruction that happens when their students are independently engaged. They also need to understand the difference between independent busy work and independent work, such as inquiry projects, that will help students become independent and strategic readers. If teachers are going to link learning centers with guided reading as the primary answer to the question, "What do we do with the rest of the kids?," can learning centers truly be *learning* centers? Can we move teachers to centers that are grounded in the needs of the learners and the demands of the curriculum, that are accessible but also meaningful, and that not only create excitement about reading and writing but actually engage children in additional practice with reading and writing? This could make the instruction away from the teacher as powerful as the instruction with the teacher.

How Are Learners Assessed during Guided Reading?

If scaffolded instruction is at the heart of guided reading, the ability to make fluid, flexible grouping decisions is critical. While the ability to make appropriate grouping decisions depends on the teacher's ongoing assessment of learners, even more importantly, the ability to make appropriate instructional decisions depends on ongoing assessment. Small group reading instruction of the past often relied solely on end-of-level assessments built into programs, but teachers implementing guided reading need to gain expertise at conducting ongoing assessments and interpreting results. The findings of this survey indicate that four assessment tools seemed to be the most critical. More than 70 percent of the teachers reported using daily observation, running

Can we move teachers to centers that are grounded in the needs of the learners and the demands of the curriculum, that are accessible but also meaningful, and that not only create excitement about reading and writing but actually engage children in additional practice with reading and writing? This could make the instruction away from the teacher as powerful as the instruction with the teacher.

records, and/or informal reading inventories to assess students. Forty-five percent of the teachers also used the assessments built into their reading programs. Twenty-one percent of the teachers informed their thinking by reviewing students' records on file from previous years. Running records have received much attention as an assessment tool for guided reading programs. Teachers were fairly evenly divided in their use of reading records: monthly (32 percent), more than monthly (33 percent), and less than once a month (36 percent).

The discovery that teachers use at least four assessment techniques (daily observation, running records, informal reading inventories, and basal reading program assessments) provides evidence about the importance of informal assessment when making decisions about how to help all children maximize their reading potential. But make no mistake: Assessment is still an issue that requires additional professional development. The first issue is that reading is a complex behavior, and a variety of assessment techniques must be used to tap these different behaviors. For example, attitude and interests significantly impact reading performances but are virtually ignored in guided reading assessment practices. Assessing each area would put teachers in a better position to make decisions about their students. Not only are some aspects of reading under-assessed, other dimensions may be over-assessed or assessed separately. For example, assessing word accuracy and speed as separate from the analysis of actual miscues may lead to interventions that assist some but may not help others. Again, the critical issue for professional development may begin with preparing teachers to administer assessment tools but cannot end until teachers feel competent and comfortable analyzing assessment results and using those insights to plan better guided reading instruction for the students.

Given the limited amount of allocated instructional time and the many mandates placed on teachers, how do we help teachers understand the variety of assessments that are available to them? How do we show them how these can be integrated into a manageable system that they will actually use to inform their thinking and impact their instruction? Another area of concern has to do with some assessments that are less than helpful yet are mandated. How do we help educators understand how best to assess components of reading such as fluency and why the assessment of it might be important?

What's Next?

What did we learn from asking teachers to discuss issues and ideas related to their practice of guided reading? We began with five critical questions about purposes, techniques, texts, instruction, and assessment. As you can see, the interpretation of these survey results raised at least as many issues as it provided answers. Reeves' (2011) survey results echoed similar areas in need of more attention: clarity of purpose and format, techniques for instruction with and away from the teacher, and integration with content areas. The concerns surfaced may be used to frame an evaluation of existing guided reading practices in an effort to make them stronger and more powerful. Figure 1B on page 32 provides key questions to help guide that discussion. The next chapters in this book will also provide additional insights and ideas.

Figure 1B: Examining Where We Are and Where We Need to Go Next with Guided Reading

Area of Concern	Questions to Explore
Purpose	• Is the purpose for the use of guided reading appropriate and clear? • Is the focus on using guided reading to help learners grow? • Are we focused on doing guided reading lessons or conducting guided reading sessions (following the lesson with little consideration of the learner vs. using the lessons to meet the needs of the learners)? • Is scaffolded instruction at the heart of what is done during guided reading? • When are demonstrations used during guided reading, and do they reflect the best use of instructional time? Would they be better positioned in whole group instruction? • How is response generated and utilized during guided reading lessons? Is there enough balance between focus on words (accuracy) and beyond the words (comprehension)?
Integration	• Is guided reading connected to other critical parts of the literacy program? • Is what is learned during guided reading transferred by students to other reading and writing experiences?
Grouping Techniques	• Are the students receiving the appropriate amount of support they need from guided reading? • Is the membership of guided reading groups examined regularly and changed to reflect the needs of the learners?
Texts	• Do the texts being used during guided reading present appropriate, increasingly complex demands for instruction? • Is there a balance in the texts being used to help learners meet the demands of a variety of text structures, features, and formats?
Schedule	• Is enough time allocated for guided reading? • Could the language arts block time be structured differently? • Does the rotation allow those with the greatest needs to receive the support warranted?
Time Away from the Teacher	• What are students doing away from the teacher? • Does the power of those activities rival the power of instruction with the teacher? • Does engagement in those activities increase the value of time away from the teacher? • Does engagement in those activities lead to growth for the learners?
Assessment	• How are formative assessments being used during guided reading? • Are we learning what we need to know with the assessments we are using? • How are we using what we are learning from the assessments to inform our subsequent instruction with learners?

CHAPTER TWO:
Why Is Guided Reading Still Important? What Is the Purpose of Guided Reading?

> Differentiation champions an atmosphere in which teachers strive to do whatever it takes to ensure that [all students] grow as much as they possibly can each day, each week, and throughout the year.
>
> *Tomlinson, 1999*

Having looked at where we have been and where we are at with guided reading, it is important to make sure guided reading is clearly defined as we discuss its purpose and why it is still important. Let's remember that Fountas and Pinnell (1996) defined guided reading as "an instructional context for supporting each reader's development of effective strategies for processing novel texts at increasingly challenging levels of difficulty" (p. 25). As previously stated, most experts describe guided reading as planned, intentional, focused instruction where the teacher helps diverse students, usually in small group settings, learn more about the reading process (Ford & Opitz, 2011). Knowing this, I want to help clarify this description by looking closely at what guided reading is and what guided reading is not. (See Figure 2A on page 34.) In doing so, the purpose and value of guided reading will become even more apparent. Similarly, others have identified the misunderstandings and new understandings of guided reading (Burkins & Croft, 2010) as well as the romance and reality of decades of guided reading (Fountas & Pinnell, 2012). My list begins with an important reminder that guided reading is not the same as the traditional use of ability-based small groups of the past. If you need to convince yourself or others that guided reading is distinguishable from traditional reading groups, see detailed comparisons others have made (e.g., Schulman & daCruz Payne, 2000; Fountas & Pinnell, 1996; and The Wright Group, 1996). My list ends with another important reminder that guided reading is not an end in and of itself. Guided reading is a means toward an end defined by the ultimate goal of moving learners toward independence (Fountas & Pinnell, 1996).

Figure 2A: The acronym GR is used to represent "guided reading" in this chart.

What Guided Reading IS NOT	What Guided Reading IS
GR IS NOT the same as the homogeneous small groups (robins, bluebirds, and crows) of the past.	GR IS a dynamic, flexible use of small groups to target specific needs and scaffold learning for students.
GR IS NOT the entire reading program; GR IS NOT the only time during the day that the teacher is teaching reading.	GR IS part of a comprehensive literacy program that focuses on teaching reading and writing throughout the school day.
GR IS NOT something you do by following a script or a program outline.	GR IS an opportunity for responsive teaching in which we teach to the needs of the students.
GR IS NOT an intervention.	GR IS an essential element of universal instruction made available to all learners within high-quality, regular classroom instruction. Varying the frequency, duration, intensity, or focus of GR can reposition it as an intervention.
GR IS NOT a separate component of the literacy program.	GR operates best when it IS connected to other aspects of the classroom literacy program, including read-alouds, shared reading, content instruction, and independent reading.
GR IS NOT solely what is done at the table with the teacher.	GR must be conceptualized to include what IS done independently by students away from the table.
GR IS NOT instruction focused exclusively on word-level strategies and accurate oral reading.	GR IS focused on both word-level and text-level strategies (i.e., accuracy with meaning making).
GR IS NOT one model of instruction that works for students at any developmental level.	GR IS tailored to the developmental needs of the readers with whom it is being used. GR includes different models to meet these needs.
GR IS NOT exclusively taught with leveled texts.	GR IS a time to use a wide variety of appealing and high-quality texts in lessons for readers.
GR IS NOT an end in and of itself. Its intent is NOT to make good guided readers.	GR IS a means to an end. The end is always to develop independent readers.

What Are the Purposes of Guided Reading?

Richardson (2009) argued that the extra time, energy, and effort that implementing guided reading requires is worth it. "Students differ in their reading development. Because students differ, teachers must use a variety of assessments to discover what their students need to learn. They must also provide differentiated small group instruction that targets those specific needs" (p. 267). Fountas and Pinnell (1996) echoed that message when stating guided reading "gives children the opportunity to develop as individual readers while participating in a socially supportive activity" (p. 1). For me, that is why guided reading matters.

When used effectively, guided reading:

- Targets similar specific needs across learners in small groups;

- Targets specific needs for individual learners within small groups;

- Scaffolds learning to accelerate the growth of similar learners in small groups;

- Scaffolds learning to accelerate the growth of individual learners within small groups;

- Provides opportunities for teachers to observe similar learners in small groups and provide responsive teaching;

- Provides opportunities for teachers to observe individual learners within small groups and provide responsive teaching;

- Can be positioned for greater intensity and impact by adjusting frequency, duration, focus, and monitoring;

- Can be restructured as an intervention when added as an additional layer beyond universal instruction;

- Supports and enhances other aspects of the comprehensive literacy program (read-alouds, shared reading, and independent reading);

- Encourages learners to use inherent text-based supports and face new manageable challenges through the use of a variety of texts that are carefully matched to learners and needs (Hornsby, 2000);

- Allows the teacher to focus attention on the learners' application of strategic behaviors at both the word and text level to lead learners toward independence in problem-solving and meaning making as readers and writers; and

- Sends a message to all learners that they are capable of becoming proficient readers while acknowledging the varying rates of development of different learners (Schulman & daCruz Payne, 2000).

Why Is Guided Reading Still Important?

For me, the rationale for guided reading is grounded in the need for differentiated instruction. P. David Pearson (2009) observed: "Kids are who they are. They bring what they bring. And we need to stop seeing this as an instructional inconvenience." It would be nice if all kids showed up at the classroom perfect, but they don't. Students arrive with different instructional needs and as soon as they cross into the classroom space, it becomes our responsibility to meet those specific needs. All teachers need tools, structures, and resources to help them meet those needs. Guided reading remains one of the most important means for bringing differentiated instruction into the classroom.

In her book, *The Differentiated Classroom*, Tomlinson (1999) initially theorized that differentiated instruction (DI) could be accomplished by thinking about three elements of instruction: the content, the process, and the product. This model suggests DI is mainly about doing different things

Students arrive with different instructional needs and as soon as they cross into the classroom space, it becomes our responsibility to meet those specific needs.

for different learners. In the end, it leads to an unwieldy vision of DI with teachers juggling a variety of different activities for all kids but doing very little meaningful instruction for any (Schmoker, 2010). DI is not just about teachers doing different things for different learners. DI is about teachers doing the right different things for different students.

The problem with the Tomlinson model for literacy instruction is when content is critical for becoming a more proficient reader and writer, the content is probably needed by all learners. Unlike some subject areas where a teacher can differentiate content by asking some students to learn about one country and other students to learn about another country, it is harder to do that in literacy. You can't tell some students to learn about these sounds and others to learn about other sounds since knowing all sounds is critical for all readers. The critical literacy content needs to be accessible for all. Differentiation is not just about switching content for different learners. Differentiation is about knowing what critical content some students know and others don't, so you can target the content individuals need most in your instruction.

Similarly, it is not as easy to differentiate processes for learning during reading and writing. Readers and writers get better at reading and writing by reading and writing. In some subject areas, students' processes for learning could be differentiated. For example, in studying countries, some students might read about them, others might view video excerpts to learn about them, and some might even visit those countries (actually or virtually). But we need to be careful about varying the processes for learning in literacy programs. For example, if some students are asked to make meaning by reading the text independently and others are allowed to listen to the text on an audio source, one needs to acknowledge that these are two entirely different experiences. One leads to a greater impact in moving learners toward greater proficiency in reading. The other outsources the reading (Hiebert, 2014). The audio allows the learner to make meaning, but it falls short of teaching him or her how to make meaning. Likewise, if one writer makes meaning by orally dictating a story recorded by the teacher, it will lead to a different impact than a child who makes meaning as he or she records his or her own story. While we may use these different techniques for children at different points of development, eventually all learners need to do their own reading and writing.

But producing products that consume significant amounts of instructional time without providing too many opportunities for using reading and writing—even when those products can be differentiated—might need to be re-examined.

Finally, differentiating products—what the students are expected to produce during reading and writing—allows for some variation for different learners. Products that involve responding with reading and writing provide more opportunities to practice reading and writing. Other products might involve less reading and writing. They might involve more art, music, or performance. These alternatives can create excitement about what has been read or written. That excitement can lead to more reading and writing as well. But producing products that consume significant amounts of instructional time without providing too many opportunities for using reading and writing—even when those products can be differentiated—might need to be re-examined. Is that the best way to differentiate when instructional time always seems to be so limited?

A different way to look at differentiation within a literacy block is to switch from looking at content, process, and products and to look more closely at texts, grouping patterns, and levels of support. These are three critical things to consider when making decisions to target literacy instruction for different learners. Decisions about texts, grouping arrangements, and levels of support are usually within the control of the classroom teacher. In considering these three factors, differentiation can become less daunting and more do-able (Opitz & Ford, 2008).

In exploring these factors, four basic models emerge. (See Figure 2B on page 39.) If the teacher uses a common text for all learners for whatever reason—practicality, community, universal instruction—then differentiation can take place, but it requires adjusting the grouping formats and the levels of support given to different students. One model that addresses differentiation within whole class models is the Grouping without Tracking model (Paratore, 1990). The lesson starts together during the pre-reading phase. When the gradual release model moves closer to the independent takeover by the learners, the teacher asks a critical question: "Which of my students are now ready to take over the reading on their own, and which of my students will need additional support to take over the reading?" This allows for an adjustment in the grouping pattern. The whole class divides into two groups. One group will begin working independently, indirectly guided by the teacher. This group will use the structures put in place during the pre-reading phase, where the focus, process, tools, and expectations were laid out and modeled for the students. The other group, which hopefully will be smaller, could flow into a guided reading group led directly by the teacher with the possibility of additional needed support through targeted, scaffolded instruction.

A second model is the Jigsaw model (Aronson, 1979). This too often involves a common text but one that can be easily divided into parts. Consider a nonfiction text that might be about a specific topic (rain forest animals) and then presents descriptions of specific examples (different rain forest animals). The text does not have to be read in a linear fashion. Different students can read about different animals and report out to synthesize the entire text. Again, the lesson can start in the pre-reading stage with common instruction about the topic and text. After a good foundation has been built, the teacher can develop a jigsaw plan, asking a slightly different question: "Which students should work together and on which part of the text?" Once groups are formed, the teacher will guide some indirectly by the focus, process, tools, and structures put in place and modeled during the common instruction. This allows the teacher to guide other groups more directly. One or two guided reading groups can flow out of the common instruction. Groups of students in need of some additional support get a piece of the text that is more manageable and have access to support from the teacher to help meet the expectations given to other groups. Every group has a piece of the text and their own information to share when the class comes back together to share what they've learned, with the goal of going more deeply into the topic.

By intentionally varying the text, the grouping assignment, and the level of support (how long and how often the group meets with the teacher), differentiation becomes more do-able than daunting. This clearly positions guided reading as a critical component in providing differentiated instruction within the classroom literacy program.

A third model is what is usually seen in Guided Reading components of literacy programs. What if you have access to multiple copies of the same texts at different difficulty levels? The best way to differentiate instruction would be to give different titles to different groups of readers. This allows for even more targeted instruction to be provided. By intentionally varying the text, the grouping assignment, and the level of support (how long and how often the group meets with the teacher), differentiation becomes more do-able than daunting. This clearly positions guided reading as a critical component in providing differentiated instruction within the classroom literacy program. It is one of the important purposes of guided reading and a strong reason why guided reading is still important. Other small group models like Literature Circles (Daniels, 2002) and Comprehension Focus Groups (Dorn & Soffos, 2011) can be used in this manner.

A final model would be created by having unlimited texts. This way, teachers could vary the text assignments even more effectively in matching a reader and a book. The teacher can consider level, interest, and other individual reader factors. Common instruction can be provided to all readers, especially when topics, procedures, skills, and strategies seem to apply across a wide variety of texts and readers. Application of what was taught during the common instruction can happen during time set aside for independent reading of the individual texts. This approach is popularized in the Reader's Workshop model. In this model, the teacher can bring together students with similar needs in a small guided reading group to provide additional support. The instruction and support can be similar because application is possible, even with different readers reading different texts. Targeted instruction could be even further differentiated by conferring with students individually as they show ability to use what was learned during the common instruction.

Each of these models—varying texts, grouping patterns, and levels of support—makes more sense as a way to provide differentiated instruction than differentiating content, process, and products. These four models already exist in many classrooms or are easily adaptable to structures that already exist. They present do-able ways to think about differentiated instruction. Interestingly, each model has the potential for small group instruction guided directly by the teacher to provide targeted, scaffolded instruction with a whole class text, part of a whole class text, a small group text, or an individual text. While the third model clearly reflects what many consider to be guided reading, all the models provide an expanded vision of what the purpose of guided reading could be and additional reasons why it is so important.

Figure 2B: Models of Differentiation (Modified from Opitz & Ford, 2008)

	Grouping without Tracking	Jigsawing	Guided Reading Literature Circle Comprehension Focus Groups	Reader's Workshop
Vary Texts	One common text	One common text but easily divided into parts	Different groups of texts for different groups of readers	Different texts for individual readers
Vary Grouping Arrangements	Whole class to start but divided into two groups for independent phase of gradual release	Whole class to start but divided into small groups (one per part of the divided text) for the independent phase of the gradual release	Class divided into small groups of similar abilities to receive similar instruction through direct support of the teacher	Readers work independently; however, the teacher can bring small groups of readers with similar needs together
Vary Levels of Support	One group receives indirect support as they work independently; the other group receives more direct support as they are guided by the teacher	Most groups receive indirect support as they work independently; one or more groups receive more direct support as needed with guidance from the teacher	Support can vary in length and frequency, but all groups receive some direct support from the teacher specific to their needs using the intentionally selected text	Support can be given by conferring with any reader who has needs or by bringing small groups of readers with similar needs together for specific targeted instruction
Role of Guided Reading	Guided reading flows out of the whole class lesson for those students in need of greater support as they work to complete the instruction directly guided by the teacher	Guided reading flows from the whole class lesson for any group that needs more direct teacher support to process their assigned part of the text	Guided reading is structured so that all groups receive at least some direct support from the teacher, though some groups may receive support for longer periods or with greater frequency	Guided reading can be used to provide targeted instruction to a small group of students with similar needs that can be applied across levels of texts and readers

What Are Other Purposes of Guided Reading?

If we are teaching readers, then even after we have selected the texts, made the grouping assignments, and decided how much support the readers need, we need to listen carefully to the readers so that we can respond appropriately.

Differentiated instruction doesn't end once decisions about the texts, grouping, and level of support are made. Differentiation is also about what happens at the table with the readers. In Chapter One, I stressed that guided reading is more than teaching texts in small groups. Guided reading is at its core the teaching of readers—finding and addressing those differences that Pearson observed every student brings through the door. If we are teaching readers, then even after we have selected the texts, made the grouping assignments, and decided how much support the readers need, we need to listen carefully to the readers so that we can respond appropriately. We must remember that it is the individual children—not the group—who learn to read (Lose, 2007). Clay (1998) pointed out that even when learners are headed toward similar outcomes, they may reach those points by different pathways. Teachers must be ready to acknowledge this by setting up observations of and interactions with readers at the table. When planning for a guided reading session, the teacher must always be very intentional about the general focus of the lesson (i.e., the similar outcomes the learners need) but also about planning activities that allow the observing of readers as they interact with texts. Those observations may reveal the individual pathways the learners take in trying to achieve those outcomes. It's at this point that the teacher's intentional planning detours a bit to be responsive to the individual needs.

Let's look at three readers. All are reading the same text, *I Go Up* by Jay Dale (Capstone Classroom, 2012). The students are all at the A level. The teacher completes a formative assessment to guide instruction during the session. The teacher uses a running record to record the oral reading of each student. She times the reading to capture a sense of the reading rate and asks for a retelling of the story with a holistic measure of under-standing (none, limited, somewhat acceptable). In looking at the three readers' results, it is clear responsive teaching means not only knowing their levels, but also their needs. (See Figure 2C.)

Figure 2C: Profiles of Readers

Text	Charli	Elle	Whit
I go up.	I go up.	I go up.	I go up.
I go up the stairs.	I go up the steps.	I go up the stars.	I go up the (omitted).
I go up the ladder.	I go up the ladder.	I go up the ladder.	I go up the ladder.
I go up the rope.	I go up the rope.	I go up the rope.	I go up the rope.
I go up the hill.	I go up the grass.	I go up the heel.	I go up the (omitted).
I go up the tree.	I go up the tree.	I go up the tree.	I go up the tree.
I go up the mountain.	I go up the snow.	I go up the mont.	I go up the (omitted).
I go up...up, up, up.	I go up...up, up, up.	I go up...up, up, up.	I go up...up, up, up.
Rate	34 seconds	40 seconds	44 seconds
Errors	3 (92 percent)	3 (92 percent)	3 (92 percent)
Miscues	stairs, hill, mountain	stairs, hill, mountain	stairs, hill, mountain
Retelling	General understanding	Limited understanding	General understanding

Let's look Charli. She read with fluency and understanding but had three uncorrected miscues. Each miscue made sense in the story, and each miscue sounded right syntactically in the grammatical structure of the sentence ("steps" for "stairs," "grass" for "hill," and "snow" for "mountain"), but two miscues showed little visual similarity to the words in the text ("grass" for "hill" and "snow" for "mountain"). The remaining miscue ("steps" for "stairs") shared a visual similarity to the word in the text, especially in the beginning.

If we look more closely at Elle, she read with less fluency and understanding. She had three uncorrected miscues. Like Charli, all were substitutions. She substituted "stars" for "stairs," "heel" for "hill," and "mont" for "mountain." In all three cases, the substitutions did not make sense. With "stars" and "heel," she did substitute nouns for nouns, so syntactically the miscues were grammatically acceptable. In all three cases, the miscues had a visual similarity ("stars" for "stairs," "heel" for "hill," "mont" for "mountain").

Finally in Whit's case, he read with understanding but with less fluency. He too had three uncorrected miscues, but in all cases, they were omissions, not substitutions. He made enough meaning from the pictures and the words he knew that he could satisfy retelling requirements.

One way to start responsive teaching is to consider broadly what the reader did. Eight key observations can guide thinking about the readers:

1. The reader read the text correctly with understanding.

2. The reader read the text with corrections and understanding.

3. The reader read the text with corrections but not complete understanding.

4. The reader read the text with understanding but not complete accuracy.

5. The reader read the text with accuracy but not complete understanding.

6. The reader attempted to read the text but without complete accuracy or understanding.

7. The reader stalled in attempting to read.

8. The reader resisted the attempt to read.

If we use the general framework to think about the three students, what we observe with Charli is profile 4. She read with understanding but not complete accuracy. Elle is more like profile 6. She attempted the reading but without accuracy or understanding. Like Charli, Whit is also profile 4. He read with understanding but not complete accuracy. All are reading at the same level, but they have variations that must be responded to differently by the teacher. The guided reading instruction needs to lead each individual student forward. If the three students are all taught the same lesson about *I Go Up* without any attention to their individual needs, the lesson may help some but will probably fall short of helping all.

It is interesting to look closely at the data collected by the teacher in three quick assessments of accuracy, fluency rate, and general understanding. (See Figure 2D.) If the teacher focuses exclusively on accuracy levels by reporting percentages of words right, these three readers look the same. Accuracy levels alone failed to detect a critical variation between these students. One might assume they are the same, and instruction that follows may not truly respond to their needs. If the teacher only focuses on the number of errors the readers made or the actual words missed, again no critical variations are detected. Instruction could focus on teaching those three words in isolation, but it falls short of teaching the strategies each student needs to be able to figure out words like these independently. It is only when the teacher observes closely what each student is doing, strategically revealed by their miscues, that critical information is obtained. This information can be used to inform subsequent responsive instruction.

It is only when the teacher observes closely what each student is doing, strategically revealed by their miscues, that critical information is obtained. This information can be used to inform subsequent responsive instruction.

Figure 2D: Assessment Results for Students

Data	Results	Importance
Accuracy level	Same for all readers	Measuring accuracy did not detect critical variations.
Number of errors	Same for all readers	Measuring number of errors did not detect critical variations.
The actual errors	stairs, hill, mountain	Noting the errors did not detect critical variations.
Miscues	Different for all readers	Noting miscues detects critical variations.
Rate	Different for all readers	Noting rate detects a variation that may be critical or not.
Comprehension check	Different for all readers	Noting general understanding detects variation that may be critical.

If I take Elle to the first page, point to the word "stairs," and ask her if "stars" makes sense, she might rethink her miscue and work toward a word that makes sense. If I do the same thing with Charli, she would tell me that "steps" does make sense. It will require a different type of responsive interaction to help Charli. We might have to stretch out the word "steps" and get her to realize it has a /p/ sound in it, and the word on the page does not have the letter that makes that sound. It's a much different interaction. I might even ask if that is the best miscue to target with Charli. Charli might be better helped by looking at the word "hill" and discovering that it is not "grass."

Whit presents a different challenge. He also missed "stairs," but an omission reveals less about his ability. His rate seems to suggest that he slowed down to look at those tough words. Perhaps he was over-relying on picture clues without success. His strategy was to basically skip the word and not worry about going back. Perhaps he got enough from what he saw and read that he was able to make sense of the text. In his case, I might take him back to the first page and if he stops on the word "stairs" again, I might guide him through some questions to see what he is trying to do strategically:

1. Tell me what you are trying to do.

2. Show me the part you are working on.

3. Is there a tricky sentence?

4. Is there a tricky word?

5. Is there a tricky part of a word?

6. Is there a tricky sound or letter?

7. (Once the tricky part is identified) Let's see if we can use what you know to figure this out.

> *Guided reading is important because it provides that significant opportunity to closely listen to and observe readers in a small group and then provide targeted, scaffolded instruction at that critical moment to move the readers forward.*

Guided reading is important because it provides that significant opportunity to closely listen to and observe readers in a small group and then provide targeted, scaffolded instruction at that critical moment to move the readers forward (Schwartz, 2005). The key is being able to surface critical variations and address those during the guided reading session. You'll notice that some measures may reveal variations between readers like measuring their rate, but differences in rates may not be that critical unless they reveal a strategic difference with a practical implication. With these three readers, the difference may not be that important, even though Charli read at a greater pace than Elle and Whit. In the end, what is the practical implication if one child reads it in 34 seconds and another reads it 40 seconds? If Elle and Whit were slowing down to try to sound out a word or use another strategy, that might be more important to note and think about. Yes, big differences in rate may have more meaning than small differences, but caution must be used in sorting children based on rate data alone, especially where variation is slight.

Finally, the check for understanding also showed differences between the readers. While Elle's limited ability to make meaning does raise a red flag, Charli's and Whit's ability to understand may be for different reasons. If Charli is making meaning from reading the words on the page and Whit is making sense by looking closely at the pictures, they are at different places strategically. To move each forward requires a different interaction. Children like Charli, Elle, and Whit are sitting at guided reading tables every day. In her study of second graders, Halladay (2012) described three readers all reading at the same level: Ben, Sarah, and Dante. Ben made a number of miscues that interfered with his comprehension. Sarah made a number of miscues, but her lack of accuracy did not interfere with her comprehension. Finally, Dante read the text accurately, but his accuracy did not lead him to comprehension. Halladay's research shows again that while students at one level may have "predictable patterns," they also have "individual pathways" (Hornsby, 2000, p. 15). The purpose of guided reading is to provide close-up observation of students, the ability to assess for critical variations, and opportunities to respond with targeted teaching. All of this is possible when effective guided reading is a part of a comprehensive literacy program. A guide to assist responsive teaching is contained in Figure 2E.

Figure 2E: A Guide to Responsive Teaching

Observed behavior	What pattern would be observed	What is working? Praise the reader as needed specifically for ...	What needs work? Instruction for the learner ...	What should be considered for future instruction?
The reader read the text correctly with understanding.	No errors	Confidence, competence, and/ or comfort level with this text	Let's look closely at your instructional goals. What do you feel you need to work on next?	Should the difficulty level of the material being read be increased? Should the instructional goals for the reader be adjusted?
The reader read the text with corrections and understanding.	All errors self-corrected while meaning was maintained	Monitoring meaning while reading	Let's look closely at a few of your self-corrections. What was the word on the page? What was the word you said? How did you make the decision to self-correct? Did you need to self-correct to keep the meaning clear?	Would stronger, more automatic word strategies reduce the need for self-corrections to focus more attention on meaning making? Does the student focus too much on accuracy with potential to eventually interfere with fluency or comprehension?
The reader read the text with corrections but not complete understanding.	All errors self-corrected but meaning was compromised	Monitoring accuracy while reading	Let's look closely at a few of your self-corrections. What was the word on the page? What was the word you said? How did you make the decision to self-correct? Did you need to self-correct to keep the meaning clear?	Would stronger, more automatic word strategies reduce the need for self-corrections to focus more attention on meaning making? Does the student's focus on accuracy interfere with fluency and/or comprehension?

continued on next page

Figure 2E: A Guide to Responsive Teaching *continued*

Observed behavior	What pattern would be observed	What is working? Praise the reader as needed specifically for …	What needs work? Instruction for the learner …	What should be considered for future instruction?
The reader read the text with understanding but not complete accuracy.	Meaning-based miscues	Making meaning while reading	Let's look closely at a few of your miscues. You said…. Does the word on the page look like the word you said? Can you use what you know about sound and letter clues to figure out the word on the page that would also make sense?	Is the reader over-relying on syntactic and semantic cues?

Does the reader need to be more accurate as he/she makes meaning?

(Be careful about overemphasizing accuracy, which could interfere with making meaning.) |
| The reader read the text with accuracy but not complete understanding. | No errors, but meaning was compromised—often seen in "word callers." These students are often very good oral readers, reading with few mistakes but demonstrating little understanding of what they have read. | Reading accurately | Let's reread, and we will stop along the way and check for understanding. You read to the end of page __. Think about what you are reading, and I will ask you a question to see if you understand. | Is the reader over-relying on decoding to the detriment of fluency and comprehension?

Would "stop and process" strategies help the student build meaning as he or she reads? |
| The reader attempted to read the text without accuracy or understanding. | Non-meaning-based miscues | Making attempts and maintaining stamina | Let's look closely at a few of your miscues. You said…. Does that make sense? Can you use what you know about sound and letter clues to figure out the word on the page that would also make sense? | Is the reader over-relying on graphophonemic cues to the detriment of fluency and comprehension?

How do we help the reader improve accuracy as he or she makes meaning? |

continued on next page

Figure 2E: A Guide to Responsive Teaching *continued*

Observed behavior	What pattern would be observed	What is working? Praise the reader as needed specifically for ...	What needs work? Instruction for the learner ...	What should be considered for future instruction?
The reader stalled in attempting to read.	Reading falters in progress	Making an attempt	Can you tell me what you are working out? Show me where the problem is? Is it...? (Keep focusing the child until he or she can articulate the problem, and then scaffold support at that level.)	Should the material being read be rethought? Should the instructional goals for the reader be adjusted?
The reader resisted the attempt to read.	Reading not attempted	The last successful attempt	Let's work on this together. I will start the reading and when you see a part where you can take over, let me know.	Should the material being read be rethought? Should the instructional goals for the reader be adjusted? Should the level of support be readjusted?

I want to make sure that I haven't made this seem simple and easy. In my example, we looked at three different readers reading the same Level A text with 39 words. We collected just a little data on each and looked at what we learned to inform our instruction about how to target subsequent instruction. Each time I work with children like these, I am stunned by the complexity of what is revealed about what readers can and cannot do. Schwartz (2005) describes the complexity of these teaching decisions even more comprehensively in assisting teachers to respond to primary students during guided reading.

Schwartz demonstrates this complexity by looking at a single miscue. Think about a child who substitutes the word "home" for "house." If a teacher focuses primarily on accuracy, the miscue is treated as something that needs to be corrected. If a teacher focuses primarily on meaning, the miscue might be ignored. Schwartz recommends that the decision also needs to consider "previous observations of the student and an assessment of his or her literacy" (p. 436). Schwartz borrows from a framework by Brown (1982) to explain four factors that need to be considered when providing responsive instruction to individuals during guided reading:

1. Response history of the learner: As you have observed the reader over time, what is the typical strategy on which the reader relies? Does the reader have a shifting pattern of response that would indicate the development of an effective processing system? Or does the reader have a more static pattern of response that would indicate the need for support in applying additional strategies to improve the effectiveness of the processing system?

2. Cues: What cues did the reader use, notice, or neglect? What does the reader do with print cues (visual and phonological)? Sentence structure cues (oral language and book language)? Meaning cues (picture and context)? What cues lead the reader to create sound-letter expectations?

3. Strategies: How does the reader use monitoring strategies? Searching strategies? And cross-checking strategies? Remember, an effective system equips the reader with the ability to know when something is not right, to search for cues to make something right, and to cross-check to verify something is right.

4. Prompts: Does the reader need a low level of support (struggled but succeeded) or high level of support (struggled without success) from the teacher to move forward? Can the reader be prompted toward independence? ("Were you right? What else can you try?") Or should you prompt to extend strategic behaviors? ("Does that look right, sound right, or make sense? Get your mouth ready, think about what would sound right, or think about what would make sense.")

Schwartz (2005) reminds us of the complexity of responsive teaching. He provides important things to consider in targeting instruction during guided reading. An appropriate response may need to consider the history of the learner, the cues he or she uses, and the strategies he or she knows. We can begin to achieve a vision of very effective differentiation as the teacher grows in the ability to provide this type of instruction. He concluded: "The guided reading lesson format provides a rich opportunity for teachers to observe and investigate early literacy. Listening to a student read a text that is only partially familiar allows us to apply and refine our theories of literacy learning and instruction" (p. 442).

Can Guided Reading Help Accelerate Growth of Learners?

It is clear that guided reading is still important because it addresses the need for critical small group instruction in an overall comprehensive literacy program. The use of guided reading provides a vehicle for adjusting texts, grouping arrangements, and levels of support to differentiate instruction for different groups of readers. Guided reading also provides one of the best opportunities to closely observe readers in small groups so developmental patterns and individual pathways can be addressed

An appropriate response may need to consider the history of the learner, the cues he or she uses, and the strategies he or she knows. We can begin to achieve a vision of very effective differentiation as the teacher grows in the ability to provide this type of instruction.

through responsive teaching. This targeted instruction can even further differentiate instruction for individual students. In many classrooms, however, differentiation needs to carry one more responsibility.

For some students, making an academic year's worth of progress in an academic year's worth of time will not help close the gap between them and their classmates. They need to receive instruction that accelerates their growth to make more than an academic year's worth of growth in an academic year's worth of time. What we do with different readers needs to be carefully considered so that a more challenging outcome is also achieved. Acceleration is often overlooked as an important dimension of differentiation. Sometimes we are too focused on differentiation as merely doing different things for different students. Other times, we are too focused on helping readers make progress but lose sight of helping them achieve proficiency (Opitz & Ford, 2014).

So how can schools focus on acceleration in a comprehensive literacy program? Dorn and Soffos (2011) recommend that teachers, schools, and districts clearly indicate expected entry and exit levels for readers at each grade level. The identification of those levels allows the teacher to clearly project a path of expected growth needed for proficiency by the end of the year. That path influences how guided reading and other supports are structured and paced. Periodic embedded benchmark assessments will allow teachers to monitor the progress of their students along the way to make sure they are on the trajectory toward proficiency. That defined path, however, only really works for the students coming in at expected entry levels.

What happens if a student, for whatever reason, enters below expected entry levels? If that student is placed on a path of linear growth that parallels the typical grade-level trajectory, the student will make progress, but the gap between that student and classmates will not narrow. A gap between the student's performance and expected proficiency levels will still exist. This student's trajectory needs to be plotted differently. The linear path needs to be a much steeper incline to make sure the learner is on a path that will lead to grade-level proficiency. Just setting a path, however, will not accelerate the growth of a learner. Instructional decisions have to be made to support the learner along that journey to accelerate growth.

Differentiated instruction that supports accelerated growth begins with effective regular classroom instruction. High-quality guided reading plays a critical role in building that foundation. I hope that the recommendations provided in this book will help us look at current practices in guided reading and tighten them up so that we can get more bang for our buck from the time and energy we set aside for guided reading. Remember, that might begin with greater fidelity to proposed guided reading instruction principles and practices, but sometimes fidelity to a practice can limit teachers from using their expertise to make it even more powerful (McMaster, et al, 2014). Fidelity should always be to the students with whom the teacher is working—not just a program. With my colleague Kathryn Glasswell (2010), we reminded teachers to get more power out of

> *Acceleration is often overlooked as an important dimension of differentiation. Sometimes we are too focused on differentiation as merely doing different things for different students. Other times, we are too focused on helping readers make progress but lose sight of helping them achieve proficiency.*

guided reading by rethinking some aspects instead of just rigidly adhering to perceived essential aspects of guided reading. For example, a teacher could move toward organizing small groups around instructional needs rather than exclusively by levels, especially for those who have the most critical instructional needs. Select texts that provide more reading mileage (greater word counts) for those who need the most practice, and scaffold the movement from easier texts by intentionally selecting multi-level text sets that share connected content, formats, and language. This can help learners move more quickly to more complex texts. (We will look more closely at text selection issues in Chapter Four.)

Differentiation that accelerates growth goes beyond tightening up guided reading. Acceleration also means paying particular attention to the pacing of guided reading sessions. Historically, there has always been a tendency to slow down instruction for those with the greatest needs (Allington, 1991), but the exact opposite is probably necessary. If a student's need for growth is greater, guided reading sessions may have to be intentionally modified to provide more time for needed instruction. Longer sessions, more frequent sessions in the class rotation, and additional sessions at other times ("double dosing," as some schools now call it) may be needed. Acceleration also means considering the need for something beyond classroom-provided guided reading. Models such as Guided Reading Plus (Dorn & Soffos, 2011) and Leveled Literacy Instruction (Fountas & Pinnell, 2014) may be added as additional layers of support. Careful monitoring would be done to make sure this layer of instruction is contributing to the acceleration of growth in the student. (We will look more closely at intervention issues in Chapter Seven.)

While acceleration means looking at practices that would deliver more bang for our buck, I would offer one caution in light of current discussions. Recently, there has been a lot of attention on the analysis of effect sizes across studies of certain practices documented in research. These are called meta-analyses, and so many meta-analyses exist now that some have also looked across those to determine effect sizes of certain instructional practices (Hattie, 2013). Effect sizes are quantitative measures of the strength of a certain practice—the larger the effect size, the stronger the potential impact from the practice. A popular interpretation of this research is to use those instructional techniques that have the greatest effect sizes in our instruction. Given a choice between two practices—one with a strong effect size and one with a weak effect size—why not choose the one that has a track record of getting better results? While this work can certainly inform our thinking, educators need to remember that a meta-analysis averages data across many studies. Studies are given different weights when averages are being computed, but, in the end, these averages can mask outlier studies. A meta-analysis of a practice with a high average size effect may include studies of that practice that had smaller effect sizes. The reverse can also be true. A meta-analysis of a practice with a low effect size average may include some studies of that practice that had higher effect sizes. It is very important to remember that variations exist and the contexts in which the studies were conducted matter. For example, schools with significant professional development and ample access to resources may have large effect sizes from the implementation of reader's/writer's workshop approaches, but others without those supports may not. What might work in one school setting may not work the same way in another.

Research suggests that there is one important element that can transcend different schools, and that is whether the instruction is delivered by an expert teacher. Teachers with expertise often have instructional practices that impact positively on the learners in their classrooms. Acceleration is not just about picking the right practice, but using practices that can accelerate the growth of the individual learner. Lose (2007) recommended that it is teachers with the most expertise that will accelerate the growth of students who may be struggling the most. "The child who is challenged by literacy learning requires a knowledgeable teacher who can make moment-by-moment teaching decisions in response to his or her idiosyncratic literacy competencies" (p. 277).

> *Acceleration is not just about picking the right practice, but using practices that can accelerate the growth of the individual learner.*

What Does the Research Say about Guided Reading?

The final question I want to address in making the case for guided reading is: What does the research say about guided reading? Guided reading practices are based on research. The research base for guided reading as an instructional approach has been articulated by Pinnell and Fountas (2010) as it relates to eight key principles. Research supports guided reading sessions that:

1. Have the ultimate goal of teaching comprehension

2. Support individual progress on a sequence of high-quality, engaging texts with increasing text difficulty

3. Increase the quantity of independent reading

4. Provide explicit instruction in fluency

5. Provide daily opportunities to expand vocabulary

6. Expand students' ability to apply phonemic awareness and phonics understanding to process print

7. Provide the opportunity to write about reading

8. Create engagement in motivation for reading

There is a difference, however, between a research-based practice and a research-tested practice (Duke & Martin, 2011). It is clear that the development of guided reading is based on theory, research, and expert opinion. But what does the research say about the efficacy of guided reading? Does it work? Denton and colleagues (2014) contend that there has been limited experimental research on guided reading. Results are mixed at best and limited, often by the lack of description on how the guided reading practices were implemented. After searching, two studies surfaced. Tobin and Calhoon (2009) compared a guided reading approach with a more explicit instruction program with first-grade students from two different schools. Guided reading students showed significant increases across time in three narrowly assessed areas: phoneme segmentation fluency, nonsense word fluency, and oral reading fluency. Guided reading had greater gains than explicit instruction in the area of phoneme segmentation fluency, though explicit instruction had stronger results on the oral reading fluency measure. Nayak and Sylva (2013) looked at young learners in Hong Kong. They compared guided reading groups, e-book groups, and no-treatment groups. Only guided reading groups showed a significant gain in both accuracy and comprehension compared to the no-treatment group.

Other studies have focused on adding elements to guided reading to see if that increased its power. Kamps and others (2007) looked at both first- and second-grade English language learners and English-only students. A balanced literacy approach that included guided reading combined with explicit instruction in decoding and fluency resulted in better outcomes than the balanced literacy program without the explicit instruction component. Hall, Sabey, and McClellan (2005) looked at focusing attention on text structures with second graders within guided reading groups. When that instruction was added with well-structured texts, greater comprehension in expository texts was seen; however, earlier research by Dymock (1998) demonstrated that general instruction through guided reading groups actually was just as effective in impacting reading comprehension on standardized tests as small group instructions that focused exclusively on text structures.

In light of the limited research, Denton and colleagues (2014) structured a more comprehensive design to compare guided reading as an intervention versus more explicit skill instruction (phonics and word skills) for at-risk second graders. While acknowledging the limitations of the study, results indicated that both guided reading and explicit instruction improved outcomes from typical classroom instruction. Outcomes did not differ significantly between the interventions, though the researchers found some added value in explicit instruction to accelerate growth in decoding, fluency, and comprehension. In the end, the efficacy of guided reading is probably best researched in the classrooms in which it is used. Teachers should be able to demonstrate a positive impact from guided reading, using outcomes their learners need to make progress.

Is Guided Reading Still Important?

In this chapter, I provide a clearer vision of what guided reading should be. When guided reading is implemented within that vision, it becomes quite clear that it still has a relevant role in classroom literacy programs. Guided reading is a viable small group structure for needed differentiated instruction in a comprehensive literacy program. Guided reading provides an important systematic means to closely observe, assess, and respond to the common patterns in learners. Guided reading can be positioned to play a vital role in accelerating the growth of learners in need of closing the gap with their peers. Grounded in research-based principles, we can see the original promise of guided reading. Now we need to make sure that promise is achieved. Let's start by looking at how guided reading can best fit with the other aspects of the literacy program in the next chapter.

CHAPTER THREE:
How Does Guided Reading Fit into the Rest of the Literacy Program?

> Read aloud, shared reading, guided reading and independent reading are connected and equally important in supporting students as they establish a reading process that focuses on meaning making.
>
> *Burkins and Croft, 2010*

At a workshop I was conducting on flexible grouping, a reading coordinator approached me during a break. Questioning my suggestions that some grouping arrangements could focus on something other than leveled texts, she argued for the need for a plan like her school had recently implemented. In her school, they guaranteed that every day every child would read appropriate leveled text for 30 minutes. They worked to reorganize the school so that children could move between classrooms to appropriate groups based on their reading levels and often to work with other teachers during that 30-minute block. While acknowledging the importance of their effort to guarantee that every child received at least 30 minutes of guided reading instruction with appropriate texts was important, I did wonder what happened to each child during the balance of the day in that school. After all, even after that 30-minute period, there were six hours of instruction remaining in the school day.

Guided reading works best when it is part of a comprehensive literacy program. Routman (2000) pointed out that no matter how powerful small group guided reading sessions can be, they are just one element of a comprehensive literacy program. No one "component" can carry the burden of accelerating the growth of all readers. In telling her story, Cathy Mere (2005) said that she had to remind herself that, in her classroom, teaching and learning happened all day—not just during guided reading. "If I haven't met with a child in a guided reading group, it doesn't mean that I haven't taught that child" (p. 124). Burkins and Croft (2010) noted the number one misunderstanding about guided reading is that it is the only time reading is taught. They challenged the idea that what a teacher did during guided reading was any more important than what a teacher did during the read-aloud, shared reading, and independent reading components of the literacy program. "Guided reading, however, is most valuable when we strategically support it across the gradual release of responsibility" (p. 11).

> *...a comprehensive literacy program can often be summed up in three words: "to," "with," and "by." You need to read **to** your students, you need to read **with** your students, and you need to have your students read **by** themselves.*

It is important to start with the assumption that if teachers are going to accelerate the growth of all readers, effective instruction needs to be a focus throughout the literacy program (and the school day)—not just relegated to one daily 30-minute period. Borrowing the language of Margaret Mooney (1990), I often tell the pre-service teachers with whom I work that a comprehensive literacy program can often be summed up in three words: "to," "with," and "by." You need to read *to* your students, you need to read *with* your students, and you need to have your students read *by* themselves. This also means you will sometimes use *large groups* for reading to and with your students during read-alouds and shared reading; *small groups* for reading with students during guided reading; and *individualized approaches* to encourage students to read by themselves. It also means that there are some things *the teacher does* like read-alouds, some things *the teacher and students do together* like shared and guided reading, and some things *the students do by themselves* like independent reading. A comprehensive literacy program acknowledges that all grouping arrangements are critical because they have different purposes, different available levels of support, and/or a different literacy focus.

This becomes even more apparent when we look at what happens in a typical day in an elementary literacy program. In the last chapter, I built a case for the continued importance of guided reading as a critical dimension of the literacy program, but children still spend significant time in the large group setting (Kelly & Turner, 2009). This shouldn't be surprising because, for teachers, the most efficient use of time and resources is with a whole group setting—working with all children at the same time using the same materials. This is typically represented by what we call "universal instruction" in RtI frameworks. It makes sense in a literacy block for activities like read-alouds and shared reading. In a gradual release model, this is also the best setting for modeling and demonstrating skills and strategies needed by all students. In a two-hour literacy block, it is often recommended that approximately 30 minutes be allocated for that purpose. However, in most cases in whole group instruction, the teacher uses a text at or above grade level. When that text is set aside, it is accessible to students who read at or above level but not to those students who would struggle to read at that level. If teachers are not required to consider how to support all learners during whole group instruction, they may be less successful in reaching those students who may need the instruction the most.

Once the teacher moves to guided reading, there is more intentionality about considering how to support all learners. As the survey results revealed, the teacher may schedule an additional hour or so to meet with three to four guided reading groups. The teacher carefully selects texts at the level of the readers in that group so that instruction can be targeted to the learners' needs. This part of the literacy block usually supports students the most. However, the small group work is only part of the time during this block. The teacher must also be very intentional in considering how to support all learners when they are working on their own. The students will typically spend most of this time working independently away from the teacher. If this time is to be successful in reaching all students, especially those in need of the most support, the teacher must carefully consider how to structure this time. Without that consideration, guided reading might not be an effective use of instructional time. (Chapter Six looks more closely at how to do that.)

When the teacher moves to the content areas, it often means a return to whole class instruction with the same text for all students. If that is another 30-minute block of time, students in need of the most support are spending even more time with texts that are not within their reading levels. As Figure 3A reveals, by the end of a typical two-hour instructional block, students in need of the most support often receive the least amount of instructional time with texts within their levels. If teachers are not intentional about the independent time the learners get, the amount of time with appropriate texts erodes even further. Finally, if the teacher walks away from guided reading for whatever reason, it is easy to see how some students could move through the entire block with virtually no time with appropriate text. Clearly, guided reading cannot carry the burden of accelerating the growth of all readers, especially those who might need our help the most. In fact, if more attention is given to fostering the conditions for learning in the classroom and to the other critical elements of a literacy program, the need for guided reading might actually be reduced. Let's look closely at those conditions and elements and how to attend to them.

Figure 3A: Typical Time Allocations for Accessible Appropriate Texts

	Readers Above Level	Readers At Level	Readers Below Level
Shared Reading	30 minutes	30 minutes	0 minutes
Guided Reading	20 minutes	20 minutes	20 minutes
Independent Reading	40 minutes	40 minutes	40 minutes
Content-area Reading	30 minutes	30 minutes	0 minutes
Total Minutes with Appropriate Accessible Text	120 minutes	120 minutes	60 minutes

Conditions of Learning

How does a teacher start maximizing the impact of guided reading with other critical dimensions of a comprehensive literacy program? She might begin by considering the conditions that lead most learners to become successful readers and writers. There is a helpful framework by Brian Cambourne (1995), who identified eight critical conditions for language learning. Reflecting on each of these eight conditions often leads me to see aspects of literacy programs that are strong and others that can be strengthened. By attending to those conditions in need, teachers may actually improve the power of other aspects of the literacy program like guided reading. Guided reading is only as strong as the other elements that surround it.

> Guided reading is only as strong as the other elements that surround it.

Cambourne theorized that to become a language learner (and I might argue to become a learner of any skill or process from athletics to music, from hobbies to occupations), there are eight conditions that must be present. The list that follows is my interpretation of what is important in each of these conditions:

1. *Immersion:* The learner needs to be surrounded with what is needed for learning to become a reader and writer. This means having access to the materials and resources needed for reading and writing and being placed in a physical environment that facilitates growth as a reader and writer.

2. *Demonstrations:* On the cognitive side, the learner works with an expert, who can provide effective models of how reading and writing skills, strategies, and processes work. On the affective side, the learner establishes a relationship with someone who is passionate about reading and writing in his or her life.

3. *Practice:* The learner is provided time to engage in reading and writing processes to show the ability to apply and use what was taught.

4. *Feedback:* The learner works with an expert coach, who provides guidance as he or she practices reading and writing tasks, seizing at-the-moment teaching opportunities to help the learner move forward. When the learner works independently, targeted response is provided when the teacher meets with the learner to scaffold him or her from one point to another.

5. *Approximations:* The learner is encouraged to perform while becoming increasingly competent. The learner is allowed to—even encouraged to—take risks in learning to read and write as developmentally appropriate without a demand for accuracy or perfection. Developmental leaps are not dismissed or marginalized but celebrated as steps in the journey to becoming a reader and writer. The emotional climate of the classroom provides a safe atmosphere for the learner to take these risks.

6. *Expectations:* The learner works with adults who see him or her as a reader and writer. The program works with an asset model focused on what a learner can do and avoids focusing on what a learner can't do. Language used in the classroom positively shapes a learner so he or she sees him- or herself as a reader and writer. Everyone is an inside player in the reading and writing club.

7. *Engagement:* There's a saying that "you can't lead a horse to water, but you can salt the hay." Teachers can surround a learner with the other conditions, but the learner must actually participate in the task. He or she must move from the instruction to the application. Engagement usually results when the learner is motivated about, interested in, and passionate about the reading and writing opportunities. Engagement is what the teacher does to salt the hay. The learner must know he or she can succeed, want to succeed, and know how to succeed (Opitz & Ford, 2014).

Engagement usually results when the learner is motivated about, interested in, and passionate about the reading and writing opportunities.

8. *Responsibility:* But ultimately, the horse must drink the water. The learner must take hold of the opportunity to read and write. He or she moves beyond compliance and develops an internal force that propels him or her toward reading and writing without external motivations (Schlechty, 2002). The learner has a sense of urgency and takes charge of his or her reading and writing life (Boushey & Moser, 2006). The learner IS a reader and writer and finds the joy in those activities beyond the school walls throughout his or her life.

In Figure 3B on page 60, I have provided a grid that can be used to help teachers evaluate the power of the conditions of language learning in their classroom literacy programs. Remember that if these conditions are being met in a classroom, guided reading will operate in a context that should enhance its use.

Figure 3B: Evaluating Literacy Program Conditions Critical to Developing Readers and Writers

Condition	Questions to Ask	Evaluation of My Comprehensive Literacy Program
Immersion	Do all learners ... • have easy access to accessible and appropriate texts at their level? • have access to the materials, resources, and technology needed to support them as they read and write? • learn in print-rich classroom environments that facilitate their growth through strategy-embedded displays and other artifacts? • live in a school environment in which reading and writing are seen as important?	
Demonstrations	Do all learners... • work with expert teachers who can effectively model critical skills and strategies in reading? • work with expert teachers who can effectively model critical skills and strategies in writing? • have relationships with role models who are passionate about reading and writing?	
Practice	Have all learners... • been provided adequate time for authentic reading experiences? • been provided adequate time for authentic writing experiences?	
Feedback	Do all learners... • work with expert teachers who can coach effectively while practicing reading tasks and processes? • work with expert teachers who can coach effectively while practicing writing tasks and processes? • receive appropriate targeted responses when completing a reading experience? • receive appropriate targeted responses when completing a writing experience? • have opportunities to confer with the teacher about reading experiences? • have opportunities to confer with the teacher about writing experiences?	

continued on next page

Figure 3B: Evaluating Literacy Program Conditions Critical to Developing Readers and Writers *continued*

Condition	Questions to Ask	Evaluation of My Comprehensive Literacy Program
Approximations	Do all learners... • work in classrooms with expert teachers who understand developmental stages and appropriate efforts in reading? • have instruction that allows, encourages, and celebrates developmentally appropriate efforts that increase competence in reading? • work in classrooms with expert teachers who understand developmental stages and appropriate efforts in writing, including spelling? • have instruction that allows, encourages, and celebrates developmentally appropriate efforts that increase competence in writing, including spelling? • feel safe as they work in classrooms?	
Expectations	Are all learners... • held to high expectations? • seen as readers and writers? • viewed through a "can do" lens? • recipients of classroom language that positively impacts their views of themselves as readers? • recipients of classroom language that positively impacts their views of themselves as writers?	
Engagement	Do all learners... • know they can succeed as readers? • want to succeed as readers? • know how to succeed at reading? • know they can succeed as writers? • want to succeed as writers? • know how to succeed at writing? • have access to instruction in which issues of motivation are intentionally addressed as a part of the lesson? • have access to instructional programs in which choice plays a role in reading opportunities? • have access to instructional programs in which choice plays a role in writing opportunities?	
Responsibility	Are the learners... • internally motivated as readers? • building strong positive identities as readers? • finding joy in reading? • internally motivated as writers? • building strong positive identities as writers? • finding joy in writing? • READING and WRITING?	

Elements of the Literacy Block

It becomes increasingly obvious that if the conditions are right in a classroom, literacy instruction will help most students become the readers and writers we desire. Guided reading becomes an instructional tool to reach those in need of additional support, but it does not have to carry that responsibility for the entire literacy block. This is especially true if the conditions are operationalized across elements within the block. In this section, we'll look at how to strengthen three other key elements of the literacy block: read-alouds, shared reading, and independent reading.

Read-alouds

As time becomes the biggest constraint on classroom instruction, it often influences decisions to reduce or even eliminate instruction that is not essential. I would argue like others (Layne, 2015; Fox, 2013) that we need to rethink the read-aloud component of the literacy block. The traditional image of the teacher sitting down with children after lunch and reading from a specially endeared chapter book for 30 minutes a day needs to be reconceptualized.

Every book that a teacher reads aloud is a book that remains in the head of the child.

When considering the conditions of language learning, read-alouds are a critical vehicle for immersing learners in reading and thus increasing the power of guided reading. Every book that a teacher reads aloud is a book that remains in the head of the child. Read-alouds provide many opportunities for teachers to demonstrate to students how the reading process works and put the teacher's love of reading on display. There is time during a read-aloud in which approximations are made (sometimes risks and celebrations occur naturally, sometimes more intentionally), so a teacher can show how performance, not perfection, is the goal in reading. Read-alouds are the time to convey expectations that everyone can do this and everyone should be engaged in doing this. Structured right, read-alouds actually can invite students to take over the responsibility for reading the text being shared.

Here are some tips in strengthening the read-aloud time, so it can provide support for the guided reading that follows.

1. If time is a constraint, move beyond the one-period-a-day vision of read-alouds and think about sprinkling shorter read-alouds throughout the day (Oczkus, 2012). Using a short read-aloud can actually be a great way to also add power to transitions during guided reading.

2. Be more intentional about the selection of the read-aloud titles. Laminack and Wadsworth (2006) suggest at least six purposes for read-alouds: address standards, build community, demonstrate craft, enrich vocabulary, model fluent reading, and entice children to read independently. Consider selecting texts that make connections to instruction that will follow during guided reading groups or to independent work away from the teacher.

3. Select texts at multiple levels for your read-alouds. The use of easier texts, including picture book formats, with older learners will help make these books seem more acceptable and less stigmatized. The end result is when these texts are included in guided reading, they are met with less resistance.

4. Select texts that will lead to independent reading habits. Start a series, introduce an author (especially one who writes at different levels), or sell a genre or format the students haven't experienced. This can lead to greater engagement in read-to-self opportunities when away from the teacher.

5. Consider how to use read-aloud choices to move students to increasingly complex texts and/or to expand their reading habits. Sometimes students self-select in a manner that keeps them rooted in easy texts when they can handle something more complex for their reading habits. This may open up acceptance of texts used during guided reading that might be different from the readers' current habit.

6. Use the read-aloud time to help students expand their visions of who readers are and what texts are by choosing alternative formats (i.e., readers read magazines, newspapers, pamphlets, brochures, graphic novels, comic books, online texts, etc.). Send a message that readers read lots of different things. It will strengthen the identities of readers who do not see themselves within the typical "readers read books" image. Students with positive identities will find greater value in guided reading instruction.

7. Plan your read-aloud moments so they leave students wanting more. Think about stopping points that would create interest in returning to the text either with you or on their own. Consider whether a read-aloud can be finished during guided reading.

8. Make sure that you are prepared for the read-aloud time. Invest in simple techniques to improve your read-aloud abilities so that your love of reading is always on display. It can start simply by varying your pace, volume, and pitch to add variety to your voice (Fox, 2008). Make sure the students know you are passionate about what you are teaching them to do using guided reading.

9. Put your reading life on display during the read-aloud time (Morgan, Mraz, Padak & Rasinski, 2009). Talk about why, when, and where you read. Share how you keep track of your reading. (I archive on Goodreads.com.) Tell where you find and keep your books. Identify who influences your choices and with whom you share what you are reading. The stories of your reading life can spill over to guided reading sessions and encourage students to share similar aspects of their reading lives. This will ultimately help them as they shape stronger identities as readers.

10. Select read-aloud texts that have central characters who embrace reading. Find characters who have a sense of urgency about reading, reveal strategies about their reading, or use reading to learn. Always consider the message you are sending to students about reading,

school, and learning in the texts you share with students. (See Figure 3C.) For older students, you might read about some characters who struggle a bit with their reading as a catalyst for conversations about how to strengthen their reading identities. (See Figure 3D.)

Figure 3C: Read-aloud Titles Featuring Characters with a Love of Reading

Again! by Emily Gravett (Simon & Schuster, 2011) A young dragon becomes a bit agitated when he can't convince his tired mother to read his favorite bedtime story over and over again.	*Lola at the Library* by Anna McQuinn (Charlesbridge, 2006) Tuesday is Lola's favorite day because she gets to go to the library with her mom and bring home new books to read.	*Roger Is Reading a Book* by Koen Van Biesen (Eerdmans Books for Young Readers, 2012) Roger must figure out a way to quiet down his neighbor so he can concentrate on his reading.
Calvin Can't Fly: *The Story of a Bookworm Birdie* by Jennifer Berne (Sterling Books, 2010) Calvin decides he would rather read than learn to fly, which comes in handy when the birds find themselves flying right into a hurricane.	*Look!* by Jeff Mack (Philomel Books, 2013) Trying to get attention from a boy whose eyes won't leave the screen, a gorilla finds a book might be the best way to start the bonding.	*The Snatchabook: Who's Stealing All the Stories?* by Helen Docherty (Sourcebooks Jabberwocky, 2013) A mystery is solved when a bunny stays up late to see who has been stealing all the bedtime stories and a new creature is discovered.
Cat Secrets by Jef Czekaj (Balzer and Bray, 2011) A mouse waits patiently for unsuspecting cats to let go of their book so the mouse can read about the cats' secrets.	*Margo and Marky's Adventures in Reading* by Thomas Kingsley Troupe (Picture Window Books, 2011) These two friends prove you can have any exciting adventure you want as long as you read.	*This Book Just Ate My Dog!* by Richard Byrne (Henry Holt and Co., 2014) The dog is only the first thing that is swallowed by a book and disappears in the center of the book as the character tries to figure out how to get it back.
Duncan the Story Dragon by Amanda Driscoll (Knopf, 2015) Duncan's imagination always catches fire when he reads (and so does his books). So he goes in search of the right buddy who will help him read.	*My Pet Book* by Bob Staake (Random House, 2014) A young boy decides a book may be a better pet than an animal but panics when his book goes missing.	*We Are in a Book!* *(An Elephant and Piggie Book)* by Mo Willems (Disney Hyperion, 2010) Elephant and Piggie discover the joy of being in a book, and a reader is reading their story.
How Rocket Learned to Read by Tad Hills (Schwartz & Wade, 2010) Rocket the dog finds his way through the alphabet and words as he learns to read.	*Ninja Bunny* by Jennifer Gray Olson (Knopf, 2015) A bunny reads his book, listing rules about becoming a ninja while learning the value of not working alone.	*You Should Read This Book* by Tony Stead (Capstone, 2015) This book actually helps kids decide what books they may want to read next.

Figure 3D: Read-aloud Books with Characters Strengthening Their Reading and Writing

Babymouse: Puppy Love by Jennifer L. Holm and Matthew Holm (Random House, 2007) Make sure you can project this graphic novel as you share it aloud. *Babymouse's* reading selections like *Charlotte's Web* and *National Velvet* guide her decisions about getting the best pet.	*Escape from Mr. Lemoncello's Library* by Chris Grabenstein (Random House, 2013) Kyle wins an overnight stay in a new library designed by his favorite game maker, but escape becomes dependent on solving a high-stakes series of clues and puzzles.	*Nightmare at the Book Fair* by Dan Gutman (Simon and Schuster, 2008) Trip hates to read, but he does help the PTA set up the book fair. Unfortunately, a stack of boxes fall on Trip, and his dreams start coming in a variety of genres. With a different genre featured in each chapter, it's a great way to introduce the categories as students figure out what they like.
Diary of a Wimpy Kid: Dog Days by Jeff Kinney (Amulet Books, 2009) Greg's mom starts a summer reading club called Reading Is Fun Club for the neighborhood boys.	*George Brown, Class Clown: Trouble Magnet* by Nancy Krulik (Grosset & Dunlap, 2010) George uses his reading to learn about Hawaii when he is assigned a class project on the state. His desire to provide a model of Hawaii's volcanoes keeps the learning moving forward.	*Squish: Brave New Pond* by Jennifer L. Holm and Matthew Holm (Random House, 2011) Like with *Babymouse*, make sure you can project this graphic novel as you share it aloud. Squish is always reading his favorite comic about Super Amoeba, who provides inspiration and insight for life's problems.
Diary of a Wimpy Kid: The Long Haul by Jeff Kinney (Amulet Books, 2014) Students might enjoy Greg's defense of his favorite reading series that he takes with him on a long family road trip. His strong defense of *The Underpants Bandits* series may give students some ideas for advocating for their favorite authors.	*Lunch Lady and the League of Librarians* by Jarrett J. Krosoczka (Knopf, 2009) As the kids' excitement about reading grows with an upcoming book fair and read-a-thon, the Lunch Lady tries to figure out what is going on with the librarians, whose demeanors have all suddenly changed.	*Star Time* by Patricia Reilly Giff (Wendy Lamb Books, 2011) The after-school program kids, better known as the Zigzag Kids, use their reading and writing to get ready to put on a show.

continued on next page

Dying to Meet You (43 Old Cemetery Road) by Kate Klise (HMH Books for Young Readers, 2009) Through a series of letters, notes, and memos, readers learn that a bestselling author moves into an old house hoping to crack his writer's block but doesn't know that a young boy, his cat, and a ghost already live there.	*Moxy Maxwell Does Not Love Stuart Little* by Peggy Gifford (Yearling, 2007) So what happens when one postpones summer reading until the day before school starts? You have to suffer the consequences. Such is the case for Moxy, who learns the hardest thing about summer reading is getting it started. Great book to start the year and talk about the importance of choice in our book selections.	*The Ellie McDoodle Diaries: New Kid in School* by Ruth McNally Barshaw (Bloomsbury, 2008) Ellie negotiates all the obstacles at being the new kid in school and finds solace in her reading and writing. Those talents lead new friends to her.
Eleven by Patricia Reilly Giff (Wendy Lamb Books, 2008) The discovery of contents in a locked box in his attic hint at the fact that Sam may have been kidnapped. This motivates him to get help with his reading from his friend Caroline so they can discover what happened in his past.	*My Life as a Book* by Janet Tashjian (Henry Holt, 2010) Central character and reluctant reader Derek uses a strategy of drawing little cartoons in the margins of his book (and they are in this book) to help him remember hard vocabulary words. His reading takes off when he tries to solve a mystery about his past.	*The Island of Dr. Libris* by Chris Grabenstein (Random House, 2015) Billy's summer island vacation takes an interesting turn when the books from a special library actually have characters that come to life.

Shared Reading

Guided reading may not be the most efficient way to provide instruction if the students across small groups often share similar needs and perform at similar levels. One teacher I observed during guided reading time had divided her young readers into multiple groups and prepared things for them to do while they were working away from her. I watched her rotate through her groups and conduct essentially the same lesson with each small group. The advantage may have been that she could attend to individual children when they were in small groups or perhaps the students could attend to the instruction when they were in small groups, but this teacher could have packed more into her day if she used a whole group model.

Shared reading, whole class instruction, and large group settings are a more efficient model for providing universal instruction, or initial instruction needed by all learners.

Shared reading, whole class instruction, and large group settings are a more efficient model for providing universal instruction, or initial instruction needed by all learners. It allows the teacher to conserve on both the amount of resources and class time needed for instruction. With all students in the same place at the same time using the same resources, effective shared reading may help support the guided reading dimension of the literacy block.

Considering the conditions of language learning can help strengthen shared readings. Shared readings are a time to create, add to, and interact with resources in an interactive classroom environment. Shared readings are designed for demonstrating and modeling. Learners can be shown how reading works, can stay with the teacher as they practice together, and can be observed by the teacher as they practice on their own. As students practice under the watchful eye of the teacher, feedback can be given and instruction adjusted. License can be given for approximations and can be judged immediately in case additional instruction is needed. Like read-alouds, shared readings provide another opportunity to establish the expectations that everyone can do this and should be engaged in doing this. The shared readings can be intentionally designed so that by the end of the lesson, the learner can take responsibility for finishing the reading experience.

Here are some tips for strengthening the universal instruction in your shared readings so it can support the guided reading that follows.

1. When teaching specific strategies, skills, or behaviors, plan universal instruction so that it follows a gradual release of responsibility model. Have modeling followed by opportunities for students to practice collectively with your guidance and independently under your watchful eye. Boyles (2004) reminds teachers that there is a need for both structured practice (teacher does while students help) and guided practice (students do while the teacher helps). In some cases, the actual guided practice might be during the guided reading lesson. When this occurs, link the large group lesson to the small group lesson (Burkins & Croft, 2010).

2. With explicit instruction, structure the lesson to include declarative knowledge (what the strategy is), conditional knowledge (why and when the strategy should be used), and, most important, procedural knowledge (how the strategy is actually done, step-by-step). This will better prepare students to apply the strategies during guided reading sessions.

3. Using explicit instruction, show that multiple strategies are used at the same time. Any one text offers opportunities to show that you could and should use many ways to think about the text in understanding and responding to it. Boyles (2004) recommends the integration of kid-friendly language in thinking aloud to model strategic thinking: "I'm *noticing, figuring out, picturing, wondering, guessing, making connections*," etc. This provides learners with language to use in articulating their strategic thinking during guided reading sessions.

4. Try to capture what is taught in hard copy. The lesson will then lead to a resource that can be added to the classroom environment and referred to at other times for additional instruction or student use. Strategy-embedded charts or posters work well and can be referred to during guided reading lessons as well. Clear step-by-step processes may be most useful.

Using explicit instruction, show that multiple strategies are used at the same time.

5. Select the texts you use for shared readings, or mentor texts, with greater intentionality. Shared readings are another opportunity to feature texts at multiple levels, in a variety of formats, from a variety of authors, and across a variety of genres. Use the shared experiences to continue to expand the vision of who readers are and what they read, so more texts become acceptable during guided reading sessions.

6. Consider the use of alternative modes (pictures, music, video) to introduce a strategy in a more concrete and accessible manner than with just a text-based example. A strategy like compare/contrast and a tool like a Venn diagram can be introduced using two pictures, two songs, or two short video clips. (Hint: Embed a hyperlink to the music or video in your Venn diagram on your interactive whiteboard.) This introduction can lay down the thinking for a print-based application during guided reading instruction.

7. Set up the shared experience so that it can be revisited during independent work time away. Provide access to the materials and resources so that it becomes a learning station that can engage some students while you're working with a guided reading group.

Independent Reading

Routman (2000) reminded us that students need to do more reading and struggling readers need to do even more reading. Her conclusion is echoed by others. "Everyone has heard the proverb: practice makes perfect. In learning to read it is true that reading practice—just reading—is a powerful contributor to the development of accurate, fluent, high-comprehension reading" (Allington, 2013, p. 43). By the end of elementary school, the greatest difference between successful readers and those who are less successful is the amount of practice in which they engage in reading (Stanovich, 1986). A classic study by Anderson, Wilson, and Fielding (1988) revealed that fifth-grade students who read at the 20th percentile reported reading 3.1 minutes per day. Those reading at the 50th percentile read 12.9 minutes a day, but those reading at the 90th percentile read approximately 40.4 minutes a day. The data are correlational, so it is easy to conclude that there seems to be some relationship between the number of minutes read and performance on traditional reading measures. Similar data emerge when we look at national and international assessments of reading performance (Allington, 2013). Unfortunately, if the relationship between time spent reading and performance extends beyond fifth grade, the gap grows wider. Those who read the most will read even more and get even better. Those who read the least will not grow stronger and will have even less reason to keep reading. One hopeful possibility rests in what could happen if we could just increase each reader's reading time 10 more minutes a day. The lowest readers would increase their reading time more than 300 percent. Yes, the other groups would also go up, but it would have its greatest impact on those who need the practice the most. It seems clear that guided

Those who read the most will read even more and get even better. Those who read the least will not grow stronger and will have even less reason to keep reading.

reading without a strong independent reading program will fall short of helping teachers close these gaps.

Reflecting on the conditions of language learning can help to evaluate independent reading programs. Independent reading programs rely on immersion in an environment in which there is virtually endless access to things to read and resources that can be used to support readers. Independent reading is the critical time to provide the practice readers need to grow their habits. To enhance the experience, consider structuring reading so peers can provide partners feedback or learners can confer with you to get that individual feedback. With encouragement, independent time provides an opportunity for learners to take chances and make approximations. And if the expectation is set that this time will be full of engagement and joy, learners will take responsibility as readers.

Let's look at some tips for bringing more power to the independent reading portion of a comprehensive literacy program so that it can support guided reading.

1. Building a classroom library is critical, but the library must be built so that almost all books can be read by almost all readers. Looking closely at one's current collection and thinking about how many titles can be read by any reader may provide a baseline for how to add to the collection. The more texts readers can read away from the teacher, the more engaged they will be during that independent time. Engagement will lead to greater stamina and more practice, which actually helps students achieve the gains desired from guided reading. (In Chapter Four, I will look more closely at texts, but remember that texts must be seen as both accessible and acceptable by the learners.)

2. Organize books with less emphasis on levels. Book centers that contain tubs of books all arranged by levels can make certain books less appealing to most students. Books organized by genres, topics, themes, authors, and formats allow different levels of books to be placed in the same tubs. This setup can lead to readers at different levels discussing their choices around the same focus, which rarely happens if the books are organized by levels. This will help take the focus off the level of the texts used in guided reading and shift attention to more important aspects like the topic, theme, format, or genre. Make sure a variety of books are displayed and promoted in the physical classroom space as well.

3. Support learners in the texts they choose to read independently. Intentionally teach learners how to select appropriate texts for their independent reading time, but don't be afraid to make suggestions. Language like "I thought you might like this" or "See what you think about this" allows for influence but leaves the final choice to the reader. Suggestions also help reduce the amount of time spent choosing books so more time is spent reading books.

> *Books organized by genres, topics, themes, authors, and formats allow different levels of books to be placed in the same tubs. This setup can lead to readers at different levels discussing their choices around the same focus, which rarely happens if the books are organized by levels.*

4. Structure guided reading so that it can lead students to texts to read during independent time. For example, consider turning the balance of the reading over to students to complete during independent reading time. Also introduce related texts for independent reading time.

5. Using explicit instruction, intentionally address what independent reading is, what ways we can read independently, what happens when we read silently, where the best places to read in the classroom are, and what the best ways to make good use of our independent reading time are (Boushey & Moser, 2006; Opitz & Ford, 2014). This will minimize management issues that can distract attention from guided reading instruction.

6. Allow time for students to share what they have been reading, thinking, and learning from independent reading time. This time to share provides a meaningful outcome for the reading activities and may encourage others to read the same books. With a greater sense of purpose, students may also be motivated to improve their reading during guided reading sessions. A small part of guided reading time could include having students share their independent reading experiences to strengthen the link between both.

7. Integrate the use of individual conferences to meet with readers about what and how they were reading. This sets up an additional opportunity to assess and interact with individual students outside the guided reading setting. It provides a chance for you and the student to discuss goals to work on during guided and independent reading time, which will keep the student focused.

8. Build in some minimal accountability for independent reading like documenting progress toward personal goals. Avoid extrinsic rewards, public displays, or tracking the number of books or number of pages read. Focus more on effort and time. This shifts the focus from what is read to reading. Independent reading is where identities about being a reader are being shaped. We want all students to come to the guided reading instruction with a positive view of who they are as readers. Social comparisons and external judgments usually interfere with that.

Other Considerations

In this chapter, I encouraged teachers to look carefully at the eight conditions needed for language learning. I also narrowed my focus by discussing ways to improve the quality of three key elements of the literacy program that go beyond guided reading. Obviously, there are other factors that can be considered in making sure guided reading fits well within a literacy program. For each of the reading elements, there is also a parallel element related to writing instruction that could be examined and strengthened as needed: writing aloud, shared writing, guided writing, and/or independent writing. Likewise, other aspects of language arts instruction (speaking, listening, viewing, and producing) could also be evaluated. The stronger each element of the language arts program is, the clearer the role and responsibility of guided reading becomes. One could also examine other places in which students receive instruction and practice: home connections, summer programs, and support programs. Manners of interaction related to classroom discourse and engagement strategies could be another focus. However, one needs to start somewhere. My suggestion is if a literacy program can at least guarantee that all learners are surrounded by the conditions of language learning and have access to effective read-alouds, shared reading, and independent reading opportunities, guided reading should be able to play an appropriate and effective role in helping all students thrive.

For school leaders and educators looking for a more thorough examination, Dorn and Soffos (2011) provide a comprehensive tool called "Environmental Scale for Assessing Implementation Levels (ESAIL)" in their book *Interventions That Work*. The tool requires that educators look at 10 criteria: literate environment, classroom organization, data-based instruction and research-based interventions, differentiation, school-wide progress monitoring, literacy coaches, collaborative learning communities, plans for systematic change, technology, and advocacy. In *Engaging Minds in the Classroom*, Michael Opitz and I (2014) provide an additional evaluative tool, which specifically targets the affective components of a school literacy program related to students, teachers, materials, assessments, and the physical environment.

> *The stronger each element of the language arts program is, the clearer the role and responsibility of guided reading becomes.*

Guided Reading: What's New, and What's Next?

CHAPTER FOUR:
How Should Texts Be Selected for Guided Reading?

> The challenge of reading instruction does not reside solely in the text, but in what each teacher does to move each reader forward.
>
> *Glasswell and Ford, 2011*

You can tell an educational practice may be getting a little too much attention when it spills over into areas you would least expect it. A commercial publisher sent me a sample of books for children it had just published. Included in the sample was a board book. Featured on its front cover almost as prominently as the title was a red circle that labeled the book as Level 3 for 12–18 months. Even board books for babies were now showing up with suggested levels on them! A lot of attention is given to the leveled texts used in guided reading; however, it is important to remember that more attention needs to be given to the child reading the text during guided reading. We are not just teaching texts, we are teaching the students reading those texts. Text selection becomes critical because, while almost any interaction a student has with a text can reveal information about that reader, specific texts may allow us to zero in on what an individual student can or needs to be able to do as an independent strategic reader. Today, teachers have a lot of sources from which to choose leveled texts. In the Appendix, starting on page 186, I have identified and described a number of publishers with potential contributions to collections to leveled texts to support classroom instruction. In this chapter, let's examine issues and ideas related to how to select the best texts for use in guided reading. Let's also look closely at how to bring and link trade books to guided reading sessions.

We are not just teaching texts, we are teaching the students reading those texts. Text selection becomes critical because, while almost any interaction a student has with a text can reveal information about that reader, specific texts may allow us to zero in on what an individual student can or needs to be able to do as an independent strategic reader.

What Level?

In guided reading, text selection decisions seem dominated by discussions of levels. Almost all models of guided reading suggest that the text be at the instructional level of the reader. If the model for guided reading is scaffolding, then instructional-level texts become the bridge between what the reader is capable of doing on his or her own (independent level) and what the reader is unable to do even with support (frustrational level). If the reader is able to do something independently, that probably does not need to be the focus of our instruction. We should always avoid doing for the student what the student can do on his or her own. Independent-level texts do offer an opportunity for students to build their comfort and confidence as readers and, ultimately, this can lead to improvement in competence as well, but the limited time we have to offer small group instruction and intervention would suggest that this might not be our top priority during guided reading. It might be a better priority for other aspects of the literacy program that support guided reading.

On the other hand, the demands of frustrational-level texts may overwhelm the students and lead to too many potential points of instruction or intervention. Frustration may actually erode confidence and comfort in the readers. Repeated experiences of this nature may interfere with readers' identities, causing them to think less of themselves as readers and writers and begin to see themselves as outsiders with little value for the instruction being offered during guided reading. So selection should focus on an instructional-level text. This type of text has enough teaching points to move the student forward in ability to operate more competently and independently without overwhelming the learner and eroding confidence and comfort with reading.

So how are instructional-level texts determined? Believe it or not, the formula to determine instructional-level texts is rooted in work by Betts that was done 70 years ago, and his framework has been relatively unchanged since then (Halladay, 2012). See Figure 4A.

Figure 4A: Betts Reading Levels

	Accuracy	Comprehension
Independent	99 percent	90 percent
Instructional	95–99 percent	75–89 percent
Frustrational	Below 90 percent	or below 50 percent

If there is one area that evolved since Betts' original work, it seems to be in regards to how to determine an instructional level. For Betts, a 95 percent accuracy rate seemed to distinguish instructional-level text from frustrational-level text. For Clay (1979), a 90 percent accuracy rate during a running record was the mark of the same distinction. Betts is suggesting that an instructional-level text would mean that the reader is missing no more than one out of 20 words as he or she reads. For Clay, it would be no more than one out of 10. So how difficult should an instructional text be? Clay finds some texts appropriate for instruction that would be considered frustrational by Betts. In his review of the research, Allington (2012) builds a case to err on the side of more accuracy versus less. Allington credits Betts with first telling us that instruction with text of high success rates (low error rates) often leads to greater gains. Allington suggests Betts' instructional-level criteria are best for guided reading sessions. He is quick to point out, however, that no matter what set of criteria is used, it needs to be used with flexibility.

Levels—Too Simple?

Why flexibility? Guided reading focuses on leveled texts at its heart, but there are some important issues to consider when placing a book in the hands of a student. Ironically, leveling systems simplify the complex interaction between the reader and text in a specific context. On the other hand, leveling systems often add a cumbersome layer of complexity by developing multiple discrete levels (Glasswell & Ford, 2011). Let's look first at how leveling systems simplify the interactions of readers and texts. In an interactive model of reading (Wisconsin Department of Public Instruction, 1986), a minimum of three critical factors are at play. First, there is the text and everything that the text demands of the reader (e.g., content, format, concepts, organization, author's purpose). Then, there is the reader and everything that the reader brings to the page (e.g., motivation, subject knowledge, background experience, vocabulary, purpose). And finally, there is the context in which the reading takes place (e.g., physical setting, activity, outcome, emotional climate) in addition to other social and cultural influences. In even minimalist models, the potential factors at play when a reader interacts with a text add up fast. If any one of those factors changes, it can make the text easier or harder for the reader. From this information, one can conclude that the successful interaction of a reader and a text in a specific context is a very complex relationship. If any single variable changes, the degree of success the reader has with the text can be affected.

The problem with leveling systems is they capture only a limited list of those factors. Most of the factors used to determine levels relate to the texts themselves since they are the most stable of the three key components. They contain elements that are easy to count (e.g., sentence length, word frequency), and even as the list of criteria that are counted and reviewed grows, leveling systems are rooted in the texts because the variations of readers and contexts are virtually impossible to capture in these formulas and rubrics. In the end, leveling systems overpromise a magical match between a text and a reader at the same level even though the level of the text never considered the potential variations of the readers to which the text is matched. In their book *Beyond Leveled Books*, Sibberson and Szymusiak (2001) pointed out that two readers with whom they worked were identified at the same level but had significant variations in what they brought to the table. Anthony and Sarah were at the same level but differed in their behaviors, interests, tastes, and abilities. Then they demonstrated how two texts identified at the same level demanded different things from the readers. *Bunnicula and Grandpa's Face* are texts at the same level but offer differing supports and challenges for readers. In the end, Anthony found one of the books easier than the other; but Sarah had just the reverse reaction—even though both the readers and the texts were all at the same level.

In her study, Halladay (2008) was working with second graders. Each second grader had a text that accuracy levels suggested was at the instructional level and another that was at the frustrational level. Then she checked each of the student's comprehension of those two texts. As to be expected, about 70 percent of the students had better comprehension on the text they read with better accuracy—the instructional-level text. However, 30 percent of the students actually had comparable or better comprehension with their frustrational-level text. How could that happen? Perhaps there were other factors at play than those that were captured by the way we assessed the level of the text and/or the child? When asked whether they enjoyed their frustrational-level texts, almost 80 percent of Halladay's second graders said "A lot!" This rivaled the positive reaction they had with their instructional-level texts. Obviously, other things must be happening when these children interacted with their books. Perhaps Halladay's second graders found as much status in being connected to their harder texts as they did to being seen with their easier texts.

Even more telling was the work of Steinkuehler (2011), who assessed fifth-grade male students using a traditional measure (the Qualitative Reading Inventory) and then assessed those students when they were reading on a self-chosen, online gaming site. In a study she called "The Mismeasure of Boys," Steinkuehler's students actually tested five grade levels higher on their websites than on the traditional measure. One of the trickiest problems in selecting texts for older readers who have been identified as reading at lower levels is finding lower-level texts that the fifth grader will find acceptable. Obviously, that was not a problem when the fifth graders brought choice and interest to the page. We will look more closely at addressing this concern later in this chapter.

So why has this complex relationship frequently been reduced to assessing a child's oral reading accuracy to determine a reading level and then matching that child to a text that has been assigned that level by some external source? It allows for an easy assumption that the best way to secure a successful transaction between the reader and the text is to match the child to a text at his or her level. In the end, lists and numbers seem to replace teacher judgment (Worthy & Sailors, 2001). I would argue that teachers need to be aware of these complexities and allowed flexibility in using professional judgment to guide a more critical use of leveled materials when making instructional decisions.

Levels—Too Complex?

In using professional judgment, teachers need to be aware of a second major problem with leveling systems. They add a layer of complexity to guided reading instruction by suggesting that there are multiple discrete levels of texts and readers. In looking at one leveling system that defined at least 26 levels of texts and readers, analysis revealed that J level texts were determined by reviewing 10 key text characteristics with 66 specific criteria. In contrast, the next level up—K level texts—used the same 10 text characteristics with 71 specific criteria. Twenty-one of the criteria were the same for both levels and others were only distinguishable by qualitative degrees (i.e., "some" or "many"). In the end, a book like *Henry and Mudge: The First Book* was assigned to the J basket, while *Frog and Toad Are Friends* found its way into the K basket.

I'm not denying there might be real differences between these two texts, but practically speaking are those differences meaningful enough to use a book at a given level with one group of readers while withholding it from another group of readers one level lower? It's even more problematic at the upper levels. In a recent conversation with a reading teacher at the intermediate grades, she discussed how she was trying to convince the teachers she supported that books listed at the R, S, and T levels are really R-ish, S-ish, and T-ish and shouldn't be treated with a type of precision that they didn't deserve.

Because of these complex systems, the idea of helping children with leveled texts has turned into a juggling act, with multiple baskets of books, assessments defining children at multiple levels, and grouping practices that become almost unmanageable (Glasswell & Ford, 2011). Perhaps efforts spent attaching levels to books and books to readers might be better spent on "making available abundant text selections that provide rich and varied reading experiences to develop students' independence and enjoyments as readers" (Dzaldov & Peterson, 2005, p. 223).

Levels Can Impact Practice

When teachers outsource the decision-making of the right text for specific readers to leveling systems, rigid fidelity can replace professional judgment. Levels are ballpark estimates but should be considered in light of what the teacher knows about the text, the goals, and the learners. If the level is the primary focus in selecting texts used during guided reading, it can actually compromise opportunities for those who might need the most practice. I realized this observing a second-grade classroom. The teacher was working with a guided reading group using a 16-page level G text that contained about 80 words (five of which were multisyllabic) in the entire book. Then the teacher moved to her N level guided reading group, which was reading 10 pages from a short chapter book. The selection had 87 words (11 of them multisyllabic) on the first page alone. I realized that by the time the N group had read the whole chapter, they would have received more than 10 times as much practice reading words than the G group, even though the G group had greater needs. Because the focus was on teaching a text at a specific level, the guided reading carried out in this classroom would do little to close the gap between the level G readers and the level N readers.

In selecting texts, especially for those readers with the greatest needs, one way to close the gap is to be more intentional about the number of words students are asked to read. Closing the gap starts with increasing awareness about the word counts of text. Texts at the same level often vary in their word count. Figure 4B on page 79 shows how wide that variation can be at a specific level. When possible, select texts that provide students with more practice. If two texts are at the same level, why not pick the text that provides the most practice? In planning the lesson, also consider how planning for rereading can increase the practice of a text with a low word count. Repeated readings of the same book will

> *When teachers outsource the decision-making of the right text for specific readers to leveling systems, rigid fidelity can replace professional judgment. Levels are ballpark estimates but should be considered in light of what the teacher knows about the text, the goals, and the learners.*

provide readers with more practice with the words in that book. You can expand the number of specific words practiced by helping students move from the guided reading text to additional related texts at the same level (introduced at the table) for independent reading away from the teacher. Reading a variety of texts at the same level will offer practice with a greater variety of words. Finally, don't outsource the reading of even more difficult texts to yourself or peers. Invite students in on accessible parts of these more challenging texts. These tips are captured in Figure 4C. For most teachers, closing the practice gap begins by becoming more aware of the issue and establishing a baseline on the number of words practiced by guided reading groups. In Figure 4D, I have looked at readers at three levels. (See Appendix page 185 for a reproducible version.) Without attention to word count gaps, those students reading at the highest level will get more practice than the other groups of readers, with almost twice as much practice than the students reading at the lowest level. By rereading the initial text with the lowest group, it raised their amount of word practice up to the level of the highest group. The same happens by jigsawing the second group's text into two parts and rereading. If I use the related text with those reading the highest level, their practice will increase further, so I have to think about how to use the related texts with my other two groups in creative ways to keep the practice comparable. In the end, I actually bring in one more text for two of the groups. They revisit previous but related texts. By the end of the sessions, those in need of the most word practice have received more reading practice. With subsequent attention to structuring their independent work once they leave the guided reading session, word practice stays on track.

This leads to the important concept of reading mileage. Advanced readers commonly process more words because they read more lengthy and dense texts, and they can read them faster. So even when a school guarantees a set time period for every child, they cannot guarantee the reading mileage that will occur in that 30 minutes. The number of words children are reading even with appropriate leveled text can contribute to a widening achievement gap. The potential gaps in word counts between different leveled texts sometimes ensure that readers who are reading lower levels receive less practice than those readers on higher levels of texts. Figure 4E on page 80 displays word count ranges in three texts at each of three consecutive levels of guided reading materials. As we see in the table, without making any adjustments, the J level group readers would read 162 more words (almost 25 percent more) than the H level group readers if they each read three texts at their level. When we do the math on this, we see the high group readers could be reading more than 800 extra words in five days. Over the course of a school year, the difference is approximately 32,000 words! In this way, the strongest readers get the most practice at reading words, and the gap between high group and low group readers can unintentionally widen. To accelerate growth, teachers need to intentionally address those instructional gaps more often and focus on helping students make significant progress through the levels in order to achieve proficiency.

Figure 4B: Difference in Word Count Ranges with Leveled Texts
from *Leveled Books, K–8: Matching Texts to Readers for Effective Teaching* (Fountas & Pinnell, 2006)

	Smallest Number of Words	Largest Number of Words
Level B	14 words	73 words
Level C	13 words	108 words
Level D	14 words	236 words

Figure 4C: Raising Word Counts

✓ Stay aware of word count differences.

✓ Select texts at the level that provides the most opportunities to read words.

✓ Make sure all readers have a chance to read the whole text.

✓ Provide opportunities for repeated readings of low count texts.

✓ Provide opportunities to read additional texts at the same level.

✓ Provide repeated readings of accessible parts of harder texts.

Figure 4D: Closing the Word Count Gap

	Group One: Level 8 (E)	Group Two: Level 11 (G)	Group Three: Level 15 (I)
Word count in group text	133	190	263
Number of times read	2	2 (jigsaw text into two parts)	1
Total	266	285	263
Word count in related text #1	152 (418)	200 (485)	296 (559)
Number of times read	2 (570)	2 (set as a reader's theater into three parts) (550)	1 (559)
Word count in related text #2	Reread related level 6 (D) (151)	Reread related level (E) book (133)	
Number of times read	1	1	
Total	151	133	
Total amount of practice	721	683	559
Other practice opportunities to raise word count	Independent practice on three guided reading texts and partner reads on the two texts with dialogue parts	Rehearse for formal presentation of readers' theater on related text	Independent reading

Figure 4E: Difference in Reading Mileage with Leveled Texts

Level	Range of Words in Books at This Level	Average Words per Book	Average Total Word Count for Three Books
H	165–247	206	618
I	201–257	229	687
J	238–282	260	780

Exposure to a variety of words over time may be a better goal than just repeated practice of a text with many of the same words. That's why moving through texts more quickly, even as you stay at one level, is more important than holding on to one text until mastered.

In addition to the number of words practiced, others have called attention to the nature of the words practiced (Murray, Munger & Hiebert, 2014). In analyzing the words in texts, a teacher may want to note how many unique words in the text are read by the reader. Again, two texts with the same number of words could differ by the number of unique words in each text. Given a choice between a text that asks readers to practice many of the same words versus a text that asks readers to practice more unique words, students may make greater gains by reading the text with the most unique words. Exposure to a variety of words over time may be a better goal than just repeated practice of a text with many of the same words. That's why moving through texts more quickly, even as you stay at one level, is more important than holding on to one text until mastered.

Hiebert (2014) makes one more critical distinction. She argues the real accelerant for growth is knowledge. The more knowledge the reader can bring to the page, the more texts the reader will be able to successfully negotiate. Knowledge is often reflected in vocabulary. Hiebert reminds us that if a child decodes a word that already exists in his or her knowledge base that he or she can already build meaning for, the decoding takes on more power. The reader now has a meaningful label for the words on the page, which helps to enhance remembering and understanding the word for future use as well.

The trouble is some leveled texts control their vocabulary to use words that target practice of specific graphophonemic patterns. Many times, the decodable words are used to name characters. Figuring out the word does little to help the reader connect a possible memorable meaning to the word to allow it to be transferred easily to future reading and writing. For example, a little storybook that features two cats named Ham and Jam allows for the practicing of the CVC pattern to impact decoding abil-ity; however, the words *ham* and *jam* get connected to the cat characters and not to the real things they represent. An informational text about what sandwiches kids like could actually use the same words. This kind of book has a few purposes, as it provides practice on the CVC pattern and, with photographic support, could help make a more powerful connection to the real meanings of those words. This can impact decoding ability and vocabulary and content knowledge.

When selecting texts, especially for young or struggling readers, teachers need to look closely at the words being practiced in two texts at the same level. More words are better. More unique words are better. More unique words that trigger actual meanings and/or add knowledge to the reader might be the best. Figure 4F on page 82 provides an analysis sheet that might assist teachers in choosing better texts, especially when both are at the same level. Beck and McKeown (1985) would call words that connect to known meanings Tier One vocabulary (*hot, cold, dry, rain*). Words that may be new labels for known concepts are Tier Two vocabulary (*scorching, frigid, arid, drizzle*), and new labels for new concepts are Tier Three vocabulary (*meteorology, steppe, tundra, climate*).

The texts selected for guided reading should focus not only on practicing an isolated word strategy, but practicing that strategy while gaining vocabulary and knowledge. Think about the quick lesson that could follow the two Ham and Jam books. Where does the learner gain the most: If we practice other CVC words, if we practice other names for cats, or if we practice other ingredients for sandwiches? It's the latter that allows for teaching points about decoding, word meaning, and adding knowledge.

The texts selected for guided reading should focus not only on practicing an isolated word strategy, but practicing that strategy while gaining vocabulary and knowledge.

Figure 4F: Word Analysis of Leveled Texts

	Text One	Text Two
Level		
Number of total words		
Number of unique words		
Number of content words that trigger known meaning for the student (known labels for known concepts)		
Number of content words that build new vocabulary for the student (new labels for known concepts)		
Number of content words that build new content for the student (new labels for new concepts)		
Other critical considerations in analyzing words in text		

Levels Are Not Needs

It has taken some time to realize that instructional levels are not the same as instructional needs. Levels are not magic bullets that ensure quality teaching in a guided reading group. My colleague Kathryn Glasswell (Glasswell and Ford, 2011) described a teacher with whom she had worked in her role as an instructional coach. In the teacher's class, there were three readers all reading at the same level. Taylor had few miscues, though he struggled with his retelling and ability to answer comprehension questions. Marita and Kimber had better comprehension but less accuracy in reading the benchmark text. But even Marita and Kimber differed in the approaches they used for word strategies. Marita's miscues showed a pattern of using initial letters in words to guess at unknown words while reading, while when Kimber came across a word she did not know, she often predicted the word from context. If the teacher focused exclusively on the level the children were reading by teaching a guided reading *lesson* with the suggested leveled text, he would have chosen to use a one-size-fits-all lesson set for readers who may all be at the same level but have very different instructional needs. Many teachers confuse reading levels with reading needs. Just because children are at the same level doesn't mean they should be taught the same. A colleague of mine once said: "Even a homogenous group is probably not that homogeneous."

> Many teachers confuse reading levels with reading needs. Just because children are at the same level doesn't mean they should be taught the same.

There's a classic example that Clay uses to share the difference between levels and needs. She profiled two children, each reading the same emergent reader text. The two children each had four miscues and, upon closer examination, they actually had miscues on the same four words (*lady, boy, bicycle, squashed*). An assessment of their accuracy rates would suggest the two learners were the same. Accuracy rate failed to catch the meaningful difference between the two readers. Recording the words they missed would suggest they were also the same. Writing down the words they missed also failed to capture a meaningful difference between the two readers. When one looked closely at their substitutions, every substitution by one student was visually similar but semantically out of sync, like Marita and Kimber above. And for the other student, every substitution was semantically compatible but had no visual similarity. They were at the same level, but how the teacher would scaffold instruction with one would have to be different from how the instruction was scaffolded for the other. You might be able to ask the first student if the miscue made sense to guide him or her to re-examine the miscue, but if you asked that same question to the second child, that child would tell you that it did.

In their classic study, Buly and Valencia (2002) looked at older learners who had not achieved proficiency on a statewide assessment exam. They wanted to know why the students had not done well on the exam. Students were reassessed to determine levels of accuracy, reading rate, and levels of understanding. Using just those three measures, Valencia and Buly identified seven profiles of readers who fell below the bar. (See Figure 4G on page 84.) By looking at the two most common profiles,

"Slow Steady Comprehenders" were clearly students who needed help with fluency. But if they were grouped with the "Slow Word Callers" because they all fell below the bar and the chosen intervention only focused on fluency, it would do little to help the second group. Would they simply learn to call words faster without any gain in comprehension? The "Slow Word Callers" might be at the same level, but they have different needs.

In looking at these examples, what is clear is that using a careful analysis of assessment data to inform one's thinking in providing flexible needs-based grouping is important. One cannot assume that knowing the right level is the same as identifying a reader's learning needs.

Figure 4G: Below the Bar Profiles
(Buly and Valencia, 2002)

Reader Profile	Accuracy	Fluency	Comprehension
Proficient	OK	OK	OK
Slow Steady Comprehenders (24 percent)	OK	Difficulties	Difficulties but OK for finished sections
Slow Word Callers (17 percent)	OK with many self-corrections	Difficulties	Difficulties
Struggling Word Callers (15 percent)	OK with laborious effort	Difficulties	Difficulties
Automatic Word Callers (18 percent)	OK	OK	Difficulties
Word Stumblers (17 percent)	Difficulties	OK	OK but missed details
Disabled (9 percent)	Difficulties	Difficulties	Difficulties

Accessible and Acceptable Leveled Texts

As previously mentioned, one of the challenges in using leveled texts is finding books that are both accessible and acceptable for readers often in need of more support. This problem is most noticeable with older students. Leveled texts are usually designed to appeal to learners who typically read at that level. For example, easier levels are designed for younger children, not for older learners who might be reading at that level. While those texts might be accessible for older struggling readers, they may find features about the texts (format, characters, topics) less than acceptable. If the text we use doesn't seem to respect the learner, the learner may quickly react, withdraw, or resist. Even the best guided reading instruction around that text will probably not engage the student who has already dismissed the text. (See Figure 4H.)

If the text we use doesn't seem to respect the learner, the learner may quickly react, withdraw, or resist. Even the best guided reading instruction around that text will probably not engage the student who has already dismissed the text.

Figure 4H: Acceptable and Accessible Texts

Older Reader	Older Reader
Easy guided reading leveled texts	*Challenging guided reading leveled texts*
Content and format often not seen as acceptable even when accessible	Content and format seen as acceptable but might not be accessible for all learners
Younger Reader	Younger Reader
Easy guided reading leveled texts	*Challenging guided reading leveled texts*
Content and format often acceptable and accessible to most but may not challenge all	Content and format often not seen as acceptable, even for those who could find it accessible

In considering the texts in the classroom, especially to use to support guided reading instruction, teachers must think about their acceptability as well as their accessibility (Fielding & Roller, 1992). It's not enough to have texts at all the levels teachers might need. They need to be texts that students would want to read, even (and maybe especially) for students in need of the greatest support. Remember, one way to make more texts seem socially acceptable in an intermediate-grade classroom is for the teacher to pervasively use texts at all levels throughout instruction, including as read-alouds and shared readings and in content areas. Also remember that with thoughtful scaffolded instruction and differentiated support, many of the texts that would be socially acceptable but academically challenging suddenly become more accessible for those readers who might struggle the most.

So are there any acceptable and accessible texts? Many transitional chapter book series serve this purpose. I have listed some of my favorites in Figure 4I on page 87. They used chapter book formats with alternative layouts, often with ample graphic or photographic support. They usually feature similarly aged kids in school-like settings with a lot of humor infused. Series often have an advantage because they share similar content, language, and layouts. Readers will make connections effectively between the texts. They don't have to renegotiate all the demands of the texts since they can carry what they have learned from reading other books in the series forward to the next book. They can work flexibly across the series, even if the single titles in the series may be at different levels. Series help to build skill and confidence to accelerate growth. Easier books with similar themes and language formats will help teachers build context for other texts that they might first have seen as too difficult for some readers (Glasswell & Ford, 2010). In guided reading materials, look for recurring characters at different levels like *Little Sea Horse* or *Min Monkey* (Capstone Classroom's Engage Literacy). Older learners will enjoy reading a new, more challenging story about a character they already know.

Remember, one way to make more texts seem socially acceptable in an intermediate-grade classroom is for the teacher to pervasively use texts at all levels throughout instruction, including as read-alouds and shared readings and in content areas. Also remember that with thoughtful scaffolded instruction and differentiated support, many of the texts that would be socially acceptable but academically challenging suddenly become more accessible for those readers who might struggle the most.

Teachers also need to discover that easier texts can be accessed in ways that make them less obvious. For example, easier texts can be found in anthologies (story collections or poetry selections), informational texts (often divided into chunks that can be read separately), newspapers and magazines (some articles are hard, but others might be right at level), and—perhaps the best tool—e-readers. The technology looks the same in every reader's hand, but what they are reading online could be at lots of different levels. Remember that in real life, readers read all kinds of things. A teacher who thoughtfully uses a variety of texts with varying degrees of difficulty is more likely to find engaging texts to put into the hands of children so that they can see themselves as readers. This may be the best way for making accessible texts seem acceptable in a classroom with children at different reading levels.

> ...remember the importance of building collections so that all readers in diverse classrooms can see themselves in the texts selected.

Finally, also remember the importance of building collections so that all readers in diverse classrooms can see themselves in the texts selected. One of the criticisms of some leveled readers is that they often vary little in sociocultural features, including the gender, race, and class of characters portrayed. Using interest inventories may provide additional insights into how to augment a collection that will reach more readers. (See the Appendix, starting on page 193.) Your familiarity with your students' identities may be just as helpful in matching texts to readers as leveled book lists (Dzaldov & Peterson, 2005).

Progressing through Leveled Texts Does Not Equal Proficiency

One of my graduate students expressed her frustration in class one night about the reading levels of her fourth graders. She works in a school with a stable population and a comprehensive literacy program that includes small group instruction with leveled texts. Half of her readers are below a fourth-grade reading level! One problem could be leveled texts. Leveling systems with multiple discrete levels often cause teachers to focus on making progress through the levels rather than staying focused on students achieving proficiency. Recently, Kathryn Glasswell and I were involved in a project to map out the trajectory of three different groups of learners using a commercially available guided reading program. Progress was plotted following the pacing recommendations suggested by the instructional materials. Each group of readers was put on a path that would lead to making progress. But the paths laid out in the pacing guide for above-, at-, and below-grade-level readers raised a confounding issue. Over the course of the year, if teachers followed the pacing guide, they would leave the below-grade-level readers far short of proficiency. What's more, if teachers in a school used the materials over multiple years, the gap between the readers who were below grade level and other readers with more skill would actually widen. For the readers below grade level, there would have been progress, but they would not achieve proficiency. So my graduate student's school likely had a kit that was part of a larger program that slowed down reading growth.

Figure 4I: Series of Acceptable and Accessible Texts

Fiction Series Texts
43 Old Cemetery Road by Kate Klise (published by Scholastic)
Alvin Ho by Lenore Look (published by Yearling)
Big Nate by Lincoln Peirce (published by Balzer + Bray)
Blogtastic! Novels by Rose Cooper (published by Delacorte Books)
Charlie Small by Charlie Small (published by David Fickling Books)
Dear Dumb Diary by Jim Benton (published by Scholastic)
Diary of a Wimpy Kid by Jeff Kinney (published by Amulet)
EllRay Jakes by Sally Warner (published by Puffin)
George Brown, Class Clown by Nancy Krulik (published by Scholastic)
Icky Ricky by Michael Rex (published by Random House)
Lulu by Hilary McKay (published by Albert Whitman)
Moxy Maxwell by Peggy Gifford (published by Schwartz & Wade)
My Life As a… by Janet Tashjian (published by Scholastic)
Raymond and Graham by Mike Knudson (published by Puffin)
The Ellie McDoodle Diaries by Ruth McNally Barshaw (published by Bloomsbury)
Zigzag Kids by Patricia Reilly Giff (published by Wendy Lamb Books)
Graphic Novels
Babymouse by Jennifer L. Holm and Matthew Holm (published by Random House)
Bean Dog and Nugget by Charise Mericle Harper (published by Knopf)
Comics Squad by various authors (published by Random House)
Dragonbreath by Ursula Vernon (published by Puffin)
Kit Feeny by Michael Townsend (published by Knopf)
Lunch Lady by Jarrett J. Kroseckra (published by Knopf)
Max Axiom STEM Adventures by Agnieszka Biskup and Tammy Enz (published by Capstone)
Mighty Mighty Monsters by Sean O'Reilly (published by Capstone)
Nickolas Flux History Chronicles by Nel Yomtov, Mari Bolte, and Terry Collins (published Capstone)
Squish by Jennifer L. Holm and Matthew Holm (published by Random House)
Stone Rabbit by Erik Craddock (published by Random House)
Superman Family Adventures by Franco Aureliani and Art Baltazar (published by Capstone)
The Flying Beaver Brothers by Maxwell Easton III (published by Knopf)
Informational Texts
5,000 Awesome Facts (About Everything!) (published by National Geographic Kids)
Guinness World Records (published by Guinness Books)
Ripley's Believe It or Not! (published by Scholastic)
TIME for Kids BIG Book of… (published by Time for Kids)

The multiple discrete levels inherent in some programs make it easy to see progress from one level to the next, especially with all the small steps that levels build into the primary grades. Teachers may get comfortable seeing this progress but lose sight of the fact that progress is a means to an end with proficiency as the end goal. End points or accepted benchmarks need to be very clear for teachers so that instruction can be paced in such a way that, as a child progresses, he or she gets closer to the goal of proficiency. This means that a teacher may need to consider how to accelerate the progress of the readers below grade level to be able to help those children achieve that end-level benchmark. For example, a child who is behind his classmates in reading by 18 months needs to make more than just an academic year's progress in one year in order to achieve proficiency.

A leveling program can be a tool in helping teachers address this time variation, but a program can also contribute to the variation. One colleague working with students with identified learning disabilities actually was looking for more levels in the system she was using. This was because some students seemed stuck at one level since each level has some range. The students may have entered on the front end of the range and moved toward the back end but stayed at the same level. More discrete levels might have captured the growth she wanted to report to the families. While that might be true, it still reflects a focus on reporting progress, and what you really want to report is proficiency.

The attention to proficiency levels has gained significant attention recently because of the conversations around College and Career Readiness Standards. One key anchor standard proposed states, "Read and comprehend complex literary and informational texts independently and proficiently" (National Governors Association Center for Best Practices & Council of Chief State School Officers, 2010). In order to accomplish that outcome, standards were set up with two-year windows. For example, in second grade, the expectation would be "by the end of the year, read and comprehend literature, including stories and poetry, in the grades 2–3 text complexity band proficiently with scaffolding as needed at the high end range," but by the end of third grade, the student should be able to "read and comprehend literature, including stories, dramas, and poetry, in the grades 2–3 text complexity band independently and proficiently." The same language defines what happens at fourth and fifth grade as well. The standards clearly have teachers looking at the complexity of the texts they are using. Do the texts lead to proficiency, especially if they are introduced earlier with teacher instructional support? Certainly that won't happen automatically.

So how do we accelerate the growth of readers to achieve proficiency in tighter, shorter time frames? In Chapter Seven, we will look more closely at how guided reading can be used as an intervention to accelerate the growth of those readers that need the most support. It begins with close monitoring. At-level texts for a student in need of accelerated growth will document the progress a student has made, but you must also use grade-level texts as benchmarks to see whether the reader has closed the gap between existing levels and proficiency levels. Figure 4J on page 90 introduces a planning guide for how to focus on a student's progress as well as proficiency.

What's Next?

The popular use of guided reading has focused a lot of attention on leveled texts. The use of leveling systems to classify readers and texts may not disappear soon; but the way teachers use them can certainly change as guided reading moves forward. The bottom line is if teachers are going to help students become readers, they should avoid using texts that will cause students to disengage from reading. When we do this, all the students get better at is figuring out ways to avoid reading. Levels help teachers find texts that might be a better fit for readers; however, keep in mind that other factors are at play in finding the right text for an individual reader. Be careful about rigidly honoring the level of a text when your professional judgment would cause a decision that might lead to a better fit. Even when guiding readers in small groups, don't let levels be the only thing that guides planning instruction and selection of texts. Consider the quantity and quality of words when selecting a text, especially for emergent and early readers. Also remember levels are not needs, so think more about selecting a text that provides practice on a skill or strategy with which the readers need help. With more flexible use of leveled texts, we can lead more readers to not just make progress, but actually become proficient.

For a description and listing of guided reading texts in the market, see the Appendix starting on page 186.

> *The bottom line is if teachers are going to help students become readers, they should avoid using texts that will cause students to disengage from reading. When we do this, all the students get better at is figuring out ways to avoid reading.*

Figure 4J: Progress and Proficiency Planning Chart

	Expected Proficiency Level	Student's Level	Gap	Pacing Schedule for Closing Proficiency Gap _____ Levels in _____ Weeks	Intervention Plan
Entry Level Beginning of the Year					
Benchmark at End of First Quarter					
Benchmark at End of Semester					
Benchmark at End of Third Quarter					
Exit Level at End of Year					Summer Plans
Additional Notes					

CHAPTER FIVE:
How Do We Support Different Types of Learners During Guided Reading?

> A simple principle—children differ—explains why there can be no one best method, material, or program. This simple principle has been reaffirmed so repeatedly in educational research that one would think that folks would have noticed it by now.
>
> *Allington, 2012*

After looking at the purposes of guided reading and why it is still important, it is clear that guided reading is a critical instructional structure. It both acknowledges and addresses the common developmental patterns of learners and their individual pathways. When learners differ, teachers matter. Teachers plan and implement the instruction needed to support those differing learners. If plans do not recognize the different needs of learners, then guided reading is just a one-size-fits-all model and its potential effectiveness is compromised. Guided reading needs to be conceptualized with different plans for different learners.

If plans do not recognize the different needs of learners, then guided reading is just a one-size-fits-all model and its potential effectiveness is compromised.

Purpose should always drive the instructional decision making of teachers. Purpose is mainly determined by the common patterns learners share. These common patterns are starting points for making decisions about small group reading instruction, including guided reading. While many educators look at stages of reading development to find these common patterns, Gentry (2015) suggests it may be more helpful to think about phases instead of stages. Stages are often seen as blocks defined by distinct ages, grade levels, or guided reading levels. Stages seem to suggest automatic leaps made by students and defined by unique separate expectations. Phases are defined by the actual performance of the learner. They acknowledge the blurry lines as students continue their trajectory toward becoming proficient readers. Phases remind us that performance varies depending on the texts being used and/or the contexts in which the reading takes place. Even adult reading ability can look quite different when given a complex text from a field in which the content is unfamiliar. Readers are always moving through phases and rarely arrive and park at a stage.

Defining Phases of Readers' Development

In thinking about common patterns, let's look at four potential phases: emergent readers, early readers, transitional readers, and fluent readers (Ellery, 2014; Richardson, 2009). It should be noted that some present continuums with additional stages often subdivide these four phases, such as pre-emergent and emergent and newly fluent and truly fluent (Saunders-Smith, 2003). For this chapter, the focus will be on four phases.

Emergent readers are trying to answer the question of how print works. They are searching for ways to make connections across various sign systems, including oral and written language. They are trying to figure out what reading is as they become immersed in worlds filled with language, including oral conversations, storybook readings, environmental print and visual graphics, and making meaning through marking on paper, among other things! The emergent reader has to come to understand concepts in how print works, phonological and phonemic awareness in discovering and manipulating sounds within language, and alphabetic knowledge in exploring why letters are important and how they work. The emergent reader is expanding the vocabulary and world knowledge needed to eventually bring meaning to the pages he or she will read. The emergent reader needs to find the joy that leads to a positive identity as a reader and writer. Keep in mind that readers at any stage can be in the emergent phase. We see this when students encounter new complex texts from fields with unusual signs and symbols. We also see this as students add a new language. Richardson (2009) suggested that some English language learners (ELLs) may not be ready for guided reading group work during this phase. This may be especially true if guided reading starts with beginning leveled texts. Saunders-Smith (2003) echoed a similar concern for some kindergartners with less experience and stamina. Both suggested that these students may benefit more from what Saunders-Smith (2003) called "bridging experiences." These include whole class shared reading and writing experiences like modeling while recording students' oral sharing during the morning meeting and inviting students to help read back the list created. Both experts suggest that for small group work to be helpful, it should focus more on working with letters and names, sounds, books, and interactive writing.

Early readers have figured out how print works. They have developed most concepts of print, a foundation in phonemic awareness, and alphabetic knowledge. They have the oral language and world knowledge they need to begin to bring meaning to the page and make meaning on a page. They have experienced enough joy to want to embrace their identities as readers and writers. While they may continue to firm up their foundations in those areas, they begin to shift attention to the question of how to figure out print. Their focus becomes acquiring the tools needed to become a reader. They move from learning about what reading is to learning about how to read. In this phase, much attention is given to the micro aspects of the texts, or what Fitzgerald (1999) called "local knowledge." They use different strategies to decode words. For example, they'll draw upon sound, visual, structural, grammatical, and semantic clues. Early readers are figuring out multiple strategies to use when searching, monitoring, and cross-checking the words they encounter or record in print (Schwartz, 2005). They get better at using what they know about sounds and letters to decode words. They begin to recognize more words automatically on sight, especially those high-frequency words they see over and over again. They are spotting patterns in words that they can chunk to assist in decoding and morphemic analysis. They grow in their ability to use context clues to figure out the meanings of unknown words. While the focus is at the word level, early readers also look beyond the word level to make meaning while they read and write. This can be seen in their oral reading as they read with greater fluency, phrasing, and expression. Boyles (2009) suggested these readers' comprehension outcomes begin at the base: identifying main idea, theme, and text elements; making predictions and drawing conclusions based on text evidence. They start to seek out others to discuss what they are reading, writing, and learning. By seizing control of their reading and writing, their self-efficacy grows. They see themselves as readers and writers. They begin to experience success, want to experience more success, and develop their knowledge base of how to continue their success (Opitz & Ford, 2014). Early readers can surface at any stage as the local knowledge needed to handle increasingly more complex text shifts, and it requires the acquisition of new strategies.

Transitional readers often have the tools they need to read the texts they encounter. For them, the challenge is not acquiring the tools but using the tools. They know strategies related to sound analysis, sight vocabulary, structural analysis, and context clues. They shift their focus from the tools to the texts. For them, the major question is how to become more sophisticated meaning makers. Goals are focused on understanding what is read and creating comprehensible texts when writing. Fitzgerald (1999) called this "global knowledge." As Boyles (2009) described, transitional readers go beyond declarative knowledge about strategies (knowing what they are) to acquiring procedural knowledge (knowing how to use them) and conditional knowledge (knowing when and why to use them). Their comprehension outcomes continue to climb. They use text elements to summarize what was read. They use their ability to identify main ideas and themes to support personal response, including genuine connections (not just coincidences). They attend to author's craft and link it to their writing.

I offer one caution in thinking about readers at this phase. Often we hear about early readers learning to read and then transitional readers reading to learn. This is a false dichotomy. Early readers are learning to read and reading to learn. Transitional readers are reading to learn and still learning to read. While the proportion of time and energy spent on each outcome might be different, we must be careful in suggesting that these expectations are exclusive to certain stages. They're not. In each phase, there should be a focus on learning to read and reading to learn. Strong identities as a reader and writer are fostered by attending to both. In fact, it may be impossible to separate the two. Learning to read is best when reading to learn is involved (Hiebert, 2014). As we read to learn, we are

> *While the proportion of time and energy spent on each outcome might be different, we must be careful in suggesting that these expectations are exclusive to certain stages.*

also learning to read better. In fact, we need to avoid conducting guided reading sessions that focus exclusively at the word level for early readers and delay focus at the text level until the transitional reader phase. If early readers receive instruction that focuses exclusively on words with a strong emphasis on accuracy, many may think that reading is just about words and getting them right. Our students will learn what we teach them. We need to think about the message our teaching sends the learners sitting at the table with us.

Fluent readers focus on being readers and writers. As they move from being transitional readers, they have acquired the tools, strategies, and desires they need to be readers and writers. They shift from focusing on primarily making meaning from texts to taking up residency in their reading and writing (Laminack, 2014). They have reached the summit (Boyles, 2009) and own comprehension outcomes that help them explore more sophisticated text structures and extend the text in new ways. They start bringing a critical lens to the authors' and characters' customs, values, and choices. They are learning how to be independent, including how to self-regulate their literate life. They are expanding their competencies with different types of texts of increasing complexity. They are able to be authentically engaged with text that has a clear meaning and immediate value to them (Schlechty, 2002). Because of their cognitive and affective strengths, they may have fewer needs than students at the other phases, but they still can benefit from interaction with the teacher. We need to remember that no matter how strong readers or writers are, they are still elementary students who can certainly benefit from interaction with the expertise of the teacher. While interaction, coaching, and guidance are still important, we need to remember what drives most proficient language users: choice, social opportunities to collaborate, time to practice, feelings of success, and intrinsic values. In other words, sometimes we need to get out of the way of this learner (Boushey & Moser, 2006). As Guthrie and Klauda (2014) theorize, it is those dimensions of instruction that lead to effort, enthusiasm, persistence, self-regulation, and ultimately—achievement. We must be careful that good intentions don't interfere with what we know is best for fluent readers. Screening tools with narrowly defined measures and interpretations sometimes misidentify proficient readers because of an inability to perform at an acceptable level on some small skill (i.e., reading nonsense words, rate on words-per-minute test). This seems to be a means-end confusion. Pearson (2006) cautions us to avoid elevating a progress indicator to the status of a curricular goal. The curricular goal should always be about creating proficient readers and writers.

We have looked at four phases of readers to define predictable common patterns and narrow the focus of instructional needs as we plan to support learners during guided reading. It is important to acknowledge the blurred lines between the phases and how the dynamic nature of interactions among readers, texts, and contexts can also impact performance. Figure 5A summarizes these phases.

Figure 5A: Four Phases of Readers

	Emergent Phase	Early Phase	Transitional Phase	Fluent Phase
Key questions	What is print? What is reading?	How do I unlock print?	How do I improve at making meaning from print?	How do I independently use print?
Major instructional focus (but not exclusively!)	Print	Tools	Texts	Being
Major areas of cognitive attention	Expand oral language Expand world knowledge Understand concepts of print Develop phonological and phonemic awareness Gain alphabetic knowledge Make meaning through shared reading and writing	Use sound analysis Increase sight vocabulary Analyze word parts through structural analysis Analyze word meanings through text analysis Use searching, monitoring, and cross-checking strategies Identify main idea, theme, and text elements Make predictions and draw conclusions based on text evidence	Use word-identification strategies with greater sophistication and automaticity Develop as a fluent reader, controlling pace and prosody while making meaning Use text elements to summarize what was read Use ability to identify main ideas and themes to support personal response, including genuine connections Attend to author's craft and link it to writing	Use word-identification strategies efficiently and automatically Be a fluent reader who controls the meaning-making process Explore more sophisticated text structures Extend the text in new ways Bring a critical lens to the authors' and characters' customs, values, and choices
Major areas of affective attention	Discovering the joy Developing a positive identity	Developing self-efficacy Knowing you can read, wanting to read, and knowing how to read	Developing confidence and comfort with increasing competence Finding intrinsic motivation	Having internalized reasons to stay engaged Developing self-regulation

continued on next page

	Emergent Phase	Early Phase	Transitional Phase	Fluent Phase
Caution	New languages, texts, and contexts can create similar circumstances	Be careful about an overemphasis on word-level knowledge with a focus on accuracy and the message it sends about what reading is	Move strategy knowledge beyond knowing what the strategy is (declarative) to knowing how, when, and why to use the strategy (procedural and conditional)	Avoid confusing ends (proficient reading and writing) with means (performance on small part assessments)
Typical GR Levels* (*Richardson, 2009)	A–C	D–I	K–P	Q→

Assessing Phases of Learners' Development

An entire book can be written (and has been) with a focus on assessing readers (Opitz, Ford & Erekson, 2011). In this section, I want to look at assessment to establish a baseline in making initial decisions about what phase is appropriate to meet each reader's needs. Once that initial decision is made, ongoing use of formative assessments will best inform decisions about instruction during guided reading sessions.

Emergent Phase

So let's start with emergent readers. How do you know when a student needs instruction typical of this phase? Five key assessments might help us to determine readers in this phase and what specific needs should be addressed during their guided reading sessions:

1. *Concepts about print checklist:* It is important to determine what the reader knows about how reading, books, and print work. Understandings about directionality (moving left to right on a page, left to right in a sentence, return sweep, moving top to bottom, starting at the beginning, finishing at the end, etc.) should be assessed. Understandings about reading (e.g., knowing print differs from pictures, has meaning, and has practical uses) should be checked on as well. One indicator includes the ability of the student to show a "voice print match" between the words on the page and the words said initially by pointing to each word and eventually relying less on pointing with a finger. The reader must have an understanding of instructional terms related to reading: "letter," "word," "page," "capital/uppercase," "small/lowercase," "cover," "title," "start," "end," "beginning," "front," "back," "first," "last," "book," "print," "picture," "line," and "sentence." Standardized concepts about print assessments exist. For example, Clay's (2006) popular An Observation Survey of Early

Literacy Achievement (OSELA) has an often used subtest to check these understandings. Clay included small books intentionally designed to check increasing sophisticated understandings about print. Many educators use similar versions of this subtest with easily accessible texts in their classrooms and programs.

2. *Phonological and phonemic awareness assessments:* An emergent reader needs to figure out that oral language is made up of groups of sounds and individual sounds. He or she needs to be able to identify, match, blend, segment, and manipulate the sounds in words, syllables, and clusters as well as individually. Phonological assessments can determine the student's ability to hear separate words in sentences, syllables within words, clusters of sounds within words, and eventually individual sounds in words. Phonemic awareness is specifically focused on the latter: individual sounds within words. These assessments are focused exclusively on auditory tasks. They are not about identifying which letters make what sounds. That comes later. Many assessments or subtests within assessments like OSELA measure phonological, including phonemic, ability. Phonological Awareness Literacy Screening (PALS) (Invernizzi, Meier, Swank & Juel, 2001) is one popular tool. Though broader than its name in what it assesses, PALS does contain subtests that are specific to phonological, including phonemic, awareness (i.e., rhyme awareness, beginning sound awareness). Many schools have also developed their own versions of similar tools to assess readers in this area.

3. *Alphabetic knowledge:* An emergent reader needs to learn what a letter is, that each letter has a name, and that a letter represents certain sounds. This understanding will be critical for building a foundation for phonics instruction that will follow later. Letter identification is a common screening tool and is a subtest in both OSELA and PALS. A set of letter flash cards can be used to check a child's knowledge in this area. For emergent students with limited knowledge in this area, check if they can notice features by matching and sorting letters. Can they find letters that match? Can they sort letters by features (circle parts, straight lines, tails, or diagonal lines)? You can also see if the child can find features of letters within words (words that start with the same letter, end with the same letter, etc.). These are quick checks to see the refinement of the child's ability to visually discriminate. Be careful to avoid visual discrimination assessments that stray too far from letters and words. Gross visual discrimination activities (i.e., finding the two animals that match) have little bearing on the child's ability to discriminate between two similar letters (*t* from *f*) or two similar words ("was," "saw").

4. *Oral language:* Reading is a language-based activity. Reading instruction requires that a student has knowledge and control over oral language structures (Dorn & Soffos, 2011). For most children, foundational knowledge of sounds, words, syntax, and stories begins by listening to and using oral language. Standardized assessments can be used to screen students' abilities in this area. Clay's and colleagues' (2015) Record of Oral Language (ROL) and Gentile's The

Oral Language Acquisition Inventory (2011) may be helpful tools in this area. These tools can help identify students with greater needs in developing their oral language abilities, which I advise working on first before moving into guided reading groups. Some have even suggested oral language small groups as a precursor or supplement to guided reading groups with emergent readers (Boquist, 2013). Separate standards and assessment tools might be helpful with ELLs, such as the WIDA standards (Gottlieb, Cranley & Cammilleri, 2007). Classroom teachers may also want to closely collaborate with speech and language experts to meet more severe needs in this area.

5. *Emergent writing:* One valuable tool to assess how students combine concepts of print, phonological awareness (including phonemic awareness), alphabetic knowledge, and oral language is to prompt a writing sample from the emergent learner. Dorn & Soffos (2011) describe a six-step process for securing a sample of writing:

   a. Child is prompted to draw a picture.

   b. Child is prompted to write about the picture "the best [he/she] can."

   c. Child is asked to read the story back.

   d. Teacher responds to the writing and reading in a positive manner.

   e. Teacher analyzes the writing.

   f. Teacher and child repeat process for two additional pieces of writing.

Multiple samples help reveal a pattern about the learner as it relates to his or her print understanding (what does the writing and reading reveal about understandings about directionality, voice-print match, word boundaries, and so on?), alphabetic understanding (do they use letter-like forms, actual letters, appropriate letters?), sounds knowledge (do symbols represent clusters of sounds, individual sounds, appropriate sounds?), and the level of his or her oral language ability, including use and understanding of academic terms. Another way to obtain a sample of writing is by using a Timed Word Writing Prompt (Dorn & Soffos, 2011). The student is given a set amount of time to write all the words he or she knows. To get some momentum going for a student who initially stalls, the teacher prompts the child to start with his or her name, then other names, and then any other words. The words that are written reveal understandings about print, letters, sounds, and the oral language of the student.

This is not an endless list of potential ways to assess a student in the emergent phase of reading, but these five measures capture the key outcomes for this phase. These measures should be able to clearly identify a student with needs in these areas and what those needs might be. Teachers can use assessment information to establish a group or groups of students who share initially similar common patterns. Students demonstrating strong competencies in these key areas may be more appropriately addressed as early readers in the next phase of the continuum.

Teachers can use assessment information to establish a group or groups of students who share initially similar common patterns.

Early Phase

With early readers, the focus shifts to the strategies the student is using to unlock and make sense of the texts he or she is reading. Assessments to establish a baseline with these readers will build on what we already know about the student's competencies based on emergent phase assessments.

Five additional assessments will be helpful in learning about students in the early reading phase.

1. *Reading level:* The first thing educators may want to know is at which level the student is reading. Dorn & Soffos (2011) suggest: "It indicates the point at which a student is most receptive to instruction (28)." It can help provide an estimate of the leveled text that would be most appropriate for instruction during an early reading guided reading session, but keep in mind the cautions previously discussed about levels. Observing a child's interaction with any text can provide information about his or her use of strategies, both at the local and global levels, but a text that is quite easy for the child would reveal less because it would not provide an observable opportunity to examine the student's strategy use. On the other hand, a text that is too difficult might provide too many opportunities to observe problem-solving. A "just right" or instructional-level text seems to be best to provide baseline information to guide instruction. Many schools use a standardized collection of reading texts or reading samples in trying to estimate the reading level of the student. These are available in leveled text systems like Developmental Reading Assessment (DRA) (Beaver & Carter, 2001) or Fountas and Pinnell Benchmark Assessment System (2008). The graded/leveled texts systems allow a teacher to gradually increase the complexity of the text in examining the student's performance. As the student reads the text, the teacher records the accuracy of the reading, monitors word-level strategy use, checks a level of understanding with a post-reading comprehension check like a retelling, and gets a sense of fluency from the child's rate and expression. Experts may differ on how accurate the text reading needs to be for appropriate instruction. Dorn & Soffos (2011) suggest for early readers an accuracy level of 90–94 percent for an instructional reading level. For older readers, 95–98 percent may be more reasonable.

2. *Oral reading sample:* While you can determine reading levels from oral reading samples, they can also be analyzed to reveal the word strategies a student uses in the context of real reading. Analysis of miscues can surface a pattern that reveals what the early reader is doing to figure out words. Coding systems can be used to capture miscues when orally reading a text. Errors include substitutions, omissions, insertions, and assisted or told words. The degree of hesitation, repetition, and self-correction can also be noted. Analysis can provide insights into what cues are being used by the reader. Is the reader relying on visual cues (graphophonemic strategies), structural

Observing a child's interaction with any text can provide information about his or her use of strategies, both at the local and global levels, but a text that is quite easy for the child would reveal less because it would not provide an observable opportunity to examine the student's strategy use.

cues (grammatically driven strategies), or semantic cues (context and meaning strategies)? The analysis both reveals what the student can do and what the student needs to be able to do, providing a critical teaching opportunity. Figure 5B presents a number of questions to consider when analyzing miscues to figure out what strategies a reader does use or needs to use. This will help target the instruction better during a guided reading session.

> *Asking early readers to decode nonsense words also sends the message that reading is not always about trying to make sense.*

3. *Phonics skills and strategies inventory:* The use of miscue analysis shows what the early reader is able to do within the context of reading. That is where strategic knowledge is the most critical. It would be difficult, however, to find a single text that would challenge the student to demonstrate ability to use all potential sound-symbol relationships. A separate phonics skills inventory will allow you to assess a more comprehensive list of graphophonemic skills and strategies. Use caution when interpreting results because the ability to identify sounds in isolation may be different from applying similar knowledge in the context of real reading and writing. Given that limitation, one such assessment is the Early Names Test (Mather, Sammons & Schwartz, 2006). Using a set of 30, one-syllable first and last name combinations selected or created to contain most of the English sound-symbol relationships, the teacher can determine the student's ability to use initial and ending single consonants, consonant digraphs and blends, short and long vowel patterns, and rimes. Looking across the results will help teachers target sound-symbol relationships with which the students need assistance. The names test provides a more realistic task than commonly used nonsense word tests, which can be confusing to early readers. Asking early readers to decode nonsense words also sends the message that reading is not always about trying to make sense.

4. *Sight-word vocabulary check:* One of the most predictable elements of the English language is the degree of frequency with which a relatively limited number of words are used in print. Ten words make up 25 percent of all words in texts: "the," "of," "and," "to," "a," "in," "that," "it," "is," "was." Checking to see if early readers are automatically recognizing these words is important in making decisions about instruction. The best way to check the student's ability to recognize sight words is to do it in the context of real reading. As with sound analysis, it might be difficult to use a single text that would contain all the sight words a teacher might want to check. Many lists of sight words exist for teachers to use in checking early readers' knowledge base, and many districts have used these to set grade-level expectations for sight-word knowledge. Dorn and Soffos (2011) present a checklist of 96 high-frequency words that can be used to assess a student's knowledge. Within this list are 25 words that should be learned by the end of kindergarten. These words may be a good starting point for assessing sight-word vocabulary of early readers. As with sounds, the recognition of words in isolation versus in context can differ.

Figure 5B: Questions to Consider in Analyzing Miscues

How many errors did the reader have?	
How many of the errors were substitutions?	
How many of the substitutions made sense?	
How many of the substitutions sound right grammatically?	
How many of the substitutions were visually similar?	
How many of the visual substitutions were similar at the beginning of the words?	
How many of the visual substitutions were similar in the middle of the words?	
How many of the visual substitutions were similar at the end of the words?	
How many of the errors were omissions?	
What types of words were omitted?	
How many omissions interrupted the meaning of the text?	
How many omissions interrupted the grammatical flow of the sentence?	
How many of the errors were insertions?	
What types of words were inserted?	
How many insertions interrupted the meaning of the text?	
How many insertions interrupted the grammatical flow of the sentence?	
How many words did the teacher assist the reader with?	
What type of words did the teacher assist with?	
What part(s) of the words did the teacher assist with?	
How many words did the teacher tell the reader?	
What type of words did the teacher tell the reader?	
How many other miscues were noted?	
How many significant hesitations did the reader have?	
What types of words followed the hesitations?	
What was the accuracy rate of words that followed hesitations?	
How many repetitions did the reader have?	
What types of words were repeated?	
What was the accuracy rate of words that were repeated?	
How many self-corrections did the reader have?	
What types of words were self-corrected?	
How many of the self-corrections were needed to restore meaning?	
How many of the self-corrections were needed to restore the grammatical flow?	
Other observations	

5. *Writing sample:* A written draft reveals a lot about what the student knows about writing and reading. Opitz, Erekson, and I (2011), developed a structure for evaluating reading skills and strategies within a student's writing sample. For example, sight words can be assessed in isolation and in the context of real reading and writing. Teachers can look at any piece of writing to assess the student's automatic use of sight-word vocabulary. Sight words written without difficulty are often read without difficulty. We can also look at the student's use of vocabulary in the writing to get a sense of whether his or her language and world knowledge seems appropriate for the grade or age. We can see if the writing sample reveals that the student knows that text needs to be comprehensible. If these elements are present within a writing sample, it indicates that the student has the same knowledge available for use when reading a text. The absence of these features in writing may indicate a direction for instruction in the early reading phase. For the early reader, one additional helpful tool is the use of written miscue analysis. Carefully analyzing what word the student was trying to write and how the student wrote it reveals what sound and letter patterns are known or still problematic.

Using these five additional measures should help teachers both identify early readers and provide baseline information to guide their instruction of those readers during guided reading sessions. Data collected with these assessments will clearly show which students are entering this phase and which students are beginning to exit this phase. Less sophisticated word strategy use seen in oral reading and writing samples and beginning sound-symbol and sight-word vocabulary knowledge reflected in skill checklists will probably be more characteristic of students performing at levels near the beginning of this phase. More balanced, automatic strategy use with greater knowledge of sound-symbol relationships and more extensive sight-word vocabularies will be more characteristic of readers at higher levels in this phase. These readers are starting to provide evidence that they are moving to the Transitional Phase.

Transitional Phase

The transitional reader has knowledge of tools to unlock texts and begins to focus on becoming a better maker of meaning using reading and writing. The focus shifts from tools to texts. Strategy use will become increasingly more complex and automatic. It will grow as the variety of texts and tasks encountered becomes more complex. That said, the transitional reader will spend the greater proportion of time toward becoming a fluent reader, making meaning with increasing comfort, confidence, and competence. In this phase, previously discussed assessments are intensified to provide insights into transitional readers to determine where readers are at, to establish baseline performances, and to inform the teacher's thinking about instruction. The following additional assessments might also provide insights into transitional readers.

1. *Phonics skills and strategies inventory:* Use of running records to capture the oral reading performance of the transitional reader will

continue to show how the student is able to address more complex sound-symbol relationships. Assessments that look at these relationships in isolation might provide a more comprehensive view in one setting of tricky sound-symbol relationships. Not surprisingly, by this phase, single consonant and vowel patterns have been fairly well mastered. More difficult combinations and representations may still need some work, especially as words grow beyond one syllable. One assessment that can be used is the Names Test (Duffelmeyer, Kruse, Merkley & Fyfe, 1994). The previously described Early Names Test was based on this assessment but designed to assess entry-level sound-symbol knowledge. The Names Test uses first and last name combinations that include multisyllabic words. The teacher can determine the student's ability to use more complex relationships like consonant digraphs and blends, vowel digraphs, schwa, and controlled vowels. The teacher can also monitor whether the student was able to "chunk" the multisyllabic words into meaningful parts to help with pronunciation. The results will assist the teacher to target sound-symbol instruction that firms up word strategies the student will need as he or she encounters longer, less familiar words.

2. *Comprehension checks:* With the attention shifting to meaning making, baseline assessments need to include more specific analysis of the strategies the transitional reader uses in making meaning to understand what is being read. Assessing comprehension can begin with a simple prompt to retell what was just read. Each statement in the retelling can be analyzed globally in four key areas: literal comprehension, inferential comprehension, engagement of schema, and self-monitoring language. The teacher can tally whether each statement reveals thinking and memory in those areas. In considering literal comprehension, the teacher listens carefully for the facts and details the child describes as stated explicitly in the story. It is what Raphael (1982) would describe as the "right there" information. For each fact and detail recalled correctly, the teacher would make a check. If the fact or detail was incorrect, the teacher might use a dash. The teacher may want to consider what details from the story would be important to remember to see if those are mentioned by the student. With inferential comprehension, the teacher listens carefully for the big ideas (e.g., mood, tone, themes, motives) as the child describes what was implicit in the story. Raphael would describe this as the "search and think" information, or what the student can read between the lines. For an appropriate inference, the teacher would make a check. For an inappropriate inference, the teacher would make a dash. Again the teacher may want to consider what big ideas from the story the student should be able to identify. With engagement of schema, the teacher listens carefully for connections that the child makes to the story. Now the reader is using information from the author and from his or her head. Connections can be personal, related to other texts, or related to the world. Boyles (2009) reminds us that there are differences between connections and coincidences, so the teacher would make a check for a significant connection. If the connection is

not a strong link to the story, the teacher would make a dash. Finally, self-monitoring language would be heard when the student thinks aloud about his or her own strategy use. The student uses metacognitive language when he or she talks about his or her own thinking. (e.g., "I didn't really understand the first part of the story until I went back and reread the first part.") By tallying the number of times this language is used during the retelling, the student reveals interesting insights. It reveals the student's thought processes when he or she tries to make meaning. That thinking shows the degree to which the student is using strategies and how that can inform instruction for guided reading sessions. See Figure 5C for a sample template of a retelling profile.

3. *Fluency:* The goal is to create fluent readers by the time students leave this phase. Fluency is not an end in and of itself. Fluency is a means to an end (Rasinski, 2003). Fluency helps transitional readers operate more efficiently so they can devote their attention and energy to comprehending the text. It is therefore appropriate to assess fluency in a broad manner to establish baseline data for readers at this phase. It helps determine how much attention should be given to fluency as part of the guided reading instruction and/or what dimension of fluency needs the most attention during guided reading. Often fluency gets reduced to measurements of rate. Oral readings are timed and words-per-minute scores are recorded exclusively as indicators of fluency. But even simple definitions of fluency (reading smoothly, quickly, and accurately) suggest that fluency needs to be thought of as a broader concept. Other factors besides speed should be considered as indicators. The Oral Reading Fluency Scale (National Center for Education Statistics, 1995) used in the National Assessment of Educational Progress (NAEP) provides a rubric with four levels of competency to more holistically assess fluency in the oral reading of a student. In the NAEP rubric, more emphasis is placed on how the student breaks the texts into phrases and uses expressive interpretation. In my work with Opitz and Erekson (2011), we created a Holistic Oral Reading Fluency Rubric that considers four elements: pace, accuracy, phrasing, and expression. Each is described on a four-point scale, allowing for an overall score that more broadly represents fluency instead of a words-per-minute computation. We also maintain that fluency cannot be separated from meaning making, so the student that has appropriate pace, accuracy, phrasing, and expression must do that while maintaining meaning. To suggest that fluency can exist separate from understanding may also send the wrong message to transitional readers by equating speed with success (Opitz, 2007).

4. *Writing sample:* Having discussed how the writing sample can be used to assess outcomes for the emergent and early readers, writing samples will also help identify transitional readers. The writing sample can provide baseline information to use in planning guided reading sessions and document changes as the student moves forward. In addition to revealing what the student knows about sight words, vocabulary, world knowledge, and understandings about

Fluency helps transitional readers operate more efficiently so they can devote their attention and energy to comprehending the text.

Name _____

Figure 5C: Retelling Analysis Grid

	Focus	Type of Thinking	Number of Appropriate Responses in Retelling	Number of Inappropriate Responses in Retelling
Literal Comprehension	Facts and details	Noticing and remembering what is right there in the text		
Inferential Comprehension	Inferences, big ideas, implied thoughts	Searching and thinking by reading between the lines to figure out more implicit information		
Engagement of Schema	Connections to self, texts, and world	Using something from the author to make a significant connection outside of the text		
Self-monitoring	Metacognitive language and strategic talk	Being able to reflect on one's thinking and articulating that to others, going beyond the author's text		
Overall reflection on data Strength(s): Area(s) in need of improvement: Other insights:				

making meaning, we can look at the way the student puts a sentence together and strings several sentences together. This reveals whether the student has an understanding of cohesive elements when reading and writing. This is what some call sentence-level comprehension (Irwin, 1986). The student's ability to use appropriate pronouns within and between sentences creates cohesion. The student's ability to use conjunctions and transitional vocabulary in stringing sentences together reflects even more knowledge of cohesive elements when writing. An ability to negotiate these cohesive elements while writing may indicate a similar ability to use these elements while reading to make meaning successfully. Similarly, we can look at the overall story or report to see whether the student has a sense of story structure or expository text structures. If these understandings are present within a writing sample, it indicates that similar tools are available to the student when comprehending. The absence of these features in writing may indicate an instructional direction for transitional readers. When using the tool of written miscue analysis and carefully analyzing what word the student was trying to write and how the student wrote it, the teacher can shift analysis to complex sound-symbol patterns, syllable structures, structural elements (prefixes, roots, suffixes, inflected endings), contextual issues (using the right homophones), and grammatical elements (possessives, contractions, capitalization).

Fluent Phase

Finally, we move to the fluent reader. The fluent reader is focused on being a reader and a writer. Fluent readers have become competent moving through phases to learn what print is, how to unlock print, and how to improve at making meaning. Paris (2005) described some skills as more constrained than others (alphabetic knowledge, sight words, sound-symbol relationships). These skills are learned quickly, mastered entirely, and, at the fluent stage, usually do not result in significant differences between readers. For the fluent reader, the more constrained skills and strategies are solidly in place. Occasionally they may have to be revisited, but, for the most part, instruction in those areas does not need to be the focus of guided reading. For the fluent reader, the focus of instruction narrows. The fluent reader attends more to the continued growth of his or her vocabulary and comprehension. These are more unconstrained since all readers can continue to learn vocabulary and improve at comprehending an ever-increasing variety of texts. It's hard to master all the vocabulary words you will ever need to know or demonstrate an ability to understand every text you will ever encounter. While the instruction narrows, the resources for instruction widen. Fluent readers benefit most from practice with many different texts for a growing list of purposes in many different contexts. That is how knowledge in unconstrained areas (vocabulary, comprehension) continue to grow and dimensions of affect (identity, internal motivations) continue to strengthen. Additional baseline assessments that might be critical in this phase include the following:

1. *Affective dimensions:* If the skill is in place, then we want to make sure the will is in place. Cognitive skills and strategies are therefore shifted to affective skills and strategies. The fluent reader's greatest need is for support of the reading habit. If the resources for instruction widen, a teacher needs to know where the student's interests are and how those interests could grow to fuel the reader's habit. In the Appendix on page 193, I provide an interest inventory that helps the teacher look at what topics are of interest to the student, what types of texts the student enjoys reading, and what some of the favorites are. (This inventory is also mentioned in Chapter Four.) This information tells us the areas in which the student is comfortable and new areas to move him or her toward. Collecting this information can inform text selection in choosing materials for guided reading sessions with fluent readers. Aggregating information from these surveys across all phases of readers can also inform thinking about what texts to feature in other parts of the literacy program, including read-alouds and shared readings. It also points to ways to develop classroom collections for independent reading experiences. In addition to interest, affective dimensions like reading attitudes and identities can be assessed through surveys or interviews (Opitz, Ford & Erekson, 2011). When the affective components are less positive than we might have thought, assessing students' perceptions about reading might give us some clues into why reading is not highly valued. Knowing how students perceive reading can help teachers clear up some misconceptions—perhaps from previous instruction—and build a clearer vision of the value of reading. Readers, who have experienced a view of reading that is almost always about getting every word right, may not find that view of reading tremendously joyful (Opitz, Ford & Erekson, 2011).

2. *Self-regulation:* Seeing how students regulate their growth as readers may be the most critical assessment to take. Self-regulation can be observed best when students are engaged in self-assessment tasks. One such self-assessment is to study their word strategies. Retrospective Miscue Analysis (Goodman & Marek, 1996) has the student monitor his or her oral reading samples. The student records an oral reading of a text. The student plays back the recording and follows along in the text. As soon as the student discovers a miscue or self-correction, the student can be given a set of questions to guide him or her in analyzing what happened:

   - What was the actual word?

   - What word did I say?

   - Did the word I say make sense?

   - Did I use context to get the meaning?

   - What clues did I use to get the meaning?

Students who internalize this process will raise their word strategy use to a more metacognitive level and have a greater awareness of how to independently resolve issues related to word strategies.

Similarly, students can record their discussions about books. After the discussion has been captured, students can play back the recording, tracking the dynamics of the conversation as well as reflecting on the kind of thinking and talk used. Students can reflect on how to improve their interactions and conversations (Opitz & Ford, 2014). More generally, fluent readers can be engaged in regularly scheduled conferences with the teacher to identify goals, discuss ways to document progress, and then provide evidence that goals were achieved (Boushey & Moser, 2009).

3. *Vocabulary strategies:* In other phases, we have looked closely at word strategies related to using sound analysis, structural analysis, and recognizing sight words. But what about the use of context clues? In an oral reading sample, the use of context clues is evident in both the number of semantic miscues where the substitution, omission, or insertion did not impact the meaning of the text. The use of context is also seen in the number of self-corrections that brought meaning back to the text after a miscue had interrupted it. But with fluent readers, reading increasingly moves to a silent mode. How can we tell if the reader is figuring out the meaning of new vocabulary as he or she reads? Modified cloze and maze procedures may help us see if the student can use word meanings and context to comprehend text (Opitz, Ford & Erekson, 2011). Teachers can select or create a modified cloze procedure by systematically leaving blanks in the passage that focus the reader in using specific context patterns to figure out the missing words. A modified maze procedure would systematically insert a choice of three possible words the students can choose from to fill in the missing text. Artley (1943) first identified nine classic context clue patterns that can be explicitly taught to and used by students to figure out the meanings of unfamiliar words. For example, unfamiliar words are often paired with a more common synonym ("arid and dry") or antonym ("arid, not humid"), so a modified cloze or maze procedure could be set up to assess the student's ability to use this pattern to figure out the meanings of unknown words. Unfamiliar words and their definitions are often linked by typographical clues like dashes ("magma—hot, melted rock inside the volcano") or parentheses "[pumice (rock that has cooled after flowing out of the volcano)]." Again, a modified cloze or maze procedure could target this pattern to assess whether the readers can strategically use it to figure out the meanings of unfamiliar words. On the other hand, a modified cloze or maze could be set up to assess the ability to use a variety of context clue patterns. Knowing where baseline knowledge is on the use of context clue patterns can provide direction for which patterns to teach more explicitly during guided reading sessions.

4. *Comprehension strategies:* Certain questions can reveal specific information about the learner's knowledge and use of common comprehension strategies. One way to assess this is through the use of targeted questions. The following questions not only show whether students understood the story, but whether they can use specific strategies to reveal their understanding of the story.

Knowing where baseline knowledge is on the use of context clue patterns can provide direction for which patterns to teach more explicitly during guided reading sessions.

- What would you predict would happen next in the story?

- What clues gave you the idea for that prediction?

- What's the main idea?

- What did you read in the story that suggests that is the main idea?

- Compare how you are alike and different from one of the characters.

- Compare and contrast how two of the characters are alike and different.

- What lesson did you learn from the story?

- Why do you think that is the most important lesson?

- Describe a picture that you visualized in your head from the story.

- What was one part of the story that was confusing?

- What did you do to handle that confusing part of the story?

- What part of the story reminded you of something from your life?

- What is another story this story reminded you of and why do you think so?

- Summarize the story in your own words.

- Whose point of view is the story written from and how do you know?

- What if the story was written from a different point of view?

- What was the biggest change a character made in the story?

- What is the theme of the story?

- What did you read in the story that suggests that is the theme?

- What was the author's purpose in writing this story?

- What happens in the story that lets you know the story could really happen or not happen?

- What was the main problem in the story?

- How was the main problem solved?

- What was your opinion about the story and why did you feel that way?

- What mood does the author create and how does the author do that?

I am not suggesting that every time a student reads a text we march him or her through a long list of questions like those above, but the selected use of four to six questions would allow the teacher to assess specific thinking strategies that might not surface in a general retelling. Thinking about a similar list of questions while reading a written response to a story could also be a means for analyzing the depth and range of strategic thinking. Assessment might even be more authentic if it is conducted while students are discussing a story. Opitz and I (2014) recommended that a teacher create a strategy grid for use during the guided reading session. The grid would list the key strategies being targeted down the left side and the names of the students in the group across the top. By listening to the discussion, the teacher can actually tally each time a student's oral contribution to the discussion reveals the use of a targeted strategy. This helps a teacher see what fluent readers are using and how a teacher can guide the discussions to move thinking to new areas or deeper levels.

Supporting Learners in Each Phase of Reading Development

The examined expectations for each of the phases of reading development give us a sense of outcomes for which instruction needs to be planned. It identifies the direction in which we are headed. Having examined a number of assessment techniques to help determine baseline information for each learner gives us a starting point for instruction. It identifies where we are at. The heart of guided reading is using instruction to build the bridge between those two points: where the readers are at (baselines) and where the readers need to be (outcomes). Building that bridge exemplifies scaffolded instruction and sets effective guided reading apart from previous small group instructional models (Boyle & Peregoy, 1998).

The heart of guided reading is using instruction to build the bridge between those two points: where the readers are at (baselines) and where the readers need to be (outcomes). Building that bridge exemplifies scaffolded instruction and sets effective guided reading apart from previous small group instructional models (Boyle & Peregoy, 1998).

1. Since the recent reemergence of guided reading, I have been on record about my belief that there is not one right way to conduct guided reading sessions (Opitz & Ford, 2001). In this section, I will present a plan for each of the phases of reading development. These should not be seen as the only way to plan guided reading instruction for each phase. They do not need to be followed rigidly. One needs to be careful about operating with orthodoxy and ignoring the responsiveness that expert teaching requires.

2. I do believe it is important to be very intentional in planning instruction for guided reading sessions. Instructional time is so precious in the classroom. We need to be careful that guided reading instruction doesn't become so routinized—following the same plan and outline day after day, no matter the students or the text—that a teacher feels thoughtful planning is not needed. Guided reading needs to be thoughtfully planned if the teacher is going to focus instruction to help students in the small group settings learn more about the reading process. While intentionality is critical, it should not preclude the teacher from being flexible. If guided reading is about common outcomes, it is also about following each individual's path. The latter requires a degree of flexibility. Guided reading plans need to be intentional but not inflexible.

3. For each phase of reading development, there are critical decisions that need to be made about teaching points, discussion opportunities, and how to foster positive affective outcomes. During any one lesson, it is not assumed that all areas identified for consideration will be needed. Part of the decision-making requires prioritizing which teaching moments are most needed. For each lesson, decisions should be made on how to sequence the instruction to assist the flow into, through, and out of the session; but sequencing might differ depending on the focus and/or detours of the instruction. Most guided reading sessions will last around 20 minutes, so instruction needs to be tightly focused and quickly paced. You can't do everything in 20 minutes, so it becomes critical to focus on what is needed most.

4. Text selection is critical for each lesson. Criteria to consider in selecting an appropriate text are embedded in each lesson guide. A range of text levels have been suggested for each phase, but remember: "The challenge of reading instruction does not reside solely in the text, but in what each teacher does to move each reader forward (Glasswell and Ford, 2010)." Some lessons might benefit from the use of multiple texts or texts chosen by the students, so these elements might also be considered in planning the session. Text selection decisions include considering whether the purpose of the session may be best achieved through the use of fiction or nonfiction texts. Even within those classifications, the formats of texts vary. Some fiction texts are predictable patterns. Others are narrative stories. Some nonfiction texts are narrative structures like a biography. Others are organized to present information like describing a topic (natural disasters) and then identifying a number of examples with that topic (volcanoes, hurricanes, earthquakes, tornadoes). Many of the demands to read a text shift when the student moves from fiction to nonfiction or from one format to another. Figure 5D on page 112 reminds us of some of those differences.

Figure 5D: Differences in Teaching Points When Using Many Nonfiction Texts

Teaching Point for Guided Reading Session	Variation for Nonfiction Texts
Concepts of print	Traditional directionality is challenged in many informational texts where reading does not have to take place in typical patterns (front to back, top to bottom, left to right)
Academic vocabulary	Informational texts introduce a number of additional academic terms: table of contents, index, glossary, table, figure, graphic, chart, caption, label
Alphabetic knowledge	Informational texts can contain non-alphabetic symbols like mathematical formulas or pictographic characters (think about a text about cave drawings)
Word analysis strategies	Informational texts contain many more multisyllabic, technical words requiring greater use of structural and context analysis strategies; use of resources (glossaries, dictionaries) come into play more
Comprehension strategies	Informational text purposes and structures differ, so different strategies are needed to acquire and use knowledge
Affective focus	Subject and topical interest can drive engagement

As needs differ, group membership should be reconsidered. Baseline assessments provide the starting points, but ongoing formative assessments are critical to monitor progress and target instruction.

5. Group membership should be considered for each session. Planning involves addressing both common patterns and individual pathways. Lesson plans have opportunities to plan for common instruction. This may be based initially on baseline assessments and needs shared by group members. These needs may determine initial membership in a group. Lesson plans also have opportunities to observe and assess individual performances. This information will reveal variations in learners. As needs differ, group membership should be reconsidered. Baseline assessments provide the starting points, but ongoing formative assessments are critical to monitor progress and target instruction. As the teacher sees a greater range of variation in needs, students may need to be regrouped. Guided reading groups are flexible groups. That doesn't require changing groups every day. Observe the students to determine stability in the growth they are making. When students have clearly demonstrated the need for different instruction, consider moving them to a new group. As I reported in the national survey results, some teachers made changes on a weekly or monthly basis. Students should be making growth if instruction is effective. If students are not making the growth needed to move to new groups, then it might be important to look at the instruction they are receiving.

6. Actual instructional activities, techniques, and resources to support instruction can come from a variety of sources. Teachers do not have to abandon current practices that are appropriate to address identified teaching targets. Teachers do need to consider whether those materials and methods send readers the kind of messages that are at the heart of effective guided reading. While isolated skill and strategy work may be needed, it is best done in the context of authentic

reading and writing. While a focus on word-level activities is certainly critical in some phases, students should also engage in text-level meaning making. The strong focus on cognitive outcomes needs to allow some consideration of positive affective outcomes.

7. Other contexts provide opportunities to use guided reading plans to structure small group instruction, such as in content areas. Students reading texts used in social studies and science, for example, may need additional support to successfully understand and use the information they contain. So what does guided reading look like in the content areas? It looks a lot like guided reading in the literacy block. It needs to acknowledge that the purpose for the reading has shifted more to the acquisition and use of the knowledge within the text, which usually means the texts are more informational (nonfiction) instead of narrative stories (fiction). Look at the lesson plan presented in the Appendix, starting on page 195. This guided reading session for transitional readers occurred during a second-grade science unit focused on habitats. The students were guided in their use of the class text that focused on seasonal changes in ponds. It is clear that reading in content areas can be the focus of a guided reading session. The context creates some differences to consider in making decisions about texts, teaching points, and instructional activities but allows for intentional, thoughtful targeted instruction to move a small group of readers forward.

Using these general principles to reflect on planning for and supporting readers during guided reading, let's also look specifically at the planning and support decisions for each phase. In this section, I will provide a decision-making guide for thinking about support needed in each phase, as well as a lesson format that can be used to write plans for guided reading sessions.

Emergent Reader Phase

Let's look at planning for and supporting the emergent reader. Guided reading instruction needs to be planned to help the learner move forward toward the following key outcomes:

- Understanding concepts of print;
- Developing phonological awareness, including phonemic awareness; and
- Securing alphabetic knowledge.

Lessons should also be planned with the intent of expanding the learners' oral language and world knowledge. Lessons should be conducted in such a manner that they help the learner discover joy and develop a positive identity as a reader and writer. Instructional considerations in this phase would include these dimensions (see Figure 5E on page 114) and could be planned using the format in Figure 5F on page 116.

Figure 5E: Instructional Considerations for Emergent Readers

Text	Format of text would clearly allow for modeling, practicing, and using...
	• book handling skills (start at the beginning and move in a linear fashion to finish at the end)
	• page directionality concepts (start at the top and move to the bottom)
	• sentence directionality (start on the left and move to the right with return sweep to the next sentence)
	• voice-print match (points to the words as read with a one-to-one match)
	• the ability to distinguish between print and pictures
	Language allows for clear practice opportunities to hear words in sentences, syllables (chunks) in words, sounds in words, and rhyming words
	Vocabulary allows for clear practice opportunities to identify, match, segment, blend, and manipulate sounds in words
	Vocabulary allows for clear practice opportunities to count, identify, match, sort, and sequence letters in words and individually
	Vocabulary allows for initial practice opportunities to match letters and sounds
	Content allows opportunity to expand students' oral language and world knowledge
	Reading experience provides an opportunity to celebrate reading and/or readers
Teaching point for developing understandings about concepts of print	Concepts of print skills, including:
	• book handling skills (start at the beginning and move in a linear fashion to finish at the end)
	• page directionality concepts (start at the top and move to the bottom)
	• sentence directionality (start on the left and move to the right with return sweep to the next sentence)
	• voice-print match (points to the words as read with a one-to-one match)
	• the ability to distinguish between print and pictures
	• the ability to retrieve meaning from pictures and/or print
	• academic language ("letter," "word," "page," "cover," "title," "start," "end," "beginning," "front," "back," "first," "last," "book," "print," "picture," "line," "sentence," etc.)
Teaching point for phonological, including phonemic, awareness	Word awareness within sentences
	Syllable awareness within words
	Rhyme
	Divide words into onsets and rimes
	Match sounds in the beginning, middle, or end of words
	Identify sounds in the beginning, middle, or end of words
	Segment sounds in words
	Blend sounds into words
	Manipulate sounds between words
	Academic language ("sound," "syllable," "chunk," "word," "sentence," "beginning," "middle," "end," "rhyming," "onset," "rime," "matching," "identifying," "blending," "segmenting," "manipulating")

continued on next page

Figure 5E: Instructional Considerations for Emergent Readers *continued*

Teaching point for alphabetic knowledge	Match letters
	Group similar letters
	Count letters in words
	Match upper- and lowercase letters
	Name letters
	Sequence letters
	Name the sounds letters make
	Academic language ("letter," "capital letter," "uppercase letter," "small letters," "lowercase letters," "word," "beginning," "middle," "end," "matching," "identifying")
Other consideration(s)	Discussion point for expanding oral language (new vocabulary? more complex syntax?)
	Discussion point for expanding world knowledge (background knowledge? new concepts?)
	Defined moment to celebrate the joy of reading
	Defined moment to foster positive identities

Figure 5F: Planning for a Guided Reading Session in the Emergent Phase

Plan for Guided Reading Session Supporting Emergent Readers	
Date of Session	
Students	
Text Selection	
Instructional Decisions	
Teaching point for developing understandings about concepts of print	
Teaching point for phonological, including phonemic, awareness	
Teaching point for alphabetic knowledge	
Discussion point for expanding oral language and world knowledge	
Defined moment to celebrate the joy of reading and foster positive identities	
Instructional Plan	
Flowing into the session	
Flowing through the session	
Flowing out of the session	

Observations of individuals in each area		
	Student One	
	Student Two	
	Student Three	
	Student Four	
	Student Five	
	Student Six	
Teaching point(s) for students for next session		
Other information		

Early Reader Phase

When planning for and supporting the early reader, guided reading instruction may need to continue with outcomes from the emergent phase, especially as students are moving from one phase to the next. This discussion will focus more directly on the early reader phase. Guided reading sessions need to be planned to help the learner in this phase move toward the following key additional outcomes:

- Ability to use sound analysis;

- Increase sight word vocabulary;

- Ability to analyze through structural analysis;

- Ability to analyze word meanings through context analysis;

- Using searching, monitoring, and cross-checking strategies;

- Identifying main idea, theme, and text elements; and

- Making predictions and drawing conclusions based on text evidence.

Sessions should also be planned with the intent of fostering the reader's self-efficacy. Self-efficacy means students believe that reading is something with which they can be successful. Knowing you can is the first step toward becoming a reader. Sessions should work to convince students that they not only know they can be successful readers, but that they should want to read. Instructional considerations in this phase include dimensions discussed in Figure 5G on page 118. Planning for this phase could be structured using the format in Figure 5H on page 120. An additional element in this plan is the identification of individual students to be assessed using running records with oral reading samples and/or writing samples. Since so much of the focus at this phase is to help students learn the tools needed to be effective readers, ongoing formative assessments will be necessary to show the degree of success with which students are acquiring these skills and strategies (Policastro, McTague & Mazeski, 2015; Opitz, Ford & Erekson, 2011).

Figure 5G: Instructional Considerations for Early Readers

Text	Format of text would clearly allow for modeling, practicing, and using…
	• sound analysis strategies (visual/graphophonemic cues)
	• structural analysis strategies (syntactic cues)
	• contextual analysis strategies (semantic cues)
	• searching, monitoring, and cross-checking strategies
	Language allows for clear practice opportunities to hear and recognize sight-word vocabulary
	Vocabulary allows for clear practice opportunities to identify, match, segment, blend, and manipulate sound-symbol relationships in words
	Vocabulary allows for clear practice opportunities to identify, match, segment, blend, and manipulate structural elements in words
	Content affords opportunity to discuss main idea, theme, and text elements
	Content allows opportunity to make predictions and draw conclusions based on text evidence
	Reading experience provides an opportunity to experience success as readers and to value reading
Teaching point for sound analysis (graphophonemic strategies)	Sound-symbol patterns in the beginning, middle, and end of words, including:
	• consistent single-letter consonants
	• variable single-letter consonants
	• single-letter vowels (CVC, CV)
	• common phonograms (word families)
Teaching point for increasing sight-word vocabulary	Confusing sight words in reading or writing
	Increased automaticity of word recognition
Teaching point for analyzing through structural analysis	Use the grammatical structure of the sentence to analyze words
	Chunk meaningful parts of words
	Understand the impact of inflected endings (-s, -es, -ed, -ing, -er, -est)
Teaching point for analyzing word meanings through context analysis (syntactic and semantic clues)	Use syntactic (grammatical) clues
	Use semantic (meaning-based) clues
Teaching point for using multiple strategies (supports students as they learn to use multiple word strategies as they read for meaning)	Searching strategies
	Monitoring strategies
	Cross-checking strategies

continued on next page

Figure 5G: Instructional Considerations for Early Readers *continued*

Teaching point for comprehension	Identify and discuss… • main idea • theme • text elements • making predictions • conclusions based on text evidence
Other consideration(s)	Defined moment to celebrate student success with reading Defined moment to identify reasons to value reading

Figure 5H: Planning for a Guided Reading Session in the Early Reader Phase

Plan for Guided Reading Session Supporting Early Readers	
Date of Session	
Students	
Text Selection	
Instructional Decisions	
Teaching point for using sound analysis (visual and graphophonemic clues)	
Teaching point for increasing sight vocabulary	
Teaching point for analyzing through structural analysis (syntactic clues)	
Teaching point for analyzing word meanings through context analysis (semantic clues)	
Teaching point for using searching, monitoring, and cross-checking strategies	
Teaching point for discussing main idea, theme, and text elements	
Teaching point for making predictions and discussing conclusions based on text evidence	
Defined moment for readers to know they can and want to read	
Instructional Plan	
Flowing into the session	
Flowing through the session	
Flowing out of the session	

continued on next page

Figure 5H: Planning for a Guided Reading Session in the Early Reader Phase *continued*

Instructional Plan *continued*		
General observations of individuals in common instruction	Student One	
	Student Two	
	Student Three	
	Student Four	
	Student Five	
	Student Six	
Teaching point(s) for students for next session		
Individual student(s) targeted for formative assessment (running record)		
Individual student(s) targeted for formative assessment (writing sample)		
Additional teaching points based on targeted formative assessments		
Other information		

Transitional Reader Phase

Guided reading instruction for transitional readers continues to build on previous instruction. The shift between early readers and transitional readers may be distinguished by degrees of automaticity, sophistication, and complexity. Early readers have acquired knowledge about word strategies and beginning comprehension strategies like identifying main idea, theme, and text elements (Boyles, 2009). Transitional readers know what the strategies are and have the ability to make automated decisions about when, why, and how to use the strategies.

Guided reading planning for transitional readers should focus on these key outcomes:

- Use word identification strategies with greater sophistication and automaticity;

- Develop fluency, controlling pace and prosody while making meaning;

- Use text elements to summarize what was read;

- Use the ability to identify main ideas and themes to support personal response, including genuine connections; and

- Attend to author's craft and link it to their writing.

Building confidence and comfort with increasing competence should also be a focus of transitional readers' sessions. Teachers should think about how to become intentional in fostering intrinsic motivations around reading. Instructional considerations at this phase are identified in Figure 5I, and planning for this phase could be structured using the format in Figure 5J on page 124. Planning also includes identifying individual students to be assessed using running records with oral reading samples and/or writing samples.

Figure 5I: Instructional Considerations for Transitional Readers

Text	Format of text would clearly allow for modeling, practicing, and using...
	• increasingly complex sound analysis strategies (visual/graphophonemic cues) with greater automaticity
	• increasingly complex structural analysis strategies (syntactic cues) with greater automaticity
	• increasingly complex contextual analysis strategies (semantic cues), including specific context clue patterns
	Allows for opportunities to demonstrate oral reading with fluency focused on controlling pace, phrasing, and expression (prosody)
	Vocabulary allows for clear practice opportunities to identify, match, segment, blend, and manipulate more sophisticated sound-symbol relationships in words
	Vocabulary allows for clear practice opportunities to identify, match, segment, blend, and manipulate more sophisticated structural elements in words
	Content allows opportunity to use text elements to summarize what was read
	Content allows opportunity to use the ability to identify main ideas and themes to support personal response, including genuine connections
	Content allows opportunity to attend to author's craft and link it to writing
	Reading experience provides an opportunity to experience success, increasing confidence and competence
	Reading experience provides an opportunity to foster intrinsic reasons to read
Teaching point for more complex sound analysis (graphophonemic strategies)	Consistent consonant combinations (blends and digraphs)
	Consistent vowel patterns (VCe, CVVC)
	Special vowel combinations (diphthongs, unique digraphs, consonant controlled)
	Syllabication patterns for pronunciation purposes
Teaching point for analyzing more complex structural analysis (syntactic strategies)	Impact of irregular applications of inflected endings (-s, -es, -ed, -ing, -er, -est)
	Impact of prefixes and suffixes on words
	Work with compound words
	Work with contractions
	Work with common roots
	Syllabication patterns for meaning purposes
Teaching point for analyzing word meanings through context analysis	Use of syntactic (grammatical) clues
	Use of semantic (meaning) clues
	Monitor for sense and sound (grammatically)
	Self-correct for sense and sound (grammatically)
Teaching point for fluency	Control and adjust pace
	Pay attention to prosodic elements using appropriate expression
Teaching point for comprehension	Use text elements to summarize what was read
	Use the ability to identify main ideas and themes to support personal response, including genuine connections
	Attend to author's craft and link it to writing
Other consideration(s)	Defined moment to experience success, increasing confidence and competence
	Defined moment to foster intrinsic reasons to read

Figure 5J: Planning for a Guided Reading Session in the Transitional Reader Phase

Plan for Guided Reading Session Supporting Transitional Readers	
Date of Session	
Students	
Text Selection	
Instructional Decisions	
Teaching point for using more complex sound analysis (visual and graphophonemic clues)	
Teaching point for analyzing more complex structural analysis (syntactic clues)	
Teaching point for analyzing word meanings through more complex context analysis (semantic clues)	
Teaching point for developing fluency, including controlling pace and prosody while making meaning	
Teaching point for using text elements to summarize what was read	
Teaching point for using the ability to identify main ideas and themes to support personal response including genuine connections	
Teaching point for attending to author's craft and linking it to writing	
Defined moment to experience success, increasing confidence, comfort, and competence with intrinsic reasons to read	
Instructional Plan	
Flowing into the session	
Flowing through the session	
Flowing out of the session	

continued on next page

Figure 5J: Planning for a Guided Reading Session in the Transitional Reader Phase *continued*

Instructional Plan *continued*		
General observations of individuals in common instruction	Student One	
	Student Two	
	Student Three	
	Student Four	
	Student Five	
	Student Six	
Teaching point(s) for group for the next session		
Individual student(s) targeted for formative assessment (running record)		
Individual student(s) targeted for formative assessment (writing sample)		
Additional teaching points based on targeted formative assessments		
Other information		

Fluent Reader Phase

In many ways, fluent readers have accomplished the goals of previous instruction. Like transitional readers, fluent readers should focus on increasing degrees of automaticity, reading sophistication, and text complexity. Strategy knowledge becomes more internalized and automatically operationalized. Guided reading planning should support fluent readers on these key outcomes:

- Use word identification strategies efficiently and automatically;

- Be a fluent reader by controlling the meaning-making process;

- Explore more sophisticated text structures;

- Extend the text in new ways; and

- Bring a critical lens to the authors' and characters' customs, values, and choices.

Since fluent readers can already operate more independently, guided reading sessions should be planned to foster—or at least not to interfere with—internalized reasons for reading. Opportunities should be provided to also foster students' abilities to self-regulate. Instructional considerations in this phase are identified in Figure 5K, and planning for this phase could be structured using the format in Figure 5L on page 129. Planning will include identifying individual students to be assessed using comprehension checks following silent reading and/or writing samples.

Figure 5K: Instructional Considerations for Fluency Readers

Text	Format of text would clearly allow for modeling, practicing, and using word-identification strategies efficiently and automatically
	Content allows opportunity to explore more sophisticated text structures
	Content allows opportunity to extend texts in new ways
	Content allows opportunity to bring a critical lens to the authors' and characters' customs, values, and choices
	Content allows for opportunities to demonstrate oral reading with fluency focused on controlling pace, phrasing, and expression (prosody)
	Reading experience provides an opportunity to foster internalized reasons to read
	Reading experience provides an opportunity to engage in self-regulation
Teaching point for enhancing efficiency and automaticity of word-identification strategies	Remaining complex sound analysis (graphophonemic strategies, e.g., complex vowel representatives like schwa)
	Remaining complex structural analysis (syntactic strategies, e.g., Greek and Latin roots)
	Syllabication patterns for pronunciation purposes and for understanding meaning
Teaching point for analyzing word meanings through context analysis	Use of typographical clues (e.g., definitions set off by dashes or parentheses)
	Use of structural/grammatical clues
	Recognition of direct definition patterns (i.e., *A* _____ *is* _____.)
	Synonym and antonym pairings
	Ability to assess mood and tone
	Use of background knowledge
	Make inferences between the lines
	Use of graphic clues
Teaching point for being a fluent reader	Additional practice while maintaining meaning on • controlling pace • increasing rate • improving phrasing • improving expression (prosody)

continued on next page

Figure 5K: Instructional Considerations for Fluency Readers *continued*

Teaching point for comprehension	Explore more sophisticated text structures
	Explore new ways to extend texts
	Bring a critical lens to the authors' and characters' customs, values, and choices
	Reinforce other key strategies... • make and support predictions • determine main ideas with support • compare and contrast elements • determine lessons and themes with support • visualize sensory images • use monitoring and fix-up strategies • make genuine significant connections to self, other texts, and world events • summarize the text in own words • identify point of view with support • distinguish reality and fantasy • identify problems and solutions with support • identify mood and tone with support
Other consideration(s)	Defined moment to experience internalized reasons to read
	Set up opportunity to self-regulate

Figure 5L: Planning for a Guided Reading Session in the Fluent Reader Phase

Plan for Guided Reading Session Supporting Fluent Readers	
Date of Session	
Students	
Text selection Single or multiple titles Who selects? Conditions for selection?	
Instructional Decisions	
Teaching point for enhancing efficiency and automaticity of word-identification strategies	
Teaching point for analyzing word meanings through context analysis (context clue patterns)	
Teaching point for developing fluent readers	
Teaching point for text structures	
Teaching point for extending texts	
Teaching point for bringing a critical lens to the authors' and characters' customs, values, and choices	
Teaching point/key questions for use of other comprehension strategies and thinking patterns	
Defined moment to experience internalized reasons to read	
Defined moment to practice self-regulation	
Instructional Plan	
Flowing into the session	
Flowing through the session	
Flowing out of the session	

continued on next page

Instructional Plan *continued*		
General observations of individuals in common instruction	Student One	
	Student Two	
	Student Three	
	Student Four	
	Student Five	
	Student Six	
Teaching point(s) for student group for next session		
Individual student(s) targeted for formative assessment (comprehension check)		
Individual student(s) targeted for formative assessment (writing sample)		
Additional teaching points based on targeted formative assessments		
Other information		

Concluding Thoughts about Planning for and Supporting Readers

In many ways, the insights and ideas in this chapter are at the heart of providing effective instruction during guided reading sessions. Guided reading depends on teachers knowing where students are at and where they need to move to. Teachers need to be able to use multiple baseline assessments to see the common patterns students share to group them appropriately for instruction. Those commonalities often help determine what phase of reading development the students may be in. Each phase has desired outcomes that help shape the instruction teachers should provide. Planning for this instruction is a series of key decisions made by the teacher to address the common needs of the students within the guided reading group. Baseline assessments also provide insights about the individual pathways of each student. This reminds teachers of the variations that exist between readers, even in the same phase of development. Planning also involves addressing these individual needs. Each instructional session provides more opportunities to observe and assess readers' performances during guided reading and that informs thinking for subsequent instruction. It leads to a powerful cycle of assessment and instruction which, in its best forms, drives effective guided reading instruction.

CHAPTER SIX:
What Is the Rest of the Class Doing During Guided Reading?

> Clearly, the power of the instruction that takes place when students are learning independently must rival the power of the instruction that takes place with the teacher if all children are to maximize their full potential as readers.
>
> *Opitz and Ford, 2001*

When classroom literacy programs returned to the use of small groups for guided reading, the focus of experts, teacher resources, and professional development was often on what to do with the students in the small group. Only limited attention was given to what to do with the rest of the class when the teacher was working with a guided reading group. Many of us remember watching recorded guided reading model lessons at professional development sessions, where it appeared no other children were in the room at the time. The question of what to do with the rest of the kids while working with a group quickly surfaced as the most frequently asked question from educators trying to successfully implement guided reading. A decade later teachers were still asking the question (Guastello & Lenz, 2005). I am guessing that teachers are still asking that question.

Guided reading must have two critical parts. First, guided reading is defined by what is done by the teacher with the students in the small group; but secondly, and just as important, guided reading needs to clearly consider what the other students are doing when they are away from the teacher. If the latter is not thoughtfully considered and addressed, the ability to focus targeted instruction with small groups is virtually impossible. An often seen series of distractions and interruptions preclude the attention needed for successful scaffolded instruction. Even in the earliest discussions of guided reading, Mooney (1990) noted: "The teacher and children should be able to think and talk and read without being distracted by, or disturbing, the rest of the children, who will probably be engrossed in other reading and writing" (p. 57). Guastello and Lenz (2005) pointed out: "The success of guided reading as an effective instructional practice is contingent upon the implementation of a classroom structure conducive to working with the guided reading group while other students are independently and actively engaged in meaningful literacy experiences" (p. 145). Bottom line: If the work away from the teacher is

First, guided reading is defined by what is done by the teacher with the students in the small group; but secondly, and just as important, guided reading needs to clearly consider what the other students are doing when they are away from the teacher.

not thoughtfully considered and addressed, the instructional model of guided reading is inherently flawed and probably doomed to fail.

The survey results presented in Chapter One revealed that, on average, teachers have four guided reading groups that they meet with for about 20 minutes three to four times a week. That means on any day, the students are actually away from the teacher more than they are with the teacher. On some days, some students may actually spend all their time away from the teacher. The sheer amount of independent time does concern some experts who see explicit instruction as more beneficial for most young readers and writers (Shanahan, 2014). This is why it is so critical that the time the students spend away from the teacher engages them in powerful work. One published model of rotation actually recommended that to manage guided reading groups, students would spend three out of five days away from the teacher; however, the learners all were engaged in standards-based, learner-focused "kidstations" away from the teacher (Guastello & Lenz, 2005). This is a good example of what Burkins and Croft (2010) said when they reminded teachers that independent work needs to increase the value of time away from the teacher. Otherwise, the effort to implement guided reading guarantees students will spend most of their time in unproductive ways. If that is the case, effective whole group instruction might actually lead to more productive outcomes for many or most students.

So what do we do with the rest of the kids? Historically for many classrooms, the work away from the teacher often involved completing every worksheet and workbook page recommended in the basal lesson (Durkin, 1978). Even though most programs suggest not using all the available skills sheets, teachers more often than not used every available sheet. Boushey and Moser (2006), in describing their evolution as classroom teachers, revealed that was what they used to manage their classrooms. It kept students busy so that a teacher might be able to meet with a small group. I remember as a classroom teacher rushing to school in the morning or staying late in the afternoon so I could use the copying machine to get my packet of seatwork ready for each of my students. Eventually, I began to question whether this was engaging my students in powerful work, but breaking the habit was difficult. I (1991) actually wrote the article "Worksheets Anonymous: On the Road to Recovery" to tell my story as a recovered worksheet user.

New educators would wonder what that ditto machine is in a museum. But they too need to be careful that the worksheets of the past that were replicated on a ditto machine are not simply electronically reproduced on today's easily accessible and increasingly popular devices. My ears perked up at a recent webinar when such devices and their apps were identified as the chosen independent work even for young students. I remember reading a feature article in my local paper about the wide use of devices in one of our local elementary classrooms. Upon closer look at the color photo accompanying the story, one could see that the app being featured was a math fact sheet that looked a whole lot like the drill and practice worksheets from the past. It's not to say that there is never a purpose for using independent seatwork, electronic or otherwise. In this chapter, we will look more closely at how to structure that work so that it retains power and leads students to make growth and solve problems.

Like Boushey and Moser's (2006) story, learning stations or centers became the next phase of many teachers' evolution. Guided reading programs became linked with centers and stations. Attention shifted away from what the teacher was doing at the table toward how to build effective centers and stations. In fact, some resources had very little attention to what the guided reading instruction would look like, only what the centers would look like (Diller, 2003, 2005). No matter how centers were conceptualized, they always seemed to require a lot of preparation and maintenance. Teachers' frustration grew as the time they spent preparing or repairing the centers seldom paid off with similar levels of engagement by the students at the centers. Burkins and Croft (2010) also pointed out that the instructional density of work at the centers was often compromised for the sake of creating a place that would keep students working independently. It was difficult to create centers around what Clay called "tasks with scope" (in Burkins and Croft, 2010). These tasks are inherently differentiated because they can benefit students regardless of level (e.g., independent reading). Many called for rethinking of centers (Opitz & Ford, 2001, 2002). Over time, some experts did focus on how to create centers with instructional density, centers that could be differentiated, or centers that focused on tasks that could apply to different texts and be done at different levels. This did lessen the frustrations of some teachers, but many kept looking for other ways to engage learners.

So as the juggling acts continued—multiple guided reading groups and multiple independent learning stations—teachers looked for ways to operate more effectively and efficiently. They began to see how the implementation of different process-oriented classroom structures allowed for time to work with individuals and small groups. Teachers discovered the value of workshop approaches. Workshop approaches build in time for:

- Individual students to engage in productive work, freeing up the teacher to work with individuals and small groups.

- Daily focus lessons at the beginning of the workshop that provide common instruction that can address the needs of many students and apply to lots of different texts.

- Students to engage in reading and writing or work with their peers in partners or small groups.

- Teachers to conference with small groups and individuals while other students were productively engaged.

- Students to come back together as a community to share across their texts with each other.

Workshop approaches are whole class structures but inherently individualized. Students could work on tasks with scope like composing stories and discussing texts at different levels, which addresses the need for differentiation.

Teachers started to see that some of the small group work time that was already built into workshop structures could be positioned for guided reading instruction as well. Some promoters of comprehensive literacy frameworks (Dorn & Soffos, 2011) showed how to build layers of small group instruction and intervention around workshop structures at the heart of the literacy program. In her book *More Than Guided Reading*, Mere (2005) discussed her return to the use of the workshop approach to accomplish goals she thought were missing in her use of guided reading. Mere actually raised the question of whether the workshop approach should support guided reading or guided reading should support the workshop approach. Burkins and Croft (2010) asked a similar question when they wondered if all learners need guided reading, especially in an effectively run workshop approach.

While many teachers achieved the effectiveness and efficiency they were looking for when integrating guided reading with workshop approaches, some felt that the big blocks of time in which learners were expected to stay engaged in productive work were too long for young readers and writers. The workshop approaches did little to teach young students how to stay engaged during these blocks of time. That led to the fourth major way of conceptualizing work away from the teacher. Boushey and Moser (2006) popularized the teaching of routines as a way to manage learners while away from the teacher. In their Daily 5 structure, Boushey and Moser recommended teaching young children how to stay engaged in five different routines: read to self, read to someone, work on writing, work on words, and listen to reading. As students were taught each of these routines with expectations and behavioral guidelines, an intentional effort was made to help young students gradually increase their stamina so that students could self-regulate behaviors while involved in these productive routines. As stamina and engagement levels increased, the teacher found the time needed to meet with small groups for a variety of purposes, including guided reading.

In this chapter, we will revisit the answers to the question, "What do I do with the rest of my kids?" We'll also examine what's new to help teachers operate more effectively and efficiently when pairing work away from the teacher with work with the teacher during guided reading.

General Guidelines

Before we implement guided reading groups, let's intentionally address what the rest of the kids will be doing when they are working away from the teacher. Let's start with this assumption: **There must be a classroom structure in place so that a teacher can work with small groups while others are purposefully engaged.**

In a recent webinar focused on guided reading practices, most experts suggested investing time up front during the first few weeks of the year to build a structure that will keep learners purposefully engaged. This occurred before starting the guided reading groups. In their original description, Boushey and Moser (2006) proposed five weeks to roll out The Daily 5 structure. Richardson (2009) suggested a six-week plan to teach routines and procedures to K–1 students. Guastello and Lenz (2005) actually recommended a span of implementation time that might extend up to seven weeks. While some may question the instructional time used to build the structure, starting without a structure virtually guarantees that learners will not be engaged and the ability to attend to learners at the table will be limited. Here are ten tips to help get started in building that structure (modified from Kane, 1995):

Tip 1: *Know your curriculum.*

Whatever structure you choose, it needs to help you move students toward the learning outcomes already identified by your grade level, school, or district. The structure is not just about keeping students engaged, but also about how to help students make growth. Studying your curriculum is the one thing any teacher can and should do in advance of starting guided reading groups. Of particular interest is knowing expected entry and exit levels of learners to be able to estimate the trajectory the learners need to be on. If your guided reading is based on a "program," then also know your program. Keep in mind your fidelity is always to your learners, but expected use of a program demands an understanding of its structure. Likewise, take time to know what specific materials you have access to in order to support learners with a variety of levels and needs.

Tip 2: *Know your learners.*

Choose a structure that fits the students who are your responsibility this year. (And they might not be the same as the ones you had last year or the ones you'll have next year.) You have to consider what might work best for them. Producing a "ready to go" structure before knowing your students sometimes works, but often the match is not the best and leads to a lot of initial disappointment when it doesn't work. Most veteran teachers have a good sense of the nature of the learners who will be in front of them, but we always need to be ready to adjust for a group of students who may not be the norm. The other thing to keep in mind is that one structure may not best meet the needs of all learners, so

adjustments may be needed. Time invested up front in assessing learners both cognitively and affectively usually pays off in the development of a structure better suited to the needs of current students.

Tip 3: *Work with the whole class initially.*

Remember the value of gradual release models not only as a way to structure single lessons, but to also conceptualize your instruction throughout the year. The beginning of the year may be a time to exercise more control. This provides you with time to explicitly and directly teach all learners about purposes and procedures for independent activity. You can model what the activities are, why they are important, and how to do them. Then you can mediate the practice of your learners with the activities while everyone is doing the activity together, evaluating effort and reflecting on how to improve next time. Instead of just expecting learners to perform at high levels of engagement with self-regulated behaviors, whole group time at the beginning of the year allows you to actually teach learners how to perform at this level with those behaviors.

Instead of just expecting learners to perform at high levels of engagement with self-regulated behaviors, whole group time at the beginning of the year allows you to actually teach learners how to perform at this level with those behaviors.

Tip 4: *Introduce the structure gradually.*

One could be too cautious in releasing the learners to operate away from the teacher. If we keep them at the carpet in the whole group until we think they have learned everything they need to know to operate away from us, they may never get off the carpet. Build learning about the structure in phases that allow the students to learn and practice part of the structure while they continue to learn other facets on how to operate productively away from the teacher. Instead of having students master five or six learning stations, different parts of the reading/writing process, or multiple routines all at the same time before trying them out, why not introduce one part and practice that to raise comfort, confidence, and competence levels before adding a new part? Get some independent activity going while you continue to teach about additional layers.

Tip 5: *Set up structure for independent use.*

Whatever structure one develops, it must be built to facilitate independent work. The activities must be achievable without the teacher's intervention. Unless the teacher can rely on dependable outside help, the structure needs to encourage students to work individually or with each other in productive ways. Part of the rollout must include teaching for transfer. Following five critical steps should help:

1. Teacher models and demonstrates
2. Teacher guides the practice of the students while together
3. Students practice together while the teacher monitors
4. Students practice independently while the teacher monitors
5. Students do monitoring themselves

If students are always asked to perform the activities with teacher guidance and support, students may expect something similar when they are on their own. Part of teaching for transfer must include independent practice observed by the teacher to see whether the students need more instruction or they truly can work on their own. Richardson (2009) reminds teachers that this is also a good time to put students in different small groups and observe which students are able to work well together. Boushey and Moser (2006) make it clear in launching each of their classroom routines what the teacher will be doing while the students are working on the routine. After introducing five routines, the students know that the teacher will be working with small groups and individuals. Some teachers use a number of creative visual signs at their table during guided reading to remind the students not to interrupt. These have included everything from a stand-up stop sign to a hat with "Not Now" on the bill—even crime scene tape (Richardson, 2009).

Tip 6: *Build a structure that provides accessible and authentic opportunities for engagement.*

One way to keep students engaged independently is to distinguish between compliance and engagement. In Schlechty's book (2002) *Working on the Work*, he reminds us that we can achieve compliance in the students we are working with, but that falls short of authentic engagement. Compliance often happens not because the students see the work in front of them as meaningful and purposeful, but because completing the work frees them from meeting some negative consequence (passive compliance). Or maybe slightly better, completing the work gains them something they desire, like perhaps a good grade (ritual compliance). But in authentic engagement, the students are "immersed in work that has clear meaning and immediate value to them." While there are plenty of days in which we would settle for compliance, it's hard to see that work that has little purpose or value for students is a good way for them to spend their time away from the teacher. On the other hand, as Mooney (1990) explained, an experience that leaves the student with a satisfied feeling, motivated to continue, and expecting the next experience will be just as enjoyable is a good way for that student to spend that time.

Tip 7: *Minimize and intensify transition time.*

In observing some classrooms, it became apparent that the time it took to get all learners to where they needed to go would almost equal the amount of time the teacher would have to work with the remaining students at the table. Transition time eats into instructional time. Even a small amount of transition time adds up over the course of a school year. Wasting five minutes while transitioning from one group to the next

results in a loss of 900 minutes of instructional time over a 180-day school year. Building a structure that has an efficient way for learners to check in and get started working away from the teacher is critical. Also important is building a structure that moves kids to and from the guided reading groups. Some teachers have become masterful at maximizing the use of transitional time to help learners get refreshed and refocused for the next activity. In Figure 6A, I have identified a number of ITs (intensified transitions) to avoid wasting a minute of instructional time. A quick inquiry about intensified transitions surfaces many sites. For more ideas, seek out: Noodle, Scholastic (search for "Brain Breaks: An Energizing Time-Out"), Pinterest (search for "Classroom Brain Breaks"), and Pottsgrove School District (search for "Pottsgrove School District" and "Brain Breaks" in your search engine).

Figure 6A: Intensified Transitions

- Sing a transition song to help students move. (See Appendix page 198.)
- Conduct a calming down routine. (See Appendix page 198.)
- Integrate a socializing moment. (See Appendix page 198.)
- Perform an action song or chant as students move.
- Recite a familiar poem as students move. (See "Miss Hocket" on page 157 in this chapter.)
- Dramatize a way to move (tiptoes, slow motion, shuffle).
- Count in a variety of ways (by twos, by fives, backward, filling in skipped numbers).
- Spell out words in a variety of ways (by chunks, backward, no vowels).
- Re-energize through a quick exercise that children do in place.
- Invite visualization through an imagined scenario (beach scene, top of the mountain, cloud watching).
- Play "Teacher Says" (like "Simon Says," but guide toward the next activity).

Tip 8: *Create equally interesting activities and provide access for all learners.*

As you build your classroom structure, make sure that it doesn't interfere with your ability to work with students individually or in small groups. Sometimes what we ask students to do independently away from the teacher is so attractive that calling someone to the table leads to groans and moans from the students. "Why do we always have to go to the table? How come we never get to work with the tablets?" Or perhaps the reverse occurs: "How come we never get to work at the table with you?" While we might need to have a lesson on the difference between what is equal and what is fair, all students should have access to high-quality and engaging learning activities. If these truly are great learning experiences for any child, then perhaps all students should have an opportunity to experience them.

Tip 9: *Focus your structure on opportunities to practice reading and writing.*

What did Mooney think the rest of the kids would be doing when she wrote about guided reading way back in 1990? "They would probably be engrossed in other reading and writing (57)." If there is one common critique of work away from the teacher, it is often that it leads to very little additional reading and writing. If the power of time away from the teacher is going to rival the time spent with the teacher, it needs to stay focused on opportunities to practice and improve on reading and writing. There are many things we can ask students to do to keep them busy, but the challenge is finding structures that keep them busy doing what they need to do most: continuing to read and write. Often the work away from the teacher resembles what some have called reading arts and crafts—response and extension projects that involve a lot of cutting, coloring, and pasting. While we know the importance of allowing students to use multiple modes, caution must be exercised to ensure that time away from the teacher engages students in what they need to practice most. Sometimes these projects create a lot of excitement about reading and writing and the ultimate outcome is more practice, but when they are just projects with no learning outcome, we might want to question their value. On the other hand, many times, if the students become excited about the reading and writing they are experiencing, they will self-initiate projects that allow them to respond to and extend the work they are doing.

Tip 10: *Always be ready to go back and re-examine structure.*

Just as we need patience to build the structure in the beginning of the year, we also need to have patience in allowing the structure to work. We need to avoid the urge to abandon our efforts too early or too fast. There is nothing wrong with stepping back from our concerns about implementation and reflecting on how to address those concerns. Re-teaching through more modeling or guided practice is sometimes warranted. It is certainly better than tossing out a structure that already consumed a lot of time, energy, and effort to put in place.

There is nothing wrong with stepping back from our concerns about implementation and reflecting on how to address those concerns. Re-teaching through more modeling or guided practice is sometimes warranted.

Structures for Engagement Away from the Teacher

So what's new, and what's next in answering the question—what do I do with the rest of the kids? Let's look at the four typical ways of answering this question.

Structure One: Routines

When asked what's new with independent work, we would have to start to look at routines. We have finally learned that no matter what structure a teacher creates to surround guided reading groups, students have to be able to stay engaged in meaningful activities for sustained periods of time. That is true whether the activity is within a workshop framework, at a learning station, or at the student's desk or table.

We have learned a lot about the value of routines and how to teach them from Boushey and Moser (2006, 2014). Since the publication of their popular text *The Daily 5*, routines have been moved to center stage for many classrooms. They described The Daily 5 as a management system that focuses on teaching students to sustain levels of engagement in five basic routines: reading to self, reading to someone, listening to reading, working on writing, and working with words. What was new in their approach? First they reminded us there is a difference between expecting behaviors and teaching students how to behave. Setting and conveying high expectations that students will be able to perform reading and writing activities can contribute to student learning. But that is only true when combined with other conditions of language learning (Cambourne, 1995, 2001). Those expectations are critical because thinking one can and wanting to succeed are starting points for motivation and engagement. (See pages 58–59 in Chapter Three for a complete list of Cambourne's conditions.) If learners are to find joy in their efforts, knowing an important adult thinks and wants them to succeed can be huge (Opitz & Ford, 2014). But thinking one can and wanting to succeed also means the learner knows how, and that is where teaching behaviors comes into play.

Secondly, Boushey and Moser (2006, 2014) point out there is also a critical difference between managing student behaviors and teaching students to manage their own behaviors. Management often suggests an external source that is present to monitor the behaviors. In a recent classroom visit, I observed a masterful teacher who was using a newly embraced management system in which she had been trained. It required pre-identifying a short list of behaviors (e.g., working quietly and staying in one place) that were going to be monitored individually or in groups during the next learning period with identification of consequences and rewards up front. In the end, there seemed to be as much attention to the monitoring of behaviors as there was to monitoring student learning. I wasn't convinced students were learning how to manage their own behaviors with such a heavy-handed, teacher-driven system. My guess is the teacher will still need to do the monitoring during the guided reading instruction.

So what routines should we teach students so they can work independently and productively while the teacher works with the guided reading group? Based on the guidelines presented, being able to read on your own often goes to the top of the list. Some caution: "Reading to self is important, but it is not as effective as reading communally with a teacher and classmates. Schools should teach reading and encourage and enable students to engage in reading beyond school" (Shanahan, November 12, 2012). Others challenge that notion and make a case for the need for students to engage in independent reading programs (Morgan, Mraz, Padak & Rasinski, 2009; Allington, 2013). And what else would be on the list? Reading to someone might have just as much value, with listening to reading close behind. In fact, if students could engage in just those three

> *Setting and conveying high expectations that students will be able to perform reading and writing activities can contribute to student learning.*

behaviors for significant periods of time, most teachers would be happy. Similarly, being able to work independently on writing would be another critical routine that would contribute to improving literacy performances. Finally, word study can keep students engaged as they explore multiple dimensions of words in fun and informative ways. Figure 6B on page 144 includes helpful routines we have discovered, using published resources such as *The Daily 5* as a guide.

Figure 6B: Tips for Improving Routines

Routine	Tips for Planning	Tips for Materials	Tips for Instruction
Read to Self	It's easy to teach students what this should look like externally (get started right away, read quietly, stay in one place, etc.), but do young children really know what they are supposed to do? You might conduct a simple interview (Opitz & Ford, 2015) with readers to see if they understand what silent reading is: 1. When someone tells you to read silently, what do you think you are supposed to do? 2. What do you actually do when you read silently? What happens inside your head? 3. How is silent reading different from oral reading? 4. Do you like to read silently? Why or why not? For students who may need to hear what they read as they read, introduce tools like curved conduit or PVC pipes to help students hear as they read to themselves. The learner can read into the device, and it directs the voice right into the learner's ear. If it is easier for students to stay on track by reading to an audience, but an audience is not available, plan opportunities for students to read to class mascots.	When teaching the three ways to read (read the picture, retell the story, and read the words), wordless picture books are a great tool as they help teach the need for reading the pictures. Since these can be quite sophisticated, all students can use books like these for improving their visual literacy. Picture books with minimal pictures are the best way to teach the importance of reading words. *The Book With No Pictures* by B.J. Novak (Dial) or *We Are in a Book!* by Mo Willems (Disney-Hyperion) are good options. Telling the story as a way of reading is easily modeled with familiar fairy tales and folktales. Check out *The Ant and the Grasshopper, Beauty and the Beast,* and *The Boy Who Cried Wolf* (Capstone Classroom). *I Hate Reading* by Arthur and Henry Bacon (Pixel Titles) is a great book to use to point out the difference between pretending to read and actually reading.	Make sure the students are actually reading appropriate texts at increasingly complex levels. Consider your goal. Independent-level texts may build comfort, confidence, and automaticity. Instructional-level texts may allow for problem-solving at the word and text levels that leads to cognitive growth. Even a frustrational-level text can have a purpose. You can position it as the student's goal book or dream book, and revisiting the harder text can show the student how he or she is improving over time. All types might be in the readers' baskets, boxes, or folders but make sure readers know which books are best for which purpose and goal.

continued on next page

Figure 6B: Tips for Improving Routines *continued*

Routine	Tips for Planning	Tips for Materials	Tips for Instruction
Reading to Someone	Preparing for performance is a good authentic reason to read with someone. Plan to teach a step-by-step approach to guide learners to work together for that outcome: 1. Leader reads the story aloud; 2. Both chorally read the story together; 3. Choose parts; 4. Practice parts on own; 5. Practice parts together; and 6. Be ready to share.	Look for multi-level texts. Poetry anthologies allow readers at different levels to find verses at their levels. Scripts allow for the assigning of different parts. Many informational texts have features at different reading levels. Journalistic texts also have easy and hard parts. Cumulative tales are also good because the strong reader can introduce the new line and the partner can repeat the familiar lines.	Training buddies to be coaches is critical. The suggested lesson of "How to Be a Good Reading Coach" needs to be emphasized. Partners that learn how to wait and let their friend work out the right answers or know how to make strategic suggestions without giving answers will lead their friend to greater growth and may learn more about the process themselves.
Listen to Reading	You can lengthen engagement levels in listening routines by planning to teach steps in listening to a recorded story: 1. Listen to the story and follow along; 2. Listen to the story and read along; 3. Turn off the story and read by yourself; 4. Listen to the story and read along again. Watch for parts you found tricky; 5. Turn off the story and read the story again to see if you can improve.	Digital texts may be the easiest way to set this up. Check out Unite for Literacy online for digital books. The easily accessible texts are free and available in nine languages.	Listening to a story may free up some readers to focus more on meaning making, so consider holding students accountable during this routine by introducing ways to respond. This can prepare them as they move to responding during silent reading.

continued on next page

Figure 6B: Tips for Improving Routines *continued*

Routine	Tips for Planning	Tips for Materials	Tips for Instruction
Work on Writing	Students should begin to see their reading materials as mentor texts of good writing. Plan to show students examples of good writing when it appears in their reading materials. Also plan for lessons that relate to writing, whether in response to reading or to mirror the author's craft under discussion.	Refer to your read-alouds during focus lessons for different types and purposes of writing [*Written Anything Good Lately?* by Susan Allen and Jane Lindaman (Millbrook Press)], formats [(*I Wanna Iguana* Karen Kaufman Orloff (Putnam) and *Diary of a Worm* by Doreen Cronin (HarperCollins)], different traits [(*Voices in the Park* by Anthony Browne (DK Children)], or mechanics [(*Punctuation Takes a Vacation* and other books by Robin Pulver (Holiday House)]	Writing instruction is critical. The lessons need to focus on what your learners need. Don't do a mini-lesson because a writing lesson is scheduled. Keep your focus on what your students need to learn as writers. Remember, any text they have created can also be the focus when you confer with the student. Then you can assess both reading and writing at the same time.
Word Work	Plan word work around key strategies. Make sure word work is appropriate for the readers: emergent (concepts of print, alphabetic knowledge, phonemic awareness), early (phonics, sight words, structural analysis, context clues), transitional and fluent (word meanings). Then match the word learning opportunity to the outcome.	Provide access through read-alouds, shared readings, and displays to books that create interest in or have fun with words. How about *Double Trouble in Walla Walla* by Andrew Clements (21st Century), *Cat Tale* by Michael Hall (Greenwillow), or the *Fancy Nancy* series by Jane O'Connor (HarperCollins)? Add riddle and pun books to the collection. Look for series from Marvin Terban, Brian P. Cleary, and Ruth Heller.	If you are already using an approach for learning about words (i.e., *Words Their Way*), bring that approach into your routine. You do not need to set up additional word work just for the sake of creating this routine.

So what's next in independent work through routines? It seems obvious, but it might be connecting routines more closely to learner outcomes. One recent critique of routines by Shanahan (2014, November 12) suggested that the routines are too focused on doing activities:

> "The Daily 5 establishes a very low standard for teaching by emphasizing activities over outcomes, and by not specifying quality or difficulty levels for student performances. Teachers can successfully fulfill The Daily 5 specifications without necessarily reaching, or even addressing, the standards .... There are lots of ways to a goal, and I deeply respect the teacher who has a clear conception of what she is trying to accomplish and the choices that entails. Starting with the activity instead of the outcome, however, allows someone to look like a teacher without having to be one."

Most critiques of any program are often based on the way the programs are interpreted and implemented. Many would suggest that this is really a critique of a poor implementation of one program. Again, published programs like *The Daily 5* are management structures. Their content can be driven in many purposeful ways to address stated concerns.

So how would goal-oriented routines look? Shanahan (2014, May 24) identifies four critical goals: word learning, oral reading fluency, writing, and reading comprehension. He reluctantly adds one affective goal (love of reading and writing). Now imagine if the launching lessons were focused on goals, why each was important, what you can do to improve in each area, and how you would know if you are making progress. (See Figure 6C on page 148.) The daily conversation would revolve around discussion like these:

- Tell me what goal area you are going to work on.

- Tell me what "I can" statement in that goal area you are working toward.

- Tell me what you are going to do to make progress toward your goal.

- Tell me how you are going to know if you made progress.

- Is there anything you need from me to get started?

I will just point out, however, that this conversation does sound a lot like the conversations recommended by Boushey and Moser (2009).

Figure 6C: Goal-oriented Launching Lesson

Goal Area	Word Learning
"I can" statement	I can quickly read the 100 most common words without a mistake.
Why I want to accomplish this goal	It will help me read more smoothly and quickly. If I am not stopping to figure out these words, I can focus more on meaning when I am reading or writing.
How I can accomplish this goal	I can work on learning these words by using Look-Say-Write-Check. I can play flash card games with my buddy. I can use a sight word app on a tablet. I can record myself saying the words and listen to see how many I got right and how fast I went. I can read some books from the sight word basket. I can look back at my writing to find sight words and see if they were right.
How I will know that I am meeting my goal	I will work with a partner who will check and time me as I work through the list of words. He or she will help me count how many I got right and how fast I went. I will record this on my chart.

So what else is next in independent work based on routines? Freebody and Luke (1990) provide another framework by which we can move the use of routines forward and perhaps in a direction that might be more appropriate with older learners. Freebody and Luke's Four Resources Model emerged in the 1990s to broaden our view of what reading means in a multimodal world in which sign systems include print but other auditory and visual systems as well. Think about how music, visual graphics, photographs, or oral speeches are "read" or interpreted. Freebody and Luke define literacy in terms of a repertoire of capabilities: able to decode written text, understand and compose meaningful texts, use texts functionally, and analyze texts critically. All four are of equal importance, especially since readers usually engage in several at the same time.

The five routines in The Daily 5 are primarily presented as opportunities for code breaking and meaning making. They often seem to be ends in and of themselves. Freebody and Luke also remind us of the importance of promoting the roles of text users and text critics. For text users, the functional use of reading and writing for a purpose is emphasized. One such function is to learn about something else, encouraging learners to engage in meaningful inquiry that could increase content knowledge and reading and writing performance. Another way to move these routines to a means toward ends versus ends in and of themselves is to focus on performance. Entertaining others can be another powerful way to help students purposefully use the texts they are consuming and creating.

So what would launching lessons looks like for text users? Let's look at teaching students how to engage in independent routines related to inquiry and performance following five key steps. Figure 6D illustrates specific launching lessons.

Entertaining others can be another powerful way to help students purposefully use the texts they are consuming and creating.

Figure 6D: Specific Launching Lessons

Step	Description	Inquiry	Performance
Step One: Catalyst	Metaphorically start a fire in our learners. Make the routine so attractive that the students will naturally gravitate toward it. Create a sense of joyful effort so they are chomping at the bit as soon as we step out of the way.	Share the texts that celebrate inquiry and learning like *Me…Jane* by Patrick McDonnell (Little, Brown) for younger children or *The Island* by Gary Paulsen (Scholastic) for older learners. Flood the room with related informational texts about a topic to generate interest and questions about a topic. Link these to topics being explored in social studies and science. Seize multimedia reports on a current event to surface questions worthy of future exploration.	Share the texts that celebrate performance like *ZooZical* by Judy Sierra (Knopf) or *The School Play from the Black Lagoon* by Mike Thaler (Scholastic). Flood the room with performance materials—scripts, lyrics, speeches—to generate interest and start the planning process. Seize the viewing of a live or recorded performance to encourage something similar in class.
Step Two: Life Applications	Make sure that the question of why this is important in the real world—not just the school world—is so obvious that the question of why we have to do this doesn't surface.	Discuss situations inside and outside of school when a student could use inquiry processes and procedures—from purchasing decisions to developing persuasive arguments in influencing family members.	Brainstorm careers in which oral performance is valuable—from obvious roles like actors and media reporters to less obvious roles like teachers.
Step Three: Learning Goals (How is your reading, writing, thinking going to improve?)	Link the routine to specific goals in reading, writing, and content so students can see how pursuing the routine also helps them get stronger in those academic areas.	Help students identify specific goals during the inquiry process. Examples might include: *I can grow in my ability to read different types of nonfiction texts.* *I can grow in my ability to write an informational text.* *I can improve my ability to use presentations to persuade others.*	Help students identify specific goals to improve in their performance skills. Examples might include: *I can improve my ability to use pacing, pitch, and volume to perform dialogues.* *I can better use visualization strategies to conceptualize what is needed (props, costumes, visual aids, scenes) to support the oral performance.* *I can better use physical movements (gestures, body language, dance) to enhance my oral performance.*

continued on next page

Figure 6D: Specific Launching Lessons *continued*

Step	Description	Inquiry	Performance
Step Four: Procedures	Provide a step-by-step process that provides students with intentional directions on how to carry out the routine. They should not be so inflexible that the learners cannot return to or revisit steps when new ideas emerge or original ideas are rethought.	Focus class time on the procedures involved in inquiry: 1. Generate ideas and questions. 2. Make a plan to collect information. 3. Organize and synthesize information. 4. Draw conclusions. 5. Develop presentation. 6. Deliver presentation. 7. Remember to use outside time to watch related digital media, create models, try out simulations, conduct the experiments, produce the presentation, etc.	1. Prepare script and select a mode (live, electronic, multimedia performance). 2. Practice the script. 3. Choose parts and tasks. 4. Practice parts independently and complete individual tasks. 5. Put all parts and tasks together. 6. Focus class time on rehearsal for the performances. 7. Select or create a script for the oral performance. 8. Assign parts to practice independently. 9. Assist each other in rehearsing to improve vocal features and physical movements to enhance performance. 10. Make decisions about needed visual supports. 11. Collectively rehearse together, coordinating efforts across involved students with final supports. 12. Deliver performance. 13. Remember to use outside time to create costumes, props, scenery, animations, etc.

continued on next page

Figure 6D: Specific Launching Lessons *continued*

Step	Description	Inquiry	Performance
Step Five: Problem-solving	Anticipate and address typical problems that may occur in working through the routine, so solutions have been discussed and students can continue to operate away from the teacher.	Discuss any potential areas of conflict and agree up front about solutions, including: 1. Limits on resources, supplies, and materials available to support the inquiry 2. Constraints on time available for inquiry and setting deadlines 3. A conflict-resolution technique agreed upon by the group (majority vote, random choice by flipping coin, etc.) 4. The teacher's role in the process, remembering that time is needed to work with guided reading groups 5. Discuss any remaining issues with students prior to starting the process or allow for future discussions	Discuss any potential areas of conflict and agree up front about solutions, including: 1. Limits on resources, supplies, and materials available to support the performance 2. Constraints on time available and conducting the performance 3. A conflict-resolution technique agreed upon by the group (majority vote, random choice by flipping coin, etc.) 4. The teacher's role in the process, remembering that time is needed to work with guided reading groups 5. Discuss any remaining issues with students prior to starting the process or allow for future discussions

Structure Two: Workshop Framework

Workshop frameworks provide an inherent structure that engages students in authentic individual and peer reading and writing experiences with potential to free the teacher to conduct guided reading sessions. Because of this, some (Dorn & Soffos, 2011) have placed one or more workshops at the heart of their literacy frameworks. In the national survey of guided reading practices, almost one-third of teachers reported that they had already paired guided reading groups with reader's/writer's workshop.

Structurally, the workshop framework is fairly simple in its conceptualization. The workshop typically begins with universal instruction. Often called a mini-lesson—though some prefer calling it a focus lesson since "mini" may make it seem less important. This explicit instruction provided by the teacher, usually in a large group setting for all students, is determined by curriculum demands and student needs in reading and writing. The instruction is very targeted and designed to occur in a relatively short amount of time, usually no longer than 10–15 minutes.

Universal instruction is followed by a quick check-in on the class. Atwell (1998) calls it taking a "status of the class" (p. 107). Without losing too much instructional time, the teacher sets the purpose for the independent and peer work that is to follow. Students quickly state what they will be doing during the independent time. A quick transition is made by the students to their independent reading and writing activities, with the teacher freed to begin work with identified students in guided reading. Identifying those students first often allows them to transition and be ready at the table by the time the teacher has checked in with the remaining students. Teachers may want to invest in check-in systems that identify and remind students where they are at in the process.

This leads to the heart of the workshop framework: significant uninterrupted time to engage in sustained reading and writing. The longer the students can stay productively engaged during this part of the workshop, the more opportunities the teacher has to meet with guided reading groups. If the typical guided reading group is about 20 minutes in length, one can see that as a minimum amount of time for sustained reading and writing. As previously stated, developing readers and writers to stay engaged for that amount of time begins with focusing on teaching those routines and their required behaviors. To be able to meet with two guided reading groups, the amount of needed time doubles. The expectation of some students to sustain their work for 40 minutes probably starts to push the boundaries of what can be expected in elementary literacy programs. It was this large amount of sustained activity expected by the workshop framework that caused Boushey and Moser to propose The Daily 5 as an alternative. This would break up time into smaller chunks that are more compatible with the learning characteristics of younger children.

It should be noted that students do not need to be restricted to just large amounts of sustained independent reading and writing during this part of the workshop framework. Students can also be taught how to work together so that peer partner and small group work can also help to keep students engaged. As students move through the drafting, revision, and editing phases of writing, they can be taught procedures that help them work with each other on their writing. As students read the same topic across texts, they can be taught procedures on how to help each other make sense of the materials they are reading. They can be taught how to meet away from the teacher to discuss what they are reading, thinking, and learning with each other. This part of the workshop can be like a studio in which participants are working individually and with others at various stages in the process. This vision of the workshop may make longer periods of engagement seem more possible than long periods of sustained silent reading and writing.

Another way to address the long period of needed self-engagement by students is to spend just a few minutes between two guided reading groups to recheck the status of the class. As the groups transition to and from the table for guided reading instruction, take a minute to check in on learners. In some programs, a mid-workshop lesson is conducted quickly based on something students were successfully doing, or intervening occurs to help students who are struggling. If needed, Boushey and Moser are not alone in recommending a little brain break

This leads to the heart of the workshop framework: significant uninterrupted time to engage in sustained reading and writing. The longer the students can stay productively engaged during this part of the workshop, the more opportunities the teacher has to meet with guided reading groups.

to get everyone refocused, re-energized, and ready to stay engaged for another block of time. Examples of brain breaks are listed on page 140 in Figure 6A.

The workshop framework usually ends with a few minutes set aside to bring the class back together for sharing. This sharing time serves so many purposes. Having time to share what was read, written, and learned makes the time set aside for reading, writing, and learning more purposeful. It actually contributes to higher levels of engagement. Public sharing allows the teacher to drop in on students and the work they did, which would be hard to observe while engaged in guided reading lessons. It allows the class to reflect on not just what was learned but how they are doing in meeting their goals. Finally coming back together at the end allows the teacher to rebuild the classroom community and create a culture of collaboration and celebration that permeates long after that moment in time. To eliminate this sharing time actually works against the workshop activity that precedes it and the workshop model as a whole.

With a longer block or another professional in the room, more guided reading can be added to the program. See Figure 6E. Blocks can also accommodate time allocated to specialists outside the classroom. You can reach closure on one part of the block and resume the work on the next part of the block when you return to the classroom.

One thing to remember is that guided reading is focused on scaffolded instruction for reading. Writing might be used as a tool to see what students know about print or as a vehicle to share how meaning was made through written response, but guided *reading* lessons typically do not provide scaffolded instruction in the composing process. Helping students become better writers will require the integration of small group writing conferences.

Figure 6E:
Workshop Alignment (90-minute Block)

Learners	Teacher
Focus Lesson (15 minutes)	
Status of the Class (5 minutes)	
Sustained Reading and Writing (20 minutes)	Guided Reading Group Number One
Intensified Transition/Mid-workshop Check (5 minutes)	
Sustained Reading and Writing (20 minutes)	Guided Reading Group Number Two
Intensified Transition/Mid-workshop Check (5 minutes)	
Sustained Reading and Writing (15 minutes)	Individual Conferences with Readers and Writers
Community Sharing (5 minutes)	

Learners	Classroom Teacher	Interventionist
Focus Lesson (15 minutes)		
Status of the Class (5 minutes)		
Sustained Reading and Writing (20 minutes)	Guided Reading Group Number One	Intervention Group Number One
Intensified Transition/Mid-Workshop Check (5 minutes)		
Sustained Reading and Writing (20 minutes)	Guided Reading Group Number Two	Intervention Group Number Two
Intensified Transition/Mid-Workshop Check (5 minutes)		
Sustained Reading and Writing (20 minutes)	Guided Reading Group Number Three	Guided Reading Group Number Four
Intensified Transition/Mid-Workshop Check (5 minutes)		
Sustained Reading and Writing (15 minutes)	Individual Conferences with Readers and Writers	Individual Interventions
Community Sharing (10 minutes)		

Structure Three: Learning Stations

So what are students doing when they are not working directly with the teacher? The national survey indicated that almost three-fourths of the teachers paired their guided reading with centers. When we look at what were the most frequently used centers, they looked a lot like the routines we previously listed as important.

- Listening center

- Writing center

- Working with words centers

- Reading center

- Buddy reading center

As we stated, these centers will still require students to stay engaged for sustained periods of time. They often represent physical locations that include supplies and resources needed.

So what could I say about centers that hasn't been said by others? Lists of center ideas offered by others look more alike than different. For young students, Richardson (2009) offered these work station possibilities: book boxes, buddy reading, writing, reader's theater, timed reading, poems and songs, ABC/word study, word wall, reading the room (word hunts), oral retelling, listening, computer, overhead projector, geography, science, big books, and library. Lists like these seem to be a mix of materials, equipment, activities, and routines. But they are mostly lists of things students can do. They often are not defined as things students need to do or should be doing; rather, they are things that will keep students busy. The goal for Richardson seems to be to make sure the students can stay busy with a work station for at least 20 minutes. For intermediate students, she focuses on four activities that seem to be more purposeful: buddy reading, word study, vocabulary, and writing, but they also seem to be goal free with menus of options.

Diller (2003) provided some of the most comprehensive ways to conceptualize centers, or what she called "literacy work stations,": "an area within the classroom where students work alone or interact with one another, using instructional materials to explore and expand their literacy. It is a place where a variety of activities reinforces and/or extends learning, often without the assistance of the classroom teacher. It is a time for children to practice reading, writing, speaking and listening, and working with letters and words" (pp. 2–3). Diller is clear to point out that literacy work stations are set up for the entire year with the materials changed to reflect different levels, strategies, and topics. She also reminds us that the materials need to be differentiated for different students at different levels. They are not just things to do, but places to go to independently practice what has already been taught. In her book for teachers of young students (Diller, 2003), she identifies six major work stations: classroom library, big book, writing, drama, ABC/word work, and poetry. She adds nine additional possible work stations: computer, listening, puzzles and games, buddy reading, overhead projector, pocket chart, science, social studies, and handwriting. In the end, there are a lot of ideas, but it becomes hard to see how you create a system to engage learners that requires setting up at least six major centers, supplying each with the materials needed to meet the needs of diverse learners, introducing them so each learner knows what to do at each station, and then monitoring them so that each learner does what they need to do at each center.

Her book for teachers of older learners (Diller, 2005) does include how literacy work stations can be positioned to support goals in comprehension, fluency, phonics, and vocabulary. But again, positioning nine centers to provide independent practice for a diverse group of learners in four critical areas and making sure that happens only shows the complexity of using work stations to partner with guided reading.

Maybe the more critical discussion is not about what can be a center but about how we get more power, value, and mileage from centers or stations. Figure 6F on page 156 offers some suggestions of things to remember and things to avoid.

Maybe the more critical discussion is not about what can be a center but about how we get more power, value, and mileage from centers or stations.

Figure 6F: Center Suggestions

Remember to...	Avoid...
Create centers that are destinations for ongoing activities with an inherently individualized scope, such as a reading corner with access to resources and support or writing centers with tools, mentor texts, and reference resources.	Creating centers that require the completion of an activity, leaving the center in need of frequent changing with little possibility of transcending texts, task, and learners.
Allow spaces and tools used for large group and shared experiences to be accessible as centers where students can repeat instructional experiences that the teacher has modeled. Let students revisit whiteboard experiences, the shared reading big book, the pocket chart, or the word wall.	Restricting student use of instructional spaces and tools that could provide purposeful goal-oriented practice for the sake of "protecting" the areas or materials. Assuming that you can't teach students how to use these areas and trust that they will once taught.
Let students be involved in the organizing and decorating of the center spaces. Let their work and class-generated products that flow naturally from instruction provide the backdrop for the center.	Spending significant amounts of time and/or resources to create "beautiful" spaces. Spending your time planning instruction and analyzing assessments.
Invest in a visual display where students can independently check into centers so that a quick glance allows you to know who should be where. Set up a way for students to record how they spent their time, including what goals they were working on (contracts, punch cards, learner notebooks).	Being distracted to constantly monitor which students are at the right centers. Implementing a heavy-handed, teacher-directed monitoring system that requires time to keep track of what students have done and learned.
Have students take responsibility for straightening up the centers on a regular basis after use. Different teams of students can be assigned to different centers. Teach and trust them to do what needs to be done to leave the center in good condition.	Seeing the cleaning up of centers as your responsibility. Thinking that you can't teach and trust students how to clean up each area.
Process students' learning at the end of the language arts block. Focus on what was learned not what was done: What did you learn today? What did you do to become a better reader? Writer? What would help your learning the next time you work at the centers? (Diller, 2005)	Ending the learning when the centers end. Focusing sharing on what was not learned or completed.

Structure Four: Independent Seatwork

So what is next in seatwork? If the worksheets and the workbook pages of the past disappear, and we avoid replacing them with electronic versions of the same thing, is there any place for seatwork?

For me, the best seatwork offers opportunity to practice skills and strategies as students continue to work on growing as readers and writers. Assuming that much of that time at one's seat or table will be spent reading independently and working on writing, other activities could provide more targeted practice. Those activities would evolve naturally from instruction that has taken place in the large or small group, be self-generating, be easily accessible, and provide more purposeful ways to practice.

In my classroom, the best way to create that type of seatwork was through the use of poems. Poetry had a pervasive place in my classroom. Friendly and familiar poems that had been introduced through shared reading experiences became tools for additional practice. My students kept a poetry folder. It provided easy access to texts for practice. For each poem that had been shared in the class, purposeful practice materials were generated for the poetry folder. As an example, I will use one of our favorite poems: an anonymous limerick called "Miss Hocket":

> A young kangaroo named Miss Hocket
> Carried dynamite sticks in her pocket
> By mistake, a match
> Dropped into her hatch
> And Miss Hocket took off like a rocket.

For a little physical exercise, my class loved to crouch in the kangaroo position and jump up when Miss Hocket took off like a rocket.

Here's how the folder evolved:

1. A hard copy of the poem was given to each student, allowing for repeated readings of the poem individually and with partners. In the large group, a variety of techniques were used to model how to set a poem up for a choral reading or reader's theater performance. Rasinski (2003) identified eight ways to do choral reading: refrain, line-a-child, dialogue, antiphonal reading, call and response, cumulative, choral singing, and impromptu choral reading. You can build in poetry breaks throughout your day by inviting individuals and partners who are ready to perform a chance to share. Poetry breaks are a good way to intensify transitional time.

2. A word list was created from the vocabulary in each poem or from a part of a longer poem. Students were invited to work on improving their automaticity in saying the words. They could time themselves or each other. The list was numbered, and ways of having fun with the numbered lists were modeled in the large group. These included calling out a word and having your partner call out the number next to it, or just the reverse: calling out a number and saying the word next to it. (See Figure 6G on page 158.)

3. Word cards are created for the folder by the student. Students are given a grid (different colors for different poems) on which they write each word from the poem or part of the longer poem in one box on the grid. (See Figure 6H on page 159.) The words are cut apart to form a set of cards that can be used in a number of individual or partner activities, which have been modeled in the large group. These might include word sorts, matching games, modified card games (e.g., "War"—

> *Poetry had a pervasive place in my classroom. Friendly and familiar poems that had been introduced through shared reading experiences became tools for additional practice.*

longest word wins), rebuilding the poems, rearranging the cards to make new sentences, and other variations. (Tip: Have students put their initials on the back of each card so they can be separated as needed. Give each student a plastic bag when new cards are made.)

4. Each poem did lead to a product that could promote more reading and writing. With "Miss Hocket," students were given individual pages with one line from the poem on each page. Illustrating and sequencing the pages led to the creation of a self-illustrated book. Since all students created their own version, the class ended up with multiple sets of the book to use in independent, partner, and small group reading forums. (See Figure 6I.)

Any poem that is shared and learned as a part of large group instruction can lead to similar activities. As new poems are learned and new activities introduced, students can rotate them into their folders and "retire" older activities by taking them home. There will always be something in the poetry folder that the student can work on while waiting for a turn at the guided reading table. Teachers may find the compilation of the "12 Best Poetry Websites for Kids" from EdTech a good source for additional poems and activities, especially Giggle Poetry and Kenn Nesbitt's Poetry4Kids.

Figure 6G: Word List for "Miss Hocket"

1. a	9. Hocket	17. named
2. and	10. in	18. off
3. by	11. into	19. pocket
4. carried	12. like	20. rocket
5. dropped	13. kangaroo	21. sticks
6. dynamite	14. match	22. took
7. hatch	15. Miss	23. young
8. her	16. mistake	

Figure 6H: Word Cards for "Miss Hocket"

A	young	kangaroo	named	Miss
Hocket	carried	dynamite	sticks	in
her	pocket	by	mistake	a
match	dropped	into	her	hatch
and	Miss	Hocket	took	off
like	a	rocket		

Figure 6I: Self-illustrated Page

A young kangaroo named Miss Hocket	

Teachers can look for other self-generating, easily accessible, purposeful ways to practice reading and writing. For example, in *The Fluent Reader*, Rasinski (2003) identified a number of classroom procedures that help capture the power of repetition, providing reading practice with purpose so students don't easily tire of their texts. These include procedures that can start with the teacher in shared reading, guided reading, or individual reading conferences and can be continued or replicated by the student as independent or partner activities at their desks or tables: formal repeated reading, radio reading, corrective repeated reading, oral recitation lessons, fluency development lessons, and phrased text lessons.

What's Next?

In this chapter, I have tried to make the case that what is done away from the teacher needs to rival the value of the instruction received during guided reading. Not only does the teacher need to be able to operate without interruptions to effectively target instruction for the learners at the table, but the students need to be able to independently use their time away from the teacher to gain greater growth. As guided reading moves toward the future, the clear challenge for teachers is to create independent learning opportunities that are goal oriented and growth focused for students. To simply provide a menu of options students can do when they are not working with the teacher may keep many busy and lead to improvements, but in the end we must be more intentional. We must be able to demonstrate that those activities are also leading students toward becoming proficient readers and writers. Doing the activity and staying busy cannot be an end in and of itself. We need independent work that leaves the learner satisfied, wanting more, and motivated to try again so that growth continues and proficiency is achieved.

CHAPTER SEVEN:
How Is Guided Reading Positioned for Intervention?

> Most learning problems exist not within the child, but in the inadequacy of the system to find a way to teach him.
>
> *Fountas and Pinnell, 2009*

There is one way the educational landscape has changed significantly since the re-emergence of small group reading instruction as guided reading in 1996. A new role for guided reading has emerged—its use as an intervention. Contributing to this change was the reauthorization of the Individuals with Disabilities Education Act (IDEA) in 2004. Within this reauthorization of federal law and subsequent state policies that followed was the opportunity for states to redefine how they determined students with Specific Learning Disabilities (SLD). The identification of students with SLD has always been problematic since, unlike other disabilities (e.g., visual or auditory impairments), clearly determining the presence of SLD and distinguishing them from other learning issues that a student might have has always been difficult and debatable. Seen as less than a black and white line of distinction and more as a gray area, IDEA looked at alternative ways to address issues with identification of students with SLDs.

Historically, IDEA supported an IQ-achievement discrepancy model as the primary means to determine a student with SLD. Theorizing that a student whose academic performance was below his or her academic potential would be evidence of a learning disability, and most state policies defined formulas for determining how much of a discrepancy would indicate a learning disability. While variations existed from state to state, many times a two-year gap was identified as evidence. Many experts, however, found fault with the discrepancy model because it often meant that a student had to wait to fail before receiving needed help. It was especially difficult to capture students in need in the early grades because a two-year gap was hard to document for young students. For older learners, the two-year gap often was more reflective of the assessment tools chosen to measure performance and potential. Different measures may have led to different results. In either case, the model placed all the focus on student factors and rarely looked at the instruction the student was receiving. It documented a discrepancy but revealed little about why the gap existed. It seemed clear that the IQ-achievement discrepancy model needed to be re-examined (Messmer & Messmer, 2008).

While IDEA did not do away with the IQ-achievement discrepancy model, it provided states with another option for determining whether a student had SLD. Policies no longer could require the use of a significant discrepancy and must permit the use of a process founded on a child's response to scientifically based interventions as part of a determination of SLD. That meant that for the first time, schools could consider the student's response to instruction as a factor (along with the IQ-achievement discrepancy) or the exclusive factor (dropping the IQ-achievement discrepancy altogether) in determining if he or she had SLD. Now the student could be assessed using benchmarks reflecting where most students are to determine whether the student was where he or she should be. Then the student could be assessed in terms of growth over time to determine if he or she was making enough progress to close the gap. The case could be made that a student who was below grade level and unable to make the progress needed to close the gap when provided effective instruction may have SLD. In a relatively short time, response to instruction options became codified in Response to Intervention (RtI) frameworks as districts tried to operationalize the identification tools, rules, and processes for schools and classrooms. While often linked directly to students with SLD, RtI was envisioned as a broad framework for thinking about helping all children with needs. What is often forgotten is that RtI is a *regular* education initiative. Many professional organizations pointed to RtI as a means to needed change in both general and special education. One of the most significant paradigm shifts was the view that regular and special education staff need to work closely together. The implementation of general education interventions must be completed prior to special education identification. If a student is later identified as having SLD, special educators and general educators will have a substantial amount of data and information on which to base instructional decisions and continue to support the student.

RtI is a multilevel system of support to improve outcomes for ALL students. Mellard and Johnson (2008) pointed out that all students should be considered RtI students, and differentiated instruction focuses on the intensity of the services that a student might receive beyond initial instruction. Schools that have implemented an RtI system should find data collection, intervention implementation, progress monitoring, and data analysis much easier and smoother. Schools using an RtI system will more quickly and systematically identify students who are not making adequate progress before achievement is so low a special education referral is made. RtI had a promise of being both a way to reduce the number of students with learning problems while also more accurately identifying students with SLD (Wixson & Lipson, 2012).

So how does this happen in schools and classrooms? It should be noted that from the beginning, it was never the intent that there should be just one model of RtI. The federal law is written in such a way that states and districts should be allowed flexibility in developing systems that meet

> One of the most significant paradigm shifts was the view that regular and special education staff need to work closely together.

their local needs (The Joint Task Force on Assessment of IRA and NCTE, 2010). Bender and Shores (2007) told educators that RtI was a process of implementing quality, research-based practices based on students' needs, monitoring the progress of students, and adjusting instruction based on students' responses. That definition describes an outcome but allows many pathways for achieving the outcome. Sometimes multiple possibilities become narrowed when defined by experts in the field who are first to provide some practical ways of meeting new challenges. In this case, the standard protocol model emerged early and grew quickly in popularity. The standard protocol model suggests that all students receive the same district-selected intervention(s) as they progress through tiers. These early models gave birth to the three tiers visually represented in pyramid structures that, for some, have become the exclusive way to think about RtI frameworks. It should be noted, however, that alternatives to the standard protocol models have always been possible. Problem-solving models are one such alternative and can be seen in models like those used by the Wisconsin Department of Public Instruction (DPI, 2010). (See Figure 7A on page 177.) As stated in their guiding document:

> "[T]he three essential elements of high-quality instruction, balanced assessment, and collaboration systematically interact within **a multi-level system of support** to provide the structures to increase success for *all* students. **Culturally responsive practices** are central to an effective RtI system and are evident within each of the three essential elements. In a multi-level system of support, schools employ the three essential elements of RtI at varying levels of intensity based upon student responsiveness to instruction and intervention. These elements do not work in isolation. Rather, all components of the visual model inform and are impacted by the others" (p. 4).

So how would a problem-solving model work? Problem-solving teams would come together to discuss a student's needs and then agree on an intervention appropriate for those needs. Four critical steps would be followed:

1. Define the problem.

2. Plan the intervention.

3. Implement the intervention.

4. Evaluate student progress.

Grimes and Kurn (2003) present a visual model that is represented in Figure 7B on page 177. Bender and Shores (2007) recommend that the problem-solving cycle is essentially repeated for each intervention. This makes the problem-solving model of RtI highly responsive to the needs of students. Once adequate time has been given for the intervention to work, the team will meet to discuss relevant data. Based on that examination of the data, the team decides whether to continue the strategy, shift to a new strategy, move to a more intensive intervention, and/or remove supports and monitor the student as he or she goes back to the general curriculum. Of course, this assumes that the intervention was effectively implemented and that may need to be the first question asked by the team.

In spite of these other visions, tiered models dominate most discussions of RtI, and the models have become somewhat standardized. Tier One usually represents universal options designed to enhance success and reduce barriers for the majority of students. Tier Two represents selected options that provide supplemental support for small groups of students who have not reached proficiency levels. Tier Three includes targeted options that provide more intensive instruction as needed by students with needs that cannot be addressed fully by Tier Two interventions. While the tiers often get most of the attention in these discussions, it is the overall intent of RtI that is most important: "[W]hether or not a school chooses to conceptualize RtI in the three-tier model, what's most important is that struggling students are offered targeted, expert, and intensive reading instruction before they are labeled as students with disabilities" (Allington & Walmsley, 2007, p. ix).

The Role of Guided Reading within RtI Frameworks

So what is the role of guided reading within these frameworks? What role does guided reading play in interventions? If RtI is a regular education initiative, then it must initially focus on providing ALL students with a quality, equitable opportunity to learn. That opportunity means, as was presented in Chapter Three, the student has had access to high-quality components within a comprehensive literacy program, including read-alouds, shared reading, independent reading, and guided reading. Before guided reading can be conceptualized as an intervention, it should be included first as an effective instructional opportunity provided to all students. Sometimes the tiers are thought of in terms of Tier One being whole group, Tier Two being small groups, and Tier Three being individualized approaches. In this mischaracterization, "regular" guided reading is positioned as a small group intervention, but that needs to be rethought. Tier One is better characterized as universal instruction provided to all, Tier Two is selected for some, and Tier Three is targeted for a few. Universal instruction implies that it is provided to all students. As discussed in this book, a comprehensive literacy program would mean that, within regular classroom instruction, all students would have already received effective large group, small group (i.e., guided reading), and individualized instruction. In their study of guided reading as an intervention, Denton and colleagues (2014) were in classrooms in which only 66 percent of the teachers implemented guided reading. Again, before we look at guided reading as an intervention, it is more critical to make sure effective guided reading had been implemented for all students during universal instruction.

IDEA specifies that data used as part of the referral process must indicate that the child was provided appropriate instruction in regular education

> Before guided reading can be conceptualized as an intervention, it should be included first as an effective instructional opportunity provided to all students.

settings, and delivered by qualified personnel. The lack of appropriate instruction needs to be eliminated as a contributing factor before final SLD determinations can be made. This suggests that the best place for a teacher, grade level, or school to begin to address the needs of all learners is to look at universal instruction. Before we start to identify, label, and sort learners for layers of interventions, educators need to be able to guarantee that all students have received access to the best forms of universal instruction—large groups, small groups, and individually. Dorn and Soffos (2011) strongly recommend that interventions should always be supported by high-quality, regular classroom instruction. Unlike models in the past, where a classroom teacher could pass on the responsibility for a struggling learner to another program, RtI requires that the quality of classroom instruction is always examined when the needs of a specific child are discussed. Before looking at how a student responded to instruction, we must look at whether the student had an opportunity to learn.

Research suggests there is plenty to look at when we examine opportunities to learn. Instruction across classrooms differs in quantity and in quality, even in standardized programs, and the difference is almost always due to the teacher (Ford & Opitz, 2010). Darling-Hammond and McLaughlin (1999) also pointed out that teacher expertise is the most important factor in improving children's learning. Scanlon (2011) actually demonstrated with her research that kindergarten and first-grade teachers who received professional development on comprehensive and responsive literacy programs actually reduced the number of children who experienced learning difficulties by about 50 percent. Teachers matter, their instruction matters, and their level of expertise probably matters the most. As Johnston (2011) concluded: "The bottom line in RtI is improved instruction, which requires increasingly expert teachers with instructionally useful data on each child and on their own teaching in circumstances in which they can make optimal use of it" (p. 528).

One problem with the earliest tiered models for RtI was they were often presented with an assumption that Tier One instruction (universal instruction) should be able to reach 80–85 percent of the students with whom teachers were working. I am not sure why this became so acceptable. Where else would it be acceptable to fail to reach one out of every five clients in need of our services? If universal instruction is reaching many of the readers in front of us with most of what they need, the first question should not be "What do we do with the students we are not reaching?" The first question we should ask is "How do we move from universal instruction that reaches many to most to universal instruction that reaches all readers with everything they need?" (Ford & Opitz, 2010). Bomer (1998) pointed out that when instruction is failing to reach all those receiving it, maybe it is time to tighten up and intensify what we are doing. Could we shine more light and heat on our own practices before starting the process of sorting and labeling students? Let's make sure the instruction children are responding to is as good as it can be before assuming the problem must be rooted in the child. In the classic study, *Unfulfilled Expectations*, Snow and her colleagues (1991) reminded

The first question we should ask is "How do we move from universal instruction that reaches many to most to universal instruction that reaches all readers with everything they need?"

us that, even when students come from low-support home environments, their success rates in high-support classrooms often rival classmates from high-support homes. However, one must realize that it is hard not only for those students to maintain those success rates in low-support classroom environments, but for students from high-support homes to maintain those success rates.

Before sorting and labeling the students, educators should consider whether the learning problem is student-centered, teacher-centered, or a combination. It's interesting that when Cambourne (2001) asked the question of why some students fail to learn to read, he identified five key factors:

- The student received faulty demonstrations of how to read and write.

- The student received quality demonstrations but did not engage with them.

- The student has low expectations of him-/herself as a reader and writer.

- The student receives faulty feedback to grow stronger.

- The student will not or cannot take responsibility for his or her learning.

When looking at these issues, most are clearly teacher centered. (Who provides the demonstrations? Who provides the feedback? Who sets the expectations? Who sets up the conditions for engagement? Who releases the responsibility?) Yes, eventually the student has to engage and take responsibility, but student success is often dependent on our instruction. What has been discussed in this book, I hope, will help us take a look at that instruction as it applies to guided reading specifically and as we position guided reading within a broader program.

Beyond Universal Instruction

So what is the role for guided reading beyond Tier One universal instruction? Can it be used as an intervention for subsequent levels? Allington (2008) identified the research-based characteristics of interventions that accelerate reading growth:

- Very small groups or tutoring

- Majority of time spent reading

- Match between reader and text level

- Use of texts that are interesting to students

- Coordination with core classrooms

- Expert teacher delivers intervention

- Daily reading activity is expanded

- Focus on meaning and metacognition

The models of guided reading presented in this book align with those characteristics. The plans used to structure guided reading sessions presented in Chapter Five address most of what Allington identified as critical characteristics in interventions. Fountas and Pinnell (2009) remind us that interventions are typically intensive, short term, supplementary, low teacher-student ratio, and taught by an expert teacher who is in communication with the classroom teacher. Again, many of those characteristics are at the heart of guided reading sessions, though the last characteristic seems to suggest that the intervention would be handled by an expert outside of the classroom. So what would have to change to position guided reading as an intervention?

It might be helpful to think about RtI as a continuum of support in literacy learning. This is actually how one school district [my local school district—the Oshkosh Area School District (OASD)] structured its RtI framework. The first level of support is "universal instruction for all students." All classroom teachers are expected to provide students with the differentiated classroom instruction the students need and, of course, effective guided reading plays a role in that first level of support. The second layer of support is labeled "additional effective classroom-based strategies recommended for some students." This layer is also the responsibility of the classroom teacher. The classroom teacher would provide these interventions within the classroom. These interventions might be better characterized as adjustments. Before implementing whole-scale change or adding a layer of new interventions, aspects of the typical guided reading session could be adjusted. For example, a teacher could adjust the frequency, duration, membership, focus, student monitoring, and/or instructional monitoring of the guided reading session.

Guided reading may have greater impact if the frequency of meetings is increased. Some students may need to participate in sessions more often than would be normally offered as a part of universal instruction. Similarly, the duration of the guided reading sessions could be adjusted to provide students with greater needs more time (and instruction) with the teacher. The typical 20-minute session might be extended. Guided reading may also have greater impact by changing who is at the table. Shift the group membership by narrowing the number of students taught. This provides more targeted instruction with greater potential for engagement and less distraction than is possible in regular guided reading groups.

Another adjustment could be to the focus of the session related to the content taught and time allocation for specific content within the lesson. This would allow for instruction that might differ from the lessons typically taught in guided reading groups. For example, there may be more time and attention to word-level work for some learners with greater needs in this area. Monitoring techniques could also be adjusted so that guided reading sessions include more and/or different formative assessments that more closely monitor the progress (or lack of it). Finally, one more way to adjust guided reading is looking closely at the instruction being offered. Teaching itself could be monitored more closely either through self-reflection, including taping the sessions, or with the help of outside

Before implementing whole-scale change or adding a layer of new interventions, aspects of the typical guided reading session could be adjusted.

supervision. Teachers should always look at the instruction first to see if how they are teaching is all that it needs to be in reaching the students. Figure 7C captures key questions a teacher can ask in considering how to adjust typical guided reading sessions in universal instruction to better meet the needs of students who might not be making adequate progress.

Figure 7C: Initial Adjustments for Guided Reading for Students with Greater Needs

Adjustments	Considerations
Frequency of guided reading sessions	How often do I meet with the student during guided reading?
	Would it help to increase the number of times I meet with the student during guided reading?
	If so, how much should I increase the number of times I meet with the student during guided reading?
	Can I increase the number of times I meet with the student during guided reading by increasing the number of times I meet with the group in my regular class rotation?
	If I need additional time to meet more often with the student during guided reading, are there additional times during the day I can meet with the student?
	If I need additional time to meet more often with the student during guided reading, are there additional times outside of the regular class schedule to meet with the student?
	Do I have access to another expert teacher who can meet with the student during additional guided reading sessions?
Duration of guided reading sessions	How long do I meet with the student during guided reading?
	Would it help to increase the amount of time I meet with the student during guided reading?
	If so, how much time should I allot to meet with the student during guided reading?

continued on next page

Figure 7C: Initial Adjustments for Guided Reading for Students with Greater Needs *continued*

Adjustments	Considerations
Duration of guided reading sessions *continued*	Can I increase the amount of time by increasing the number of minutes I meet with the guided reading group in my regular class rotation?
	If I want to increase the amount of time I meet with the student during guided reading, are there additional times during the day when I can teach a longer guided reading session for the student?
	If I want to increase the amount of time I meet with the student during guided reading, are there additional times outside the regular class schedule when I can teach a longer guided reading session for the student?
	Do I have access to another expert teacher who can hold longer guided reading sessions with the student?
Membership of guided reading sessions	Who is the student currently working with during the guided reading session?
	Would it help the student to change the number of other students in the guided reading group?
	Would it help the student to change any of the other students who are in the guided reading group?
	What number of students might be best to help the student stay engaged with targeted instruction during the guided reading session?
	Are there other students who might help the student stay engaged with targeted instruction during the guided reading session?
	Should I intentionally add some students who would be good role models for the student during the guided reading session?

continued on next page

Figure 7C: Initial Adjustments for Guided Reading for Students with Greater Needs *continued*

Adjustments	Considerations
Focus of guided reading sessions	What is the student currently working on during the guided reading session?
	Would it help the student to change the instructional focus of the guided reading session?
	If so, what should the instructional focus of the guided reading session be if it is more targeted to the needs of the student?
	Is the time allocated for different parts of the guided reading instruction appropriate for the needs of the student?
	If not, how could the time allocation within the guided reading lesson be adjusted to better meet the needs of the student?
Monitoring of learners during guided reading sessions	What is used to monitor the progress of the student during the guided reading session?
	Are the tools an effective means to capture what I need to know to inform my instruction as I help the student during guided reading?
	If so, would adjusting the frequency of administering those tools provide me with more valuable information to inform my thinking?
	If not, would adjusting the tools I am using provide me with more effective ways to monitor the progress of the student during guided reading?
	Would consulting with an expert assist my interpretation of data collected so I could more effectively plan targeted instruction for the student during guided reading?

continued on next page

Figure 7C: Initial Adjustments for Guided Reading for Students with Greater Needs *continued*

Adjustments	Considerations
Monitoring of instruction during guided reading sessions	Am I satisfied with the instruction I am providing the student during guided reading? If not, would recording my guided reading sessions and reflecting on them help me to strengthen my guided reading sessions for the student? If not, would working with an outside expert who could observe my teaching during guided reading be an additional way to improve my instruction for the student?

The next layer of support in the OASD continuum is adding what they describe as "structured low-intensity interventions for *some* students." At this level, it should be remembered that adding any new intervention assumes that the student continues to receive guided reading as a part of high-quality universal instruction in the regular classroom. Decisions about adjustments for guided reading related to frequency, duration, membership, focus, and monitoring would also continue to be considered and addressed. In addition to those efforts, however, a low-level intervention would include consideration of the need for small group support in addition to what is offered by the classroom teacher. This is made available to students who are not meeting identified benchmarks. In this district, some schools have access to Title I reading services and others have in-district interventionists. In either case, a collaborative decision would be made to intentionally add additional small group work outside the classroom to support the student in accelerating his or her progress toward proficiency levels. Many times, this instruction reinforces what is done in the classroom, providing the student with greater frequency and duration of guided reading sessions, but often the guided reading sessions shift focus and provide an instructional approach that differs from traditional guided reading instruction.

There are many interventions schools can consider. Some of those interventions take topics receiving contemporary attention and situate them as interventions. In an after-school program for older learners, Fisher and Frey (2014) described how close reading was used as a successful intervention. Others have a very specific focus, such as a fluency intervention proposed by Rasinski (2003) from his book, *The Fluent Reader*. This involves lessons that employ short reading passages (poems, story segments, or other texts) that students read and reread over a short period of time. (See Figure 7D for the steps.)

Figure 7D: Rasinski's Fluency Intervention

1.	Students read a familiar passage from the previous lesson to the teacher or a fellow student for accuracy and fluency.
2.	The teacher introduces a new short text and reads it to the students two or three times while the students follow along. Text can be a poem, segment from a basal passage or literature book, etc.
3.	The teacher and students discuss the nature and content of the passage.
4.	The teacher and students read the passage chorally several times. Antiphonal reading (alternating responses between two groups of readers) and other variations are used to create variety and maintain engagement.
5.	The teacher organizes student pairs. Each student practices the passage three times while his or her partner listens and provides support and encouragement.
6.	Individuals and groups of students perform their reading for the class or other audience.
7.	The students and their teacher choose three or four words from the text to add to the word bank and/or word wall.
8.	Students engage in word study activities (e.g., word sorts with word bank words, word walls, flash card practice, defining words, word games, etc.).
9.	Students take a copy of the passage home to practice with parents and other family members.
10.	The process begins again the next school day, with the students reading the passage to the teacher or a partner who checks for fluency and accuracy.

OASD focuses on the use of an intervention model from Dorn and Soffos (2011) called Guided Reading Plus. Guided Reading Plus presents a two-day plan for targeted instruction for students with needs greater than can be addressed in typical classroom implementations of guided reading. Dorn and Soffos identify the following characteristics of Guided Reading Plus:

- Is for readers at the emergent-to-transitional levels who are lagging behind peers;

- Has the goal of acquisition of flexible strategies for solving problems in reading and writing;

- Maintains a strong focus on comprehension;

- Uses writing to enhance reading achievement by slowing down the process and increasing attention to alphabetic and phonological knowledge as the student uses motor skills to write the letters, words, and sentences; and

- Adds word study to the traditional guided reading lesson.

On day one, the lesson is structured with components that first address word work (i.e., quick activities to address needs related to sound analysis and sight vocabulary). Then time is spent to orient the students to a new text at their level. Students read the text independently under the watchful eye of the teacher at the table. Once the independent reading is underway, the teacher starts dropping in on each student with a quick conference. Day one (phase one) of the lesson ends with a follow-up discussion to the reading.

Writing can drive reading instruction, especially with young learners and learners who struggle.

When the students come back on day two (phase two) of the Guided Reading Plus lesson, the teacher begins by assessing students individually with a running record. Others are revisiting the text by reading it independently. Then the lesson moves to a writing about reading phase. For Dorn and Soffos, the "plus" in Guided Reading Plus is the addition of writing as a tool to learn even more about how texts work and how meaning is made. Dorn once remarked that, for her, the blank sheet of paper put in front of the child and the draft writing that ends up on that paper is probably the best reflection of what is going on in the head of the child. It is like a mirror reflecting what the student knows about text. After recently teaching first grade, I would agree. Writing can drive reading instruction, especially with young learners and learners who struggle. When looking at a blank sheet of paper, the student has very few supports he or she can draw upon. It's a purer reflection of what is known. When a student picks up a book, a teacher can't always know what might be supporting the performance during oral reading. Has the student seen or heard the book before? Is he or she relying on the illustrations for most of the meaning making? So the addition of writing shifts the instructional focus of the guided reading lesson. (You see this in other assisted writing interventions recommended by Dorn and Soffos, like interactive writing and writing aloud. For more complete information on interventions by Dorn and Soffos, consult their text *Interventions That Work*.) The subsequent reading and writing that follows provide an instructional experience different from the classroom guided reading lesson. Dorn and Soffos (2011) provide a framework for designing these lessons. Others like Fountas and Pinnell have provided instructional materials in intervention programs, such as Leveled Literacy Intervention (LLI), as a way to structure small group instruction outside of the regular classroom. A complete description of LLI can be found online.

The OASD continuum has two additional layers of support to consider before referring a student for special education placement. Level Four is identified as "structured moderate-intensity interventions for a few students." These interventions are provided outside of the classroom for students who are not meeting benchmarks. One such example for young learners is Reading Recovery. Level Five is identified as "targeted high-intensity intervention for very few students." These are often approved skills-focused interventions and progress-monitoring assessments, and they are required to be in compliance with state rule in identifying students with SLD. One example might be implementation of a research-tested, intensive, code-based program to improve phonics skills and strategies. The American Research Institute maintains a website that identifies and examines programs and approaches positioned as intensive interventions. Educators can see comprehensive descriptions of such programs and the research conducted on the programs.

In talking with the reading coordinator of the OASD, she explained that they will not move into that final level of support prior to a referral for special education until the other layers have been implemented. There are cases in which the linear nature of the continuum is adjusted. Sometimes educators know they need to provide more intensive support earlier. They don't wait until the student has passed through all levels of support first. For example, there was a situation in which a child came to a new district and entered third grade with limited alphabetic knowledge. The school immediately provided the student with a more intensive level of support.

Most proposed interventions offered to small groups of students focus on reading and are teacher-guided but may not follow more traditional guided reading formats. These interventions often offer additional support for learners who are not making adequate progress after accessing high-quality classroom instruction. While they are not traditional in their formats, many contain what was previously defined in Chapter One as the essential elements of guided reading and clearly satisfy the definition of instruction as "planned, intentional, focused instruction where the teacher helps students, usually in small group settings, learn more about the reading process" (Ford & Opitz, 2011). Most of these interventions match Fountas and Pinnell's (1996) description of guided reading: "an instructional context for supporting each reader's development of effective strategies for processing novel texts at increasingly challenging levels of difficulty" (p. 25). These approaches may be alternative ways to "guide" the reading of small groups of students in need. The interventions are identified on a menu of options the OASD (2013) makes available to teachers in their continuum of sup-port. (See Figure 7E on page 176.) Of course, any menu of potential interventions could be quite extensive. For this district, an effort was made to identify those interventions that were aligned with district beliefs and values about literacy programs. Those listed were also compatible with the other aspects of the district's comprehensive literacy program. Interestingly, all involve the use of small groups of students, with expert teachers providing guidance on critical aspects of reading and writing.

Figure 7E: Oshkosh Area School District Menu of Interventions

Intervention	Description
Assisted writing: interactive writing for K–2 and writing aloud for 3–5 (Dorn & Soffos, 2011)	Interventions that intensify the use of writing and its links to reading to learn more about how print works. Interactive writing is for children at emergent and early stages of development. Writing aloud is for older students who use the writing process to learn more about strategies for reading and writing.
Comprehension focus groups (Dorn & Soffos, 2011)	An intervention for children who are reading at the transitional level and beyond but are having difficulty meeting the demands for comprehending different text genres. The interventions help students develop knowledge for three major texts: literary, informational, and persuasive. In focus groups, the students participate in a unit around a specific text type or genre for a minimum of three weeks and participate in the writing process by developing an original piece of writing within the genre of the focus unit.
Writing process interventions (Dorn & Soffos, 2011)	Designed for children who are struggling with the writing process in their writing workshop classrooms. The intervention specialist provides tailored instruction that focuses on the writing process, including drafting, revising, crafting, editing, and publishing processes. In this case, the focus on writing is primarily to help students who were not making adequate progress in their writing.
Guided Reading Plus (Dorn & Soffos, 2011)	An intervention for readers not reading at level, providing additional exposure to explicit reading instruction using a planned and purposeful lesson, with a daily strategy focus selected from the previous day's running record. Attention is given to self-monitoring, self-correcting strategies, fluency, comprehension strategies, word solving, and vocabulary. Students respond to reading in written form and connect what they can do in reading to what they can do in writing.
Oral language literacy groups	Small group interventions designed for those children who need explicit instruction in storytelling and how books work. It focuses on K–1 students using talking about books, sharing stories across genres, and shared and interactive writing to strengthen understandings about concepts of print and how reading sounds (pace, expressions, and phrasing).
Emergent language and literacy groups (Dorn & Soffos, 2007)	An intervention that focuses on emergent literacy foundations and oral language to strengthen concepts of print, phonemic awareness, and language development using a variety of materials monitored through writing samples and running records as possible, with growth noted through entrance and exit performances on the observational survey, dictated story, and record of oral language.
Interactive Strategies Approach (Scanlon, Anderson, and Sweeney, 2010)	A research-supported framework for early literacy instruction that aligns with multi-tiered response-to-intervention (RtI) models. It is designed around essential instructional goals, related both to learning to identify words and to comprehending text targeting these goals with K–2 students at risk for reading difficulties.

Figure 7A: Wisconsin Department of Public Instruction Response to Intervention Problem-solving Model

Figure 7B: Problem-solving Model (Grimes & Kurn, 2003)

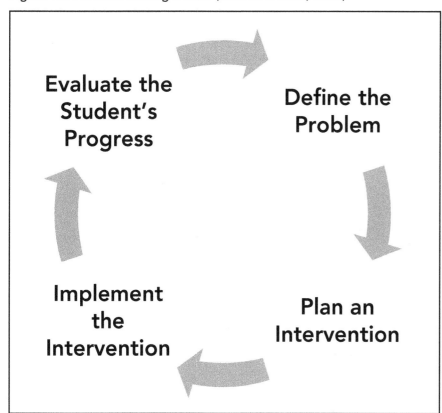

Final Thoughts about Guided Reading and Interventions

> *We must be willing to take a look at guided reading when it is not working as well as it could for some learners and reflect on whether adjustments related to frequency, duration, focus, membership, or monitoring could improve the practice.*

The reauthorization of IDEA has changed the landscape of today's classrooms. But enough time has passed that we can try to answer the question that Peter Johnston posed during a conversation: "Will Response to Intervention be a welcomed and productive change or a road map to disaster?" If we have moved forward by trying to achieve the intent of RtI to improve education for all students, it will be easy to see it as a welcomed and productive change. That would start with tightening up Tier One instruction, and effective guided reading instruction would play a featured role in high-quality universal instruction. We must be willing to take a look at guided reading when it is not working as well as it could for some learners and reflect on whether adjustments related to frequency, duration, focus, membership, or monitoring could improve the practice. We must be ready to add forms of guided reading instruction that offer an additional, more intensive type of instruction to reach even more learners in need. In the end, our willingness to move in these directions will help us resist and reduce the need to label and sort students. It presents all of us with a huge challenge.

> "When working with students who are challenging for us to accelerate and grow, we might say with great sincerity, 'I have tried everything!' That, however, should lead to another step. We need to challenge ourselves by asking, 'Is everything I have tried everything I know (which might not be extensive) or everything research suggests (which is deeper and broader)?' In other words, making sure the child isn't instructionally disabled is a necessary part of the RtI process" (p. 1)
>
> *Ford, Champeau & Andrews, 2013*

Appendix

1 CHAPTER ONE: 180

1A Guided Reading Practices Survey 180

4 CHAPTER FOUR: 185

4A Closing the Word Count Gap 185

4B Description of Guided Reading Texts 186

4C Interest Inventory 193

5 CHAPTER FIVE: 195

5A Guided Reading Session During a Science Unit . . 195

5B Sample Six-box Grid 196

5C Self-evaluation 197

6 CHAPTER SIX: 198

6A Supporting Transitions 198

CHAPTER ONE: 1A
Guided Reading Practices Survey
(Adapted from Ford & Opitz, 2008)

Consider your use of guided reading within your reading/language arts classroom instructional program. Then respond to each question based on your guided reading practices. Examine your responses closely to establish a baseline, and determine areas in need of further attention. Focus on those areas and revisit the survey after implementing changes to capture your changes. (Consider discussing your initial results with other colleagues to collectively move forward school practices related to guided reading.)

1. How much time do you typically have each day for reading/language arts instruction?

    _____ Less than 30 minutes

    _____ 30 minutes to 59 minutes

    _____ 1 hour to less than 1 ½ hours

    _____ 1 ½ hours to less than 2 hours

    _____ 2 hours or longer

2. What percentage of the instructional time you spend on your reading program is devoted to guided reading?

    _____ Do not devote any time to guided reading (skip to question 19)

    _____ 1% to 9%

    _____ 10% to 24%

    _____ 25% to 49%

    _____ 50% to 99%

    _____ Guided reading is the only element in your reading program

3. How many days a week does the instructional time for your reading program include guided reading?

    _____ Once a week

    _____ Twice a week

    _____ Three times a week

    _____ Four times a week

    _____ Daily

4. Which of the following best describes the purpose for your guided reading instruction?
    (Place a #1 next to the main purpose and then check other purposes you include.)

    _____ To provide demonstrations of skills, strategies, response, and/or procedures to students

    _____ To provide interventions around scaffolded instruction for students

    _____ To facilitate a group response between students around a shared text

    _____ To facilitate a group response between students around multiple texts

5. How often is guided reading connected to read-alouds, shared reading, independent reading/writing instruction, or content areas in your instruction?

    _____ Always

    _____ Usually

    _____ Sometimes

    _____ Seldom

    _____ Never

continued on next page

6. How many guided reading groups do you typically maintain in your reading program?

_____ None   _____ 2   _____ 4

_____ 1   _____ 3   _____ 5 or more

7. How many days per week do you typically meet with each group?

_____ Less than 1 day   _____ 2 days   _____ 4 days

_____ 1 day   _____ 3 days   _____ 5 days

8. How long do you typically meet with each guided reading group?

_____ Less than 10 minutes   _____ 15–19 minutes   _____ 25–29 minutes

_____ 10–14 minutes   _____ 20–24 minutes   _____ 30 minutes or longer

9. How many students, on average, are in your guided reading groups?

_____ 1 or 2   _____ 4   _____ 6

_____ 3   _____ 5   _____ 7 or more

10. How are your students placed in guided reading groups? (Check all that apply.)

_____ Homogeneous by developmental level   _____ Heterogeneous

_____ Homogeneous by need   _____ Homogeneous by other method (specify) _____

11. Which of the following diagnostic or assessment tools do you use to place your students in guided reading groups? (Check all that apply.)

_____ Records from the previous year   _____ Daily observation

_____ Running record or individual reading inventory   _____ Other (specify) _____

_____ Scores from reading program assessments

12. How often do you normally change the students in your guided reading groups?

_____ Never/annually   _____ 1 to 3 times per week

_____ Less than once monthly   _____ 4 or more times per week

_____ 1 to 3 times per month

continued on next page

13. Approximately what percentage of time do each of the following occur during your guided reading sessions? (Give an answer for each.)

All students read the same book _____ %   Other (specify) _____ %

Most students read the same book _____ %   Total should equal   100 %

All students read different books _____ %

14. What percentage of the books chosen for use during guided reading are narrative stories only (as opposed to informational texts)?

_____ None, use informational texts only   _____ 50% to 99%

_____ 1% to 24%   _____ 100%, use narrative stories only

_____ 25% to 49%

15. What percentage of the books used during guided reading are chosen by the students?

_____ None   _____ 25% to 49%   _____ 75% to 99%

_____ 1% to 24%   _____ 50% to 74%   _____ 100%

16. Which best describes the levels of the books chosen during guided reading? (Check only ONE.)

_____ All students read books at the instructional level.   _____ Students do not always read books at the instructional level.

17. How often do you use each of the following materials during guided reading? (Give an answer for each type.)

Basal textbooks

_____ Always   _____ Usually   _____ Sometimes   _____ Seldom   _____ Never

Supplemental basal materials

_____ Always   _____ Usually   _____ Sometimes   _____ Seldom   _____ Never

Trade books

_____ Always   _____ Usually   _____ Sometimes   _____ Seldom   _____ Never

"Little" books

_____ Always   _____ Usually   _____ Sometimes   _____ Seldom   _____ Never

Newspapers

_____ Always   _____ Usually   _____ Sometimes   _____ Seldom   _____ Never

Magazines

_____ Always   _____ Usually   _____ Sometimes   _____ Seldom   _____ Never

Poems

_____ Always   _____ Usually   _____ Sometimes   _____ Seldom   _____ Never

Other (specify) _____   *continued on next page*

18. While you are working with a guided reading group, what are the other students usually doing? (Check no more than the three most frequent activities.)

_____ Working at centers/learning stations   _____ Working in reader's/writer's workshop

_____ Working on independent seatwork   _____ Working on class routines

_____ Working with another adult in a separate guided reading group   _____ Other (specify)

_____ Working on inquiry projects   _____

If you checked "working at centers/learning stations," what are the activities students usually do at centers/learning stations while you are working with a guided reading group? (Check no more than the five most frequent activities.)

_____ Listening post (audio books)   _____ Discussion groups

_____ Performance (reader's theater, puppets, plays)   _____ Science center

_____ Reading and/or writing the room   _____ Social studies center

_____ Pocket chart activities   _____ Math center

_____ Working with word materials   _____ Computer/electronic devices

_____ Art projects   _____ Whiteboard activities

_____ Writing projects/book publishing   _____ Big book stand

_____ Buddy reading   _____ Other (specify)

    _____

19. How many days per week, on average, do you teach explicit skill instruction?

_____ Less than 1 day   _____ 2 days   _____ 4 days

_____ 1 day   _____ 3 days   _____ 5 days

20. How much time do you spend each day on explicit skill instruction?

_____ Less than 10 minutes   _____ 15 to 19 minutes   _____ 25 to 29 minutes

_____ 10 to 14 minutes   _____ 20 to 24 minutes   _____ 30 minutes

21. Which of the following skills do you teach in your explicit instruction? (Check all that apply.)

_____ Phonological and phonemic awareness   _____ Comprehension

_____ Phonics   _____ Spelling

_____ Other word identification strategies   _____ Grammar/mechanics

_____ Fluency   _____ Composition

_____ Vocabulary   _____ Other (specify)

    _____

continued on next page

22. When does explicit skill instruction usually take place in relation to your guided reading group lesson? (Check all that apply.)

_____ Skills are taught before the guided reading lesson

_____ Skills are taught during the guided reading lesson

_____ Skills are taught after the guided reading lesson

_____ Other (specify)

_____

23. Do you utilize running records to assess your students' progress?

_____ Yes   _____ No

24. If "yes," how many times per month, on average, do you complete a running record for an individual student?

_____ Less than once per month

_____ 1

_____ 2

_____ 3

_____ 4

_____ 5 or more

25. Which of the following types of guided reading leveling systems do you follow? (Check all that apply.)

_____ Fountas and Pinnell

_____ Reading Recovery

_____ Lexiles

_____ Your reading textbook levels

_____ Other (specify)

_____

26. How many leveled books do you have access to each day?

_____ Fewer than 200

_____ 200–399

_____ 400–999

_____ 1,000–1,999

_____ 2,000 or more

27. With whom do you share leveled books? (Check all that apply.)

_____ The titles you use are for your classroom only

_____ Only one other teacher

_____ All the teachers at your grade level

_____ All the teachers in primary classrooms

_____ Entire school

_____ Other (specify)

_____

28. How would you rate your knowledge base of guided reading instruction?

_____ Very well informed

_____ Fairly well informed

_____ Not very well informed

_____ Not at all informed

Closing the Word Count Gap

	Group One	Group Two	Group Three
Word count in group text			
Number of times read			
Total			
Word count in related text #1			
Number of times read			
Total			
Word count in related text #2 (as needed)			
Number of times read			
Total			
Total amount of word practice			
Other practice opportunities to raise word count (as needed)			

Description of Guided Reading Texts

I have reviewed guided reading materials from three publishers. At the end of this section is a recommended book list by level. The book list includes the books offered by the publishers as well as others I recommend.

Publisher: Abrams Learning Trends
16310 Bratton Lane
Suite 250
Austin, TX 78728

Program: Key Links Literacy: Guided Readers

Abrams Learning Trends has 212 leveled readers in its Key Links Literacy program. The texts are identified by both DRA levels and Guided Reading Levels. The texts extend through DRA level 50 to address fluent readers through fifth grade. Word counts are identified for each text, allowing teachers to consider the amount of words in each text to gauge potential reading practice. A step-by-step lesson plan is presented at the beginning of each text. Lesson directions, or ThinkLinks Panels, are actually embedded inside on each page to guide instruction before, during, and after the reading. Each text includes pages to focus follow-up activities for partner talk, writing activities, and applications in independent reading. In nonfiction texts, photographs are used to present visual support. The program has both nonfiction and fiction texts at each level with a 50–50 balance in early phases that tilts toward nonfiction in the later phases. Nonfiction texts use a variety of formats, including description, explanations, reports, and persuasive arguments. Some include a table of contents and an index. Texts are supported by digital resources, including a platform for e-books. Teacher Tools support the program to provide additional instruction and assessment resources. The program also provides a scope and sequence of appropriate skills and strategies and an alignment with the Common Core State Standards. Links to other parts of the literacy program, including the read-aloud, shared readings, and independent reading are recommended. The program includes built-in assessment materials to support running records, including scoring guides.

Publisher: Capstone Classroom
1710 Roe Crest Drive
North Mankato, MN 56003

Program: Engage Literacy

Capstone Classroom currently has 186 leveled readers in its Engage Literacy program. The texts are identified by both Reading Recovery Levels and Guided Reading Levels. Text levels extend through Guided Reading Level N. Fiction and nonfiction texts are topically paired, allowing for a 50–50 balance. Fiction books contain recurring characters that are featured in stories at different guided reading levels, allowing readers to re-encounter familiar characters in more complex texts. Word counts are identified for each text, allowing teachers to know the quantity of text in making decisions related to reading practice and reading mileage. Specific recommendations for working with words, including sight-word vocabulary (newly introduced as well as those reintroduced) and words with specific sound-symbol patterns (for phonological awareness and phonics instruction), point out potential teaching principles for word strategies. Suggested inferential questions are included with each text for potential comprehension checks and discussion points. Some nonfiction texts have picture glossaries. Nonfiction texts are presented in a variety formats and are usually illustrated with photographs featuring school age children. Nonfiction texts on unfamiliar topics use visuals to clearly present samples and examples of items featured in the texts. Many nonfiction texts provide well-illustrated steps for projects that students can replicate. Others present a logical flow into actions children can take in the classroom, school, and/or community. Engage Literacy also provides a Comprehension Strategy Kit and Benchmark Assessment Kits to support instruction. Other teacher support materials are available, including digital e-books. The Teacher's Resource for this program provides suggested lessons and instructional support materials for each level text.

....

Publisher: MaryRuth Books, Inc.
             18660 Ravenna Road
             Building 2
             Chagrin Falls, OH 44023

Program: MaryRuth Books

Even small publishers have produced resources that can be used to support guided reading programs. MaryRuth Books include 128 titles that are identified by Reading Recovery Levels A–L. The word count for each book is included so that teachers can consider the amount of text in making decisions related to reading practice and reading mileage. The stories have been carefully written with the developing reader in mind. Both fiction and nonfiction titles are written with topics and situations familiar to young children. Most of the books are nonfiction texts with most containing photographs. Many of the fiction stories use photographs as their illustrations as well. Many are focused on wild and domestic animals. Within the program, linked titles exist. For example, one series of nonfiction texts focuses on zoo animals. The fiction titles feature a series called the Danny books focused on photographed dogs named Danny and Norman. The characters reappear in different texts at increasingly complex levels. Danny even maintains a blog readers can visit. Clear thought has been given to the layout of the text and language structure used in each text. The early leveled texts present text on one side and photographs on the other with a strong link between text and visuals. The text is presented with clear attention to introducing or reinforcing concepts of print. Even more difficult texts always present print that is clearly separated from the photographs. The early level books are written with strong predictable patterns. Supporting materials, including lesson plans, are available on the company website.

Level A

I Go Up by Jay Dale, Capstone Classroom, 2012, Fiction

In the Water by Anne Giulieri, Capstone Classroom, 2012, Fiction

Look at Me by Anne Giulieri, Capstone Classroom, 2012, Fiction

The Zookeeper by Jay Dale, Capstone Classroom, 2012, Nonfiction

Up Here by Jay Dale, Capstone Classroom, 2012, Fiction

Level B

Counting Frogs Around the Pond by Mia Coulton, MaryRuth Books, 2013, Nonfiction

Look at the Animals by Jay Dale, Capstone Classroom, 2012, Fiction

My Little Toys by Jay Dale, Capstone Classroom, 2012, Nonfiction

The Farm by Mia Coulton, MaryRuth Books, 2013, Nonfiction

Up and Down by Jay Dale, Capstone Classroom, 2012, Fiction

Level C

A Goat by Mia Coulton, MaryRuth Books, 2013, Nonfiction

Danny and the Big Race by Mia Coulton, MaryRuth Books, 2014, Fiction

I Can Go to School by Anne Giulieri, Capstone Classroom, 2013, Fiction

School by Jay Dale, Capstone Classroom, 2013, Nonfiction

The Woods by Mia Coulton, MaryRuth Books, 2013, Nonfiction

Level D

Ladybug Puppet by Jay Dale, Capstone Classroom, 2013, Nonfiction

Pigs by Mia Coulton, MaryRuth Books, 2012, Nonfiction

The Little Bug by Jay Dale, Capstone Classroom, 2013, Fiction

Tummy Trouble for Danny by Mia Coulton, MaryRuth Books, 2013, Nonfiction

Turtles Around the Pond by Mia Coulton, MaryRuth Books, 2013, Nonfiction

Level E

Bananas in My Tummy by Jay Dale, Capstone Classroom, 2012, Fiction

Big Balloon by Jay Dale, Capstone Classroom, 2012, Nonfiction

Pete the Cat: Play Ball! by James Dean, HarperCollins I Can Read, 2013, Fiction

The Aquarium by Anne Giulieri, Capstone Classroom, 2012, Nonfiction

Who's in the Chicken Coop? by Mia Coulton, MaryRuth Books, 2012, Fiction

Level F

Going Buggy! by Dona Herweck Rice, TIME for Kids, 2012, Nonfiction

Pete the Cat: Pete's Big Lunch! by James Dean, HarperCollins, 2013, Fiction

Sea Life by Dona Herweck Rice, TIME for Kids, 2012, Nonfiction

The Banana Spider by Anne Giulieri, Capstone Classroom, 2012, Nonfiction

The Best Banana in the Tree by Jay Dale, Capstone Classroom, 2014, Fiction

Level G

Aaron Is Cool! by P. D. Eastman, Random House Step Into Reading, 2015, Fiction

Clean Up Shelly Beach by Kelly Gaffney, Capstone Classroom, 2015, Fiction

Giraffes at the Zoo by Mia Coulton, MaryRuth Books, 2014, Nonfiction

Recycling by Anne Giulieri, Capstone Classroom, 2015, Nonfiction

Taking Care of the Ocean by Jay Dale, Capstone Classroom, 2012, Nonfiction

Level H

Billy Brown's Cat by Elizabeth Pulford, Capstone Classroom, 2012, Fiction

Brown Bears at the Zoo by Mia Coulton, MaryRuth Books, 2014, Nonfiction

Danny and Dad Go on a Picnic by Mia Coulton, MaryRuth Books, 2014, Fiction

Danny Looks for a Honeybee Yard by Mia Coulton, MaryRuth Books, 2014, Fiction

Night-time Noises by Jay Dale, Capstone Classroom, 2015, Fiction

Level I

Play Ball! by Anne Giulieri, Capstone Classroom, 2015, Nonfiction

Race to Nome! by Amy Helfer and Kelley Beaurline, Sundance Reading Powerworks, 2004, Nonfiction

The Jobs People Do by Anne Giulieri, Capstone Classroom, 2015, Nonfiction

The Littlest Clown by Jay Dale, Capstone Classroom, 2015, Fiction

Wheels by Jacquie Kilkenny, Capstone Classroom, 2015, Nonfiction

Level J

All About Teeth by Jessica Holden, Capstone Classroom, 2013, Nonfiction

Animals with Fins, Animals with Fur by Kelly Gaffney, Capstone Classroom, 2013, Nonfiction

Fancy Nancy: Apples Galore! by Jane O'Connor, HarperCollins I Can Read, 2013, Fiction

Snorkeling with Nana by Kelly Gaffney, Capstone Classroom, 2013, Fiction

Wibbly Wobbly Tooth by Jay Dale, Capstone Classroom, 2013, Fiction

Level K

Little Lucy Goes to School by Ilene Cooper, Random House Step Into Reading, 2014, Fiction

Moving by Mia Coulton, MaryRuth Books, 2012, Fiction

Pirate Lessons by Wendy Graham, Capstone Classroom, 2013, Nonfiction

The New House by Lisa deMauro, Macmillan McGraw-Hill, 2010, Fiction

The Senses by Anne Giulieri, Capstone Classroom, 2013, Nonfiction

Level L

An Extraordinary Egg by Leo Lionni, Random House Step Into Reading 1994, Fiction

Animal Rescue Shelter by Jay Dale, Capstone Classroom, 2013, Nonfiction

Strawberry Storm by Lucinda Cotter, Capstone Classroom, 2013, Fiction

Weather Watch by Jacquie Kilkenny, Capstone Classroom, 2013, Nonfiction

Whirly Bird by Anne Giulieri, Capstone Classroom, 2013, Nonfiction

Level M

Magnetic Race Car by Anne Giulieri, Capstone Classroom, 2013, Nonfiction

Morvena the Mermaid by Jay Dale, Capstone Classroom, 2013, Fiction

Not All Birds Fly by Jaclyn Crupi, Capstone Classroom, 2013, Nonfiction

Ocean Craft by Wendy Graham, Capstone Classroom, 2013, Nonfiction

Playing Team Sports by Jessica Holden, Capstone Classroom, 2013, Nonfiction

Level N

A Dog Called Prince by Jay Dale, Capstone Classroom, 2013, Fiction

The Curious World of Beetles by Doris Licameli, Macmillan McGraw-Hill, 2007, Nonfiction

The Elephant's Boast by Susan Blackaby, Macmillan McGraw-Hill, 2009, Fiction

The Goat-Mobile by Paul Mason, Abrams Learning Trends, 2013, Fiction

Through the Lens by Paul Mason, Abrams Learning Trends, 2013, Nonfiction

Level O

A Thirsty World by Jill Eggleton, Abrams Learning Trends, 2013, Nonfiction

Future Planning by Lulu Turner, Abrams Learning Trends, 2013, Nonfiction

Go Fish by Lulu Turner, Abrams Learning Trends, 2013, Nonfiction

Judo by Rachel Blackburn, Wright Group McGraw-Hill Foundations Take Two Books, 2000, Nonfiction

Through the Eyes of Bloggers by Jill Eggleton, Abrams Learning Trends, 2013, Nonfiction

Level P

Change Happens by Jill Eggleton, Abrams Learning Trends, 2013, Fiction

Faraway Home by Ellen Dreyer, Macmillan McGraw-Hill, 2009, Fiction

Lens on Nightlife by Paul Mason, Abrams Learning Trends, 2013, Fiction

North American Snakes by Dina Anastasio, Macmillan McGraw-Hill, 2010, Nonfiction

Spooky & Spookier: Four American Ghost Stories by Lori Haskins Houran, Random House Step into Reading, 2003, Fiction

Level Q

Fiction Today—Fact Tomorrow by Jill Eggleton, Abrams Learning Trends, 2013, Nonfiction

Invisible Threads by Jill Eggleton, Abrams Learning Trends, 2013, Nonfiction

Reader's Viewpoints by Jill Eggleton, Abrams Learning Trends, 2013, Nonfiction

Tapping into Talent by Jill Eggleton, Abrams Learning Trends, 2013, Fiction

Technophobia by Paul Mason, Abrams Learning Trends, 2013, Fiction

Level R

Amazing Insect and Spider Builders by Carol Pugliano-Martin, Macmillan McGraw-Hill, (no date), Nonfiction

Blizzard by Emily Wortman-Wunder, Macmillan McGraw-Hill, (no date), Nonfiction

Coyote and the Rock by Nomi J. Waldman, Macmillan McGraw-Hill, 2009, Fiction

Team Haircut by Paul Mason, Abrams Learning Trends, 2013, Fiction

Uncle Al—Chaperone by Jill Eggleton, Abrams Learning Trends, 2013, Fiction

Level S

Built for Speed by Paul Mason, Abrams Learning Trends, 2013, Nonfiction

Crazy Challenges by Jill Eggleton, Abrams Learning Trends, 2013, Nonfiction

On the Wings of a Bird by Jill Eggleton, Abrams Learning Trends, 2013, Nonfiction

Shadows of the Past by Jill Eggleton, Abrams Learning Trends, 2013, Nonfiction

The Lost Cave by Sarah Glasscock, Macmillan McGraw-Hill, 2009, Fiction

Level T

Call Me Harry by Jill Eggleton, Abrams Learning Trends, 2013, Fiction

Gorillas and Chimpanzees by Sally Cole, Wright Group McGraw-Hill Foundations Take Two Books, 2002, Nonfiction

Looking Back—Moving Forward by Paul Mason, Abrams Learning Trends, 2013, Nonfiction

The Claw by Paul Mason, Abrams Learning Trends, 2013, Fiction

World without Trees by Paul Mason, Abrams Learning Trends, 2013, Nonfiction

Level U

All the World's a Stage by Paul Mason, Abrams Learning Trends, 2013, Nonfiction

Beyond Our Planet by Paul Mason, Abrams Learning Trends, 2013, Nonfiction

Food for Thought by Jill Eggleton, Abrams Learning Trends, 2013, Nonfiction

Hidden Horrors by Jill Eggleton, Abrams Learning Trends, 2013, Nonfiction

See Through by Paul Mason, Abrams Learning Trends, 2013, Nonfiction

Level V

Alien: The Brown Tree Snake Story by E. C. Hill, Macmillan McGraw-Hill, 2009, Nonfiction

Black Bear's Backyard by Julia Schaffer, Macmillan McGraw-Hill, 2005, Fiction

From Dragonflies to Helicopters: Learning from Nature by Manuel Aleman, 2009, Macmillan McGraw-Hill, Nonfiction

Life on the Deep Sea Floor by Melissa McDaniel, Macmillan McGraw-Hill, 2009, Nonfiction

Rachel's Choice by Sarah Glasscock, Macmillan McGraw-Hill, 2006, Fiction

Level W

100 Most Dangerous Things on the Planet by Anna Claybourne, Scholastic, Inc., 2008. Nonfiction

All About Baseball by Daniel Rosen, Macmillan McGraw-Hill, 2009, Nonfiction

Escape from the Volcano by Ann M. Rossi, Macmillan McGraw-Hill, 2009, Fiction

How to Be a Publisher by Barbara Burt, Macmillan McGraw-Hill, (no date), Nonfiction

Will the Show Go On? by Sarah Glasscock, Macmillan McGraw-Hill, (no date), Fiction

Level X

A Visit to Yellowstone National Park by Lauren Eckler, Macmillan McGraw-Hill, (no date), Nonfiction

Cesar Chavez by Johanna Ehrmann, Macmillan McGraw-Hill, 2009, Nonfiction

Earthquake by Emily Wortman-Wunder, Macmillan McGraw-Hill, (no date), Nonfiction

Eruption on the Mountain by Ann M. Rossi, Macmillan McGraw-Hill, (no date), Fiction

How Thor Got His Hammer by Nomi J. Waldman, Macmillan McGraw-Hill, 2009, Fiction

Level Y

Canine War Heroes by Sarah Jane Brian, Macmillan McGraw-Hill, 2009, Nonfiction

Fire in the Sierra Nevada by Tricia Levi, Macmillan McGraw-Hill, 2006, Nonfiction

Ida B. Wells: Woman of Courage by Judith Lechner, Macmillan McGraw-Hill, 2008, Nonfiction

Saving Alligators by Barbara A. Donovan, Macmillan McGraw-Hill, 2009, Nonfiction

Surprises in the Desert by Sofia Cruz, Macmillan McGraw-Hill, 2009, Fiction

Level Z

James Franklin: Hurricane Specialist by Heera Kang, Macmillan McGraw-Hill, (no date), Nonfiction

Talking Pictures: The Mayan Mystery by Elizabeth West, Macmillan McGraw-Hill, 2009, Nonfiction

The Smithsonian: America's Attic by Johanna Ehrmann, Macmillan McGraw-Hill, 2009, Nonfiction

The Trees of Time Past by Becky Cheston, Macmillan McGraw-Hill, 2009, Fiction

Thurgood Marshall: Civil Rights Champion by Eric Oatman, Macmillan McGraw-Hill, 2009, Nonfiction

CHAPTER FOUR: 4C

Interest Inventory

Modified from Opitz, Ford & Erekson (2011)

Check all that apply.

1. Do you like to read?

    _____ Yes, all the time   _____ Yes, sometimes

    _____ Yes, most of the time   _____ Not usually

2. What topics are you interested in (check all that apply)?

    _____ animals   _____ sports   _____ solving problems
                                                         in life
    _____ music   _____ friendships
                                                   _____ cars, trucks,
    _____ science   _____ famous people   motorcycles

    _____ art   _____ families   _____ magic

    _____ riddles and jokes   _____ different places   _____ Other topics (specify)

    _____ health and fitness _____ growing up   _____

3. What types of fiction books (make-believe stories) do you like to read (check all that apply)?

    _____ realistic stories   _____ historical fiction

    _____ mysteries   _____ fantasy

    _____ humorous books   _____ science fiction

    _____ myths, fables, and legends _____ westerns

    _____ folktales and fairy tales _____ romance

    _____ scary stories   _____ Other types of fiction books (specify)

                                     _____

4. What types of nonfiction books (true stories and informational books) do you like to read (check all that apply)?

    _____ "how to" books   _____ political topics

    _____ biographies and autobiographies _____ facts and records

    _____ events in history   _____ Other types of nonfiction
                                               books (specify)
    _____ current issues
                                         _____
    _____ science topics

continued on next page

5. Do you like books in a series?   _____ yes   _____ no

   Do you have a favorite series?

6. Do you like reading poetry?   _____ yes   _____ no

   Do you have a favorite poet?

7. Do you like reading plays?   _____ yes   _____ no

   Do you have a favorite play?

8. Do you like reading graphic novels?   _____ yes   _____ no

   Do you have a favorite author, character, or series?

9. Do you like reading magazines?   _____ yes   _____ no

   What magazines would you like to read?

10. Do you like reading newspapers?   _____ yes   _____ no

   What newspapers would you like to read?

11. Do you like…

Picture books	_____ yes	_____ no	Paperback books	_____ yes	_____ no
Chapter books	_____ yes	_____ no	E-books	_____ yes	_____ no
Hardcover books	_____ yes	_____ no	Audio books	_____ yes	_____ no

12. What helps you to choose something to read? (check up to three)

Cover	_____ yes	_____ no	Level	_____ yes	_____ no
Title	_____ yes	_____ no	Genre (Type)	_____ yes	_____ no
Author	_____ yes	_____ no	Series	_____ yes	_____ no
Format	_____ yes	_____ no	Recommendation	_____ yes	_____ no
Topic	_____ yes	_____ no			

13. What else can you tell me about your reading interests?

Guided Reading Session During a Science Unit

Flowing into the session	1. Create a six-box grid. (See sample that follows this table as 5B on page 196.) 2. Introduce key vocabulary words ("burrow," "ecosystem," "gnaw," "hibernate," "oxygen") from *A Year at the Pond* by Tisha Hamilton (Macmillan-McGraw-Hill). Ask students to predict what the book will be about in box number 1. Ask for probes on predictions. Use additional prompts to change predictions: nature's swimming pool, full of water, not too big or too deep. Move students to the book. 3. Explicitly state before introducing reading strategy: "Let's think about what else we already know about this topic. In box number 2, write down one more word you predict that will be in this book." Record on note cards and add to other word cards. Do two rounds if needed. Make links to vocabulary words ("burrow," "ecosystem," "gnaw," "hibernate," "oxygen"), if possible. 4. Use boxes number 3 and 4 ("What I Knew" and "What I Didn't Know") next. Provide one minute for a quick look and response. Discuss responses. Link to vocabulary as possible.

Flowing through the session	1. Flip the grid over. Explicitly state the strategy: "Let's walk through and see how the text is organized. Let's design our graphic organizer as we walk through the text." Start a web, "A year in the pond." Add "spring, pages 4–5," "summer, pages 8–9," "autumn, pages 10–11," and "winter, pages 12–13." Continue to link to vocabulary words as possible.
	
	2. Have students listen to pages 2–3 read aloud.
	
	3. Work through "spring, pages 4–5" together. Routine is as follows:
	  • Read, think, and write about the first two paragraphs.
	  • Explicitly model main idea and supporting details.
	  • Lead students in reading, thinking, and writing about paragraph three.
	  • Students work together in reading, thinking, and writing about paragraph four.
	  • Students work independently reading, thinking, and writing about paragraph five.
	
	4. Assign two students to do "summer, pages 8–9." They read, think, and add to web, then reflect on how they did working together independently.
	
	5. Assign two students to do "autumn, pages 10–11." They read, think, add to web, and then reflect on how they did working together independently.
	
	6. Work with two students to do "winter, pages 12–13" and assess as they read, think, and add to the web.

Flow out of the session	1. Bring students together to share summer, autumn, and winter, adding to the webs. 2. Chorally read conclusions: spring: ALL, summer: team one, autumn: team two, and winter: team three. 3. Explicitly state strategy: "Let's reflect on what we learned to help us remember the important things longer." Use boxes 5 and 6 to finish with a THINK/WINK—Things I Now Know about *A Year at the Pond* and What I Need to Know about *A Year at the Pond*. Have students report out. 4. Have students use the self-evaluation on page 197 to reflect on learning. Invite sharing of reflections. 5. Link to other resources, such as other animals and habitats books.

Sample Six-box Grid

1.	2.	3. What I Knew
4. What I didn't know	**5. THINK**	**6. WINK**

Self-evaluation

Name	+ (good) or – (needs work)	Reason
Making predictions		
Using prior knowledge		
Reading the book		
Finding important details		
Working in the small groups		
Working with my partner		

Supporting Transitions

Transition Song

(Sung to the tune of "The Ants Go Marching One by One")

It's time to change very quietly—Let's go! Let's go!

It's time to change very quickly—Let's grow! Let's grow!

We never waste a minute of time

Because we're learning all the time.

Let's make our change and get back to work and learn some more—LET'S GO!

Calming Down Routine

From Incorporating Brain Breaks:
Keeping Students Engaged, Pottsgrove School District

1. Stand or sit with the right leg crossed over the left at the ankles.
2. Take your right wrist, and cross it over the left wrist.
3. Link your fingers so that the right wrist is on top.
4. Bend the elbow out, and gently turn the fingers in toward the body until they rest on the center of your chest. Stay in this position.
5. Breathe slowly and deeply for two minutes.

Buddy Time

Adapted from Incorporating Brain Breaks:
Keeping Students Engaged, Pottsgrove School District

1. Stand up.
2. Partner up with a friend near you.
3. Take two minutes to connect with a friend in class.
4. Talk about what/how you are doing.

Resources

Allington, R. L. (1991). The legacy of "slow it down and make it more concrete." In J. Zutell & S. McCormack (Eds.), *Learner factors/teacher factors: Issues in literacy research and instruction*, (pp. 19–29). Chicago: National Reading Conference.

Allington, R. L. (2001). *What really matters for struggling readers: Designing research-based programs*. New York: Addison-Wesley.

Allington, R. L. (2008). *What really matters in response to intervention: Research based designs*. Boston: Allyn & Bacon.

Allington, R. L. (2012). *What really matters for struggling readers: Designing research-based programs, 3rd ed.* Boston: Pearson.

Allington, R. L. (2013). What really matters when working with struggling readers. *The Reading Teacher, 66*(7), 520–530.

Allington, R. & Walmsley, S. (Eds.). (2007). *No quick fix: Rethinking literacy programs in America's elementary schools (The RtI edition).* New York: Teachers College Press.

Anderson, R. C., Hiebert, E. H., Scott, J. A. & Wilkinson, I. A. G. (1985). *Becoming a nation of readers.* Champaign, IL: University of Illinois. Center for the Study of Reading.

Anderson, R. C., Wilson, P. T. & Fielding, L. G. (1988). Growth in reading and how children spend their time outside of school. *Reading Research Quarterly, 23*(3), 285–303.

Aronson, E. (1979). *The jigsaw classroom.* New York: Sage.

Artley, A. S. (1943). Teaching word meaning through context. *Elementary English Review, 20*(2). 68–74.

Atwell, N. (1998). *In the middle: New understandings about writing, reading, and learning.* Portsmouth, NH: Boynton/Cook.

Beaver, J. & Carter, M. A. (2001). *Developmental reading assessment.* Parsippany, NJ: Celebration Press.

Beck, I. L. & McKeown, M. G. (1985). Teaching vocabulary: Making the instruction fit the goal. *Educational Perspectives, 23*(1), 11–15

Bender, W. N. & Shores, C. F. (2007). *Response to intervention: A practical guide for every teacher.* Thousand Oaks, CA: Corwin.

Bergeron, B. (1990). What does the term whole language mean? *Journal of Reading Behavior, 22*(4), 301–329.

Bomer, R. (1998). Transactional heat and light: More explicit literacy learning. *Language Arts, 76*(1) 11–18.

Boquist, S. (2013). Oral language groups as intervention? Why? *The Wisconsin State Reading Association Journal, 50*(3), 39–41.

Boushey, G. & Moser, J. (2006). *The daily 5: Fostering literacy independence in the elementary grades.* Portland, ME: Stenhouse Publishers.

Boushey, G. & Moser, J. (2009). *The café book: Engaging all students in daily literacy assessment & instruction.* Portland, ME: Stenhouse Publishers.

Boushey, G. & Moser, J. (2014). *The daily 5: Fostering literacy independence in the elementary grades (2nd. Ed.).* Portland, ME: Stenhouse Publishers

Boyle, O. & Peregoy, S. (1998). Literacy scaffolds: Strategies for first- and second-language readers and writers. In M. F. Opitz (Ed.), *Literacy instruction for culturally and linguistically diverse students* (pp. 150–157). Newark, DE: International Reading Association.

Boyles, N. N. (2004). *Constructing meaning through kid-friendly comprehension strategy instruction.* Gainesville, FL: Maupin House.

Boyles, N. N. (2009). *Launching RTI comprehension instruction with shared reading: 40 model lessons for intermediate reader*s. North Mankato, MN: Maupin House.

Brown, A. (1982). Learning how to learn from reading. In J. A. Langer & M. T. Smith-Burke (Eds). *Reader meets author: Bridging the gap,* (pp. 26–54). Newark, DE: International Reading Association.

Brown, A. & Palinscar, A. (1982). Inducing strategic learning from texts by means of informed self-control training. *Topics in Learning and Learning Disabilities, 2,* 1–17.

Buly, M. R. & Valencia, S. W. (2002). Below the bar: Profiles of students who fail state reading assessments. *Educational Evaluation and Policy Analysis, 24*(3), 219–239.

Burkins, J. M. & Croft, M. M. (2010). *Preventing misguided reading: New strategies for guided reading teachers.* Newark, DE: International Reading Association.

Caldwell, J. S. & Ford, M. P. (2002). *Where have all the bluebirds gone? How to soar with flexible grouping.* Portsmouth, NH: Heinemann.

Cambourne, B. (1995). Toward an Educational Relevant Theory of Literacy Learning: Twenty Years of Inquiry. *The Reading Teacher, 49*(3), 182–190.

Cambourne, B. (2001). Conditions for literacy learning: Why do some students fail to learn to read? Ockham's razor and the conditions of learning. *The Reading Teacher, 54*(8), 784–786.

Cassidy, J. & Ortlieb, E. (2013). What was hot (and not) in literacy: What we can learn. *Journal of Adolescent & Adult Literacy, 57*(1), 21–29.

Cassidy, J. & Wenrich, J. K. (1997). What's hot, what's not for 1997. *Reading Today, 14*(4), 34.

Cassidy, J. & Wenrich, J. K. (1998/1999). Rapid Research Report: Literacy Research and Practice: What's Hot, What's Not, and Why. *The Reading Teacher, 52*(4), 402–406.

Clay, M. M. (1979). *The early detection of reading difficulties, 2nd ed.* Portsmouth, NH: Heinemann.

Clay, M. M. (1991). *Becoming literate: The construction of inner control.* Portsmouth, NH: Heinemann.

Clay, M. M. (1993). *An observational survey of early literacy achievement.* Portsmouth, NH: Heinemann.

Clay, M. M. (1998). *By different paths to common outcomes.* Portland, ME: Stenhouse.

Clay, M. M. (2006). *An observation survey of early literacy achievement (2nd Edition.)* Portsmouth, NH: Heinemann.

Clay, M. M., Gill, M., Glynn, T., McNaughton, T. & Salmon, K. (2015). *Record of oral language: Observing changes in the acquisition of language structures: A guide for teaching (New edition).* Portsmouth, NH: Heinemann.

Cunningham, P., Hall, D. & Cunningham, J. (2000). *Guided reading the Four Blocks way.* Greensboro, NC: Carson Dellosa.

Daniels, H. (2002). *Literature circles: Voice and choice in book clubs and reading groups.* Portland, ME: Stenhouse.

Darling-Hammond, L. & McLaughlin, M. (1999). Investing in teaching as a learning profession: Policy problems and prospects. In Darling-Hammond, L. & Sykes, G. (Eds.). *Teaching as the learning profession: Handbook of policy and practice.* San Francisco: Jossey-Bass Publishers.

Denton, C. A., Fletcher, J. M., Taylor, W. P., Barth, A. E. & Vaughn, S. (2014). An Experimental Evaluation of Guided Reading and Explicit Interventions for Primary-Grade Students At-Risk for Reading Difficulties. *Journal of Research on Educational Effectiveness, 7*(3), 268–293

Diller, D. (2003). *Literacy work stations: Making centers work.* Portland, ME: Stenhouse Publishers.

Diller, D. (2005). *Practice with purpose: Literacy work stations for grades 3–6.* Portland, ME: Stenhouse Publishers.

Dorn, L. J. & Soffos, C. (2007). *Comprehensive intervention model (CIM): A response to intervention model.* Little Rock, AK: Center for Literacy, University of Arkansas at Little Rock.

Dorn, L. J. & Soffos, C. (2011). *Interventions that work: A comprehensive intervention model for preventing reading failure in grades K–3.* Boston, MA: Pearson Higher Education.

Duffelmeyer, F. A., Kruse, A. E., Merkley, D. J. & Fyfe, S. A. (1994). Further validation and enhancement of the Names Test. *The Reading Teacher, 48*(2), 118–128.

Duke, N. K. & Bennett-Armistead. V. S. (2003). *Reading and writing informational text in the primary grades: Research-based practices.* New York: Scholastic.

Duke, N. K. & Martin, N. M. (2011). 10 things every literacy educator should know about research. *The Reading Teacher, 65*(1), 9–22.

Durkin, D. (1978). What classroom observations reveal about reading comprehension instruction. *Reading Research Quarterly, 14*(4), 481–533.

Durkin, D. (1981). Reading comprehension instruction in five basal reader series. *Reading Research Quarterly, 16*(4), 515–544.

Dymock, S. J. (1998). A comparison study of the effects of text structure training, reading practice, and guided reading on reading comprehension. In *National Reading Conference Yearbook* (Vol. 47, 90–102).

Dzaldov, B. S. & Peterson, S. (2005). Book leveling and readers. *The Reading Teacher, 59*(3), 222–229.

Ellery, V. (2014). *Creating Strategic Readers: Techniques for Supporting Rigorous Literacy Instruction (3rd ed.).* Huntington Beach, CA: Shell Education.

Fawson, P. & Reutzel, R. (2000). But I only have a basal: Implementing guided reading in the early grades. *The Reading Teacher, 54*(1), 84–97.

Ferguson, J. & Wilson, J. (2009). Guided reading: It's for primary teachers. In F. Falk-Ross. (Ed.), *Literacy issues during changing times: A call to action* (pp. 293–306). Arlington, TX: The College Reading Association.

Fielding, L. & Roller, C. (1992). Making difficult books accessible and easy books acceptable. *The Reading Teacher, 45*(9), 678–685.

Fisher, D. & Frey, N. (2014). Close reading as an intervention for struggling middle school readers. *Journal of Adolescent & Adult Literacy, 57*(5), 367–376.

Fitzgerald, J. (1999). What is this thing called "balance"? *The Reading Teacher, 53*(2), 100–107.

Ford, M. P. (1991). Worksheets anonymous: On the road to recovery. *Language Arts, 68*(7) 563–566.

Ford, M., Champeau, K. & Andrews, N. (2013). Response to Intervention: Expertise matters. *The Wisconsin State Reading Association Journal, 50*(3), 1–3.

Ford, M. P. & Opitz, M. F. (2002). Using centers to engage children during guided reading time: Intensifying learning experiences away from the teacher. *The Reading Teacher, 55*(8) 710–717.

Ford, M. P.,& Opitz, M. F. (2008). A national survey of guided reading practices: What we can learn from primary teachers. *Literacy Research and Instruction, 47*(4), 309–331.

Ford, M. P. & Opitz, M. F. (2010). From many and most to every and all: Research-based strategies for moving all readers forward. *Illinois State Reading Journal, 38*(1), 3–13.

Ford, M. P. & Opitz, M. F. (2011). Looking back to move forward with guided reading. *Reading Horizons, 50*(4), 3.

Fountas, I. C. & Pinnell, G. S. (1996). *Guided reading: Good first teaching for all children.* Portsmouth, NH: Heinemann.

Fountas, I. C. & Pinnell, G. S. (2001). *Guiding readers and writers grades 3–6: Teaching comprehension, genre, and content literacy.* Portsmouth, NH: Heinemann.

Fountas, I. C. & Pinnell, G. S. (2006). *Leveled books, K–8: Matching texts to readers for effective teaching.* Portsmouth, NH: Heinemann.

Fountas, I. C. & Pinnell, G. S. (2008). *Fountas and Pinnell: Benchmark assessment system.* Portsmouth, NH: Heinemann.

Fountas, I. C. & Pinnell, G. S. (2009). *When readers struggle: Teaching that works.* Portsmouth, NH: Heinemann.

Fountas, I. C. & Pinnell, G. S. (2012). Guided reading: The romance and the reality. The Reading Teacher, 66(4), 268–284.

Fountas, I. C. & Pinnell, G. S. (2014). *Level literacy instruction.* Portsmouth, NH: Heinemann.

Fox, M. (2008). *Reading magic: Why reading aloud to our children will change their lives together.* New York: Mariner Books.

Fox, M. (2013). What next in the read-aloud battle? Win or lose? *The Reading Teacher, 67*(1), 4–8.

Freebody, P. & Luke, A. (1990). Literacies programs: Debates and demands in cultural context. *Prospect: Australian Journal of TESOL, 5*(7), 7–16.

Gambrell, L. (1996). Creating classroom cultures that foster reading motivation. *The Reading Teacher, 50*(1), 14–25.

Gambrell, L. & Almasi, J. F. (Eds.) (1996). *Lively discussions! Fostering engaged reading.* Newark, DE: International Reading Association.

Gentile, L. M. (2011). *The oral language acquisition inventory.* San Antonio, TX: Pearson.

Gentry, R. (2015, July 19). *Phase observation in PreK through grade 1: Powerful formative literacy assessment and targeted teacher.* Paper presented at the 2015 International Literacy Association Convention. (St. Louis, MO).

Glasswell, K. & Ford, M. P. (2010). Teaching flexibly with leveled texts: More power for your reading block. *The Reading Teacher, 64*(1), 57–60.

Glasswell, K. & Ford, M. P. (2011). Let's start leveling about leveling. *Language Arts, 88*(3), 208–216.

Goodman, Y. & Marek, A. (1996). *Retrospective miscue analysis.* Katonah, NY: RC Owens.

Gottlieb, M., Cranley, M. E. & Cammilleri, A. (2007). *WIDA Consortium: English language proficiency standards & resource guide.* Madison, WI: WIDA Consortium.

Grimes J. & Kurn, S. (2003, December). An intervention-based system for addressing NCLB and IDEA expectations: A multiple tiered model to ensure every child learns. Paper presented at the National Research Center on Learning Disabilities Responsiveness-to-Intervention Symposium, Kansas City, MO.

Guastello, E. F. & Lenz, C. (2005). Student accountability: Guided reading kidstations. *The Reading Teacher, 59*(2), 144–156.

Guthrie J. T. & Klauda, S. L. (2014). Effects of classroom practices on reading comprehension, engagement, and motivations for adolescents. *Reading Research Quartlery, 49*(4), 387–416.

Hall, K. M., Sabey, B. L. & McClellan, M. (2005). Expository text comprehension: Helping primary-grade teachers use expository texts to full advantage. *Reading Psychology, 26*(3), 211–234.

Halladay, J. L. (2008). "Reconsidering Frustrational Level Texts: Second Graders' Experiences with Difficult Texts" Paper presented at the National Reading Conference (Orlando, Florida).

Halladay, J. L. (2012). Revisiting key assumptions of the reading level framework. *The Reading Teacher, 66*(1), 53–62.

Hattie, J. (2013). *Visible learning: A synthesis of over 800 meta-analyses relating to achievement.* New York: Routledge.

Hiebert, E. (2014, June). *The next-generation assessments: What's new, what's not?* Paper presented at the 34th University of Wisconsin Reading Research Symposium (Madison, WI).

Holdaway, D. (1979). *The foundations of literacy.* Sydney: Ashton Scholastic.

Hornsby, D. (2000). *A closer look at guided reading.* Amerdale, Vic Australia: Eleanor Curtain.

Invernizzi, M., Meier, J., Swank, L. & Juel, C. (2001). *PALS: Phonological awareness literacy screening.* Charlottesville, VA: University of Virginia Printing Services.

Irwin, J. W. (1986). *Understanding and teaching cohesion comprehension.* Newark, DE: International Reading Association.

Johnston, P. H. (2011). Response to intervention in literacy: Problems and possibilities. *The Elementary School Journal, 111*(4), 511–534.

Kamps, D., Abbott, M., Greenwood, C., Arreaga-Mayer, C., Wills, H., Longstaff, J., Culpepper, M. & Walton, C. (2007). Use of evidence-based, small-group reading instruction for English language learners in elementary grades: Secondary-tier intervention. *Learning Disability Quarterly, 30*(3), 153–168.

Kane, K. (1995). *Keeping your balance teacher's guide for guided reading in the early grades.* New York: Grolier Classroom Publishing.

Kelly, S. & Turner, J. (2009). Rethinking the effects of classroom activity structure on the engagement of low-achieving students. *The Teachers College Record, 111*(7), 1665–1692.

Kletzien, S. B. & Mariam, J. D. (2004). *Informational text in K–3 classrooms: Helping children read and write.* Newark, DE: International Reading Association.

Laminack, L. (2014, February 6). *Resident or tourists?* Paper presented at the 2014 Wisconsin State Reading Association Convention. (Milwaukee, WI).

Laminack, L. & Wadsworth, R. (2006). *Learner under the influence of language and literature: Making the most of read alouds across the day.* Portsmouth, NH: Heinemann.

Layne, S. (2015). In defense of read-aloud: Sustaining best practice. Portland, ME: Stenhouse

Lose, M. K. (2007). A child's response to intervention requires a responsive teacher of reading. *The Reading Teacher, 61*(3), 276–279.

Mather, N., Sammons, J. & Schwartz, J. (2006). Adaptations of the Names Test: Easy-to-Use Phonics Assessments. *The Reading Teacher, 60*(2), 114–122.

McMaster, K. L., Jung, P. G., Brandes, D., Pinto, V., Fuchs, D., Kearns, D. & Yen, L. (2014). Customizing a Research–Based Reading Practice. *The Reading Teacher, 68*(3), 173–183.

Mellard, D. F. & Johnson, E. S. (2008). RTI: A practitioner's guide to implementing response to intervention. Thousand Oaks, CA: Corwin.

Mere, C. (2005). More than guided reading: Finding the right instructional mix, K–3. Portland, ME: Stenhouse.

Messmer E. & Messmer, H. (2008). Response to Intervention (RTI): What teachers of reading need to know. *The Reading Teacher, 62*(4), 280–290.

Mooney, M. E. (1990). *Reading to, with, and by children.* Katonah: NY: RC Owen Publishers.

Morgan, D. N., Mraz, M., Padak, N. & Rasinski, T. (2009). *Independent reading: Practical strategies for grades K–3.* New York: Guilford Publications.

Murray, M. S., Munger, K. A., Hiebert, E. H., (earlier version of 2014 publication). An Analysis of Two Reading Intervention Programs: How do the Words, Texts, and Programs Compare? *Elementary School Journal, 114*(4), 479–500.

National Center for Education Statistics. (1995). *Listening to children read aloud.* Washington, DC: U.S. Department of Education.

National Center for Education Statistics. (2003). *International comparisons in fourth grade reading literacy: Findings from the Progress in International Reading Literacy Study (PIRLS) of 2001*. Washington, DC: US Department of Education.

National Governors Association Center for Best Practices & Council of Chief State School Officers. (2010). *Common Core State Standards for English language arts and literacy in history/social studies, science, and technical subjects*. Washington, DC: Authors.

Nayak, G. & Sylva, K. (2013). The effects of a guided reading intervention on reading comprehension: a study on young Chinese learners of English in Hong Kong. *The Language Learning Journal, 41*(1), 85–103.

Oczkus, L. (2012). *Best ever survival tips: 72 lessons you can't teach without*. Newark, DE: International Reading Association.

Opitz, M. F. (2007). *Don't speed, read! 12 steps to smart and sensible fluency instruction*. New York: Scholastic.

Opitz, M. F. & Ford, M. P. (2001). *Reaching readers: Flexible and innovative strategies for guided reading*. Portsmouth, NH: Heinemann.

Opitz, M. F. & Ford, M. P. (2008). *Do-able differentiation: Varying groups, texts, and supports to reach readers*. Portsmouth, NH: Heinemann.

Opitz, M. F. & Ford, M. P. (2014). *Classroom catalysts: 15 efficient practices that accelerate readers' learning*. Portsmouth, NH: Heinemann.

Opitz, M. F. & Ford, M. P. (2014). *Engaging minds in the classroom: The surprising power of joy*. Alexandria, VA: ASCD.

Opitz, M. F., Ford, M. P. & Erekson, J. A. (2011). *Accessible assessment: How 9 sensible techniques can power data-driven reading instruction*. Portsmouth, NH: Heinemann.

Oshkosh Area School District. (2013). *Response to intervention plan: Continuum of support*. Oshkosh, WI: OASD.

Paratore, J. (1990). *Classroom contexts for literacy training: Flexible grouping*. Paper presented at the Wisconsin State Reading Association, Eau Claire, WI.

Paris, S. G. (2005). Reinterpreting the development of reading skills. *Reading research quarterly, 40*(2), 184–202.

Pearson, P. D. (2006). Forward. In Goodman, K. *The truth about DIBELS: What it is, what it does*. Portsmouth, NH: Heinemann.

Pearson, P. D. (2009, February 5). *Reading policy in America: A checkered past, an uneasy present, and an uncertain future*. Paper presented at the Wisconsin State Reading Association, Milwaukee, WI.

Pearson, P. D. & Gallagher, M. (1983). The instruction of reading comprehension. *Contemporary Educational Psychology, 8*(3), 317–344.

Pinnell, G. S. & Fountas, I. C. (2010). Research base for guided reading as an instructional approach. *Scholastic.com*. http://teacher.scholastic.com/products/guidedreading/pdf/2.0_InYourClassroom/GR_Research_Paper_2010.pdf (retrieved July 22, 2015).

Policastro, M. M., McTague, B. & Mazeski, D. (2015). *Formative assessment in the new balanced literacy classroom*. North Mankato, MN: Capstone.

Pottsgrove School District. *Incorporating brain breaks: Keeping students engaged,* http://www.pgsd.org/cms/lib07/PA01916597/Centricity/Domain/43/Brain%20Breaks.pdf (retrieved July 11, 2015).

Raphael, T. (1982). Question-answering strategies for children. *The Reading Teacher, 36*(3), 186–190.

Rasinski, T. V. (2003). *The fluent reader: Oral reading strategies for building word recognition, fluency, and comprehension.* Scholastic Inc.

Reeves, C.A. (2011). *Teacher perceptions of guided reading.* Education and Human Development Master's Theses, Paper 63. (College of Brockport: State University of New York.)

Richardson, J. (2009). *The next step in guided reading: Focused assessments and targeted lessons for helping every student become a better reader.* New York: Scholastic Inc.

Routman, R. (2000). *Conversations: Strategies for teaching, learning and evaluating.* Portsmouth, NH: Heinemann.

Saunders-Smith, G. (2003). *The ultimate guided reading how-to book: Building literacy through small-group instruction.* Thousand Oaks, CA: Corwin.

Scanlon, D. M. (2011). Response to intervention as an assessment: The role of assessment and instruction. In A. McGill-Franzen and R. L. Allington (Eds.), *The handbook of reading disabilities research.* New York: Routledge.

Scanlon, D. M., Anderson, K. L. & Sweeney, J. M. (2010). *Early intervention for reading difficulties: The interactive strategies approach.* New York: Guilford.

Schlechty, P. C. (2002). *Working on the work: An action plan for teachers, principals, and superintendents.* San Francisco, CA: Jossey-Bass.

Schmoker, M. (2010, September 29). When pedagogic fads trump priorities. *Education Week, 30*(5), 22–23.

Schulman, M. B. & daCruz Payne, C. (2000). *Guided reading: Making it work.* New York: Scholastic.

Schwartz, R. M. (2005). Decisions, decisions: Responding to primary students during guided reading. *The Reading Teacher, 58*(5), 436–443.

Shanahan, T. (2012, November 12). "Daily Five and Common Core" http://www.shanahanonliteracy.com/2012/11/daily-five-and-common-core.html (retrieved July 11, 2015).

Shanahan, T. (2014, May 24). "How to Organize Daily Literacy Instruction—Part II." http://www.shanahanonliteracy.com/search/label/Daily%20Five (retrieved July 11, 2015).

Sibberson, F. & Szymusiak, K. (2001). *Beyond leveled books: Supporting transitional readers in grades 2–5.* Portland, ME: Stenhouse Publishers.

Snow, C. E., Barnes, W. S., Chandler, J., Goodman, I. F. & Hemphill, L. (1991). *Unfulfilled expectations: Home and school influences on literacy.* Harvard University Press.

Snow, C., Burns, M. & Griffin, P. (1998). *Preventing reading difficulties in young children.* Washington, D.C.: National Academy Press.

Soderman, A. K., Gregory, K. M. & McCarty, L. T. (2005). *Scaffolding emergent literacy: A child-centered approach for preschool through grade 5* (2nd ed.). Boston, MA: Allyn & Bacon.

Stanovich, K. E. (1986). Matthew effects in reading: Some consequences of individual differences in the acquisition of literacy. *Reading Research Quarterly, 21*(4), 360–407.

Steinkuehler, C. (2011). *The mismeasure of boys: Reading and online videogames* (WCER Working Paper No. 2011–3). Retrieved from University of Wisconsin–Madison, Wisconsin Center for Education.

Taylor, B. M., Pearson, P. D., Clark, K. F. & Walpole, S. (1999). Effective schools/accomplished teachers. *The Reading Teacher, 53*(2), 156–159.

The Joint Task Force on Assessment of IRA and NCTE. (2010). *Standards for the Assessment of Reading and Writing.* Newark, DE: International Reading Association.

The Wright Group. (1996). *Guided reading level 1: Guiding students from emergent literacy to independence (Grades K–2, Emergent/Early Literacy).* Bothell, WA: The Wright Group.

Tobin, K. G. & Calhoon, M. B. (2009). A Comparison of Two Reading Programs on the Reading Outcomes of First-Grade Students. *Journal of Direct Instruction, 9*(1), 35–46.

Tomlinson, C. A. (1999). *The differentiated classroom: Responding to the needs of all learners.* Alexandria, VA: ASCD.

Tomlinson, C. A. & Moon, T. R. (2013). *Assessment and student success in a differentiated classroom.* Alexandria, VA: ASCD.

Watson, D. (1997). Beyond decodable books: Supporting and workable literature. *Language Arts, 74*(8), 635–643.

Wisconsin Department of Public Instruction. (1986). *Wisconsin Guide to Curriculum Planning in Reading.* Madison, WI: Wisconsin DPI.

Wisconsin Department of Public Instruction. (2010). *Wisconsin response to intervention: A guided document.* Madison, WI: The Wisconsin Department of Public Instruction.

Wixson, K. K. & Lipson, M. Y. (2012). Relations between the CCSS and RTI in literacy and language. *The Reading Teacher, 65*(6), 387–391.

Worthy, J. & Sailors, M. (2001). "That book isn't on my level": Moving beyond text difficulty in personalizing reading choices. *New Advocate, 14*(3), 229–239.

Maupin House by

capstone®
professional

At Maupin House by Capstone Professional, we continue to look for professional development resources that support grades K–8 classroom teachers in areas, such as these:

Literacy	Language Arts
Content-Area Literacy	Research-Based Practices
Assessment	Inquiry
Technology	Differentiation
Standards-Based Instruction	School Safety
Classroom Management	School Community

If you have an idea for a professional development resource, visit our Become an Author website at:

http://www.capstonepub.com/classroom/professional-development/become-an-author/

There are two ways to submit questions and proposals.

1. You may send them electronically to: proposals@capstonepd.com

2. You may send them via postal mail. Please be sure to include a self-addressed stamped envelope for us to return materials.

Acquisitions Editor
Capstone Professional
1 N. LaSalle Street, Suite 1800
Chicago, IL 60602